Ellis Roberts

New York

The planting and the growth of the Empire State. Vol. 1

Ellis Roberts

New York
The planting and the growth of the Empire State. Vol. 1

ISBN/EAN: 9783337175627

Printed in Europe, USA, Canada, Australia, Japan

Cover: Foto ©Andreas Hilbeck / pixelio.de

More available books at **www.hansebooks.com**

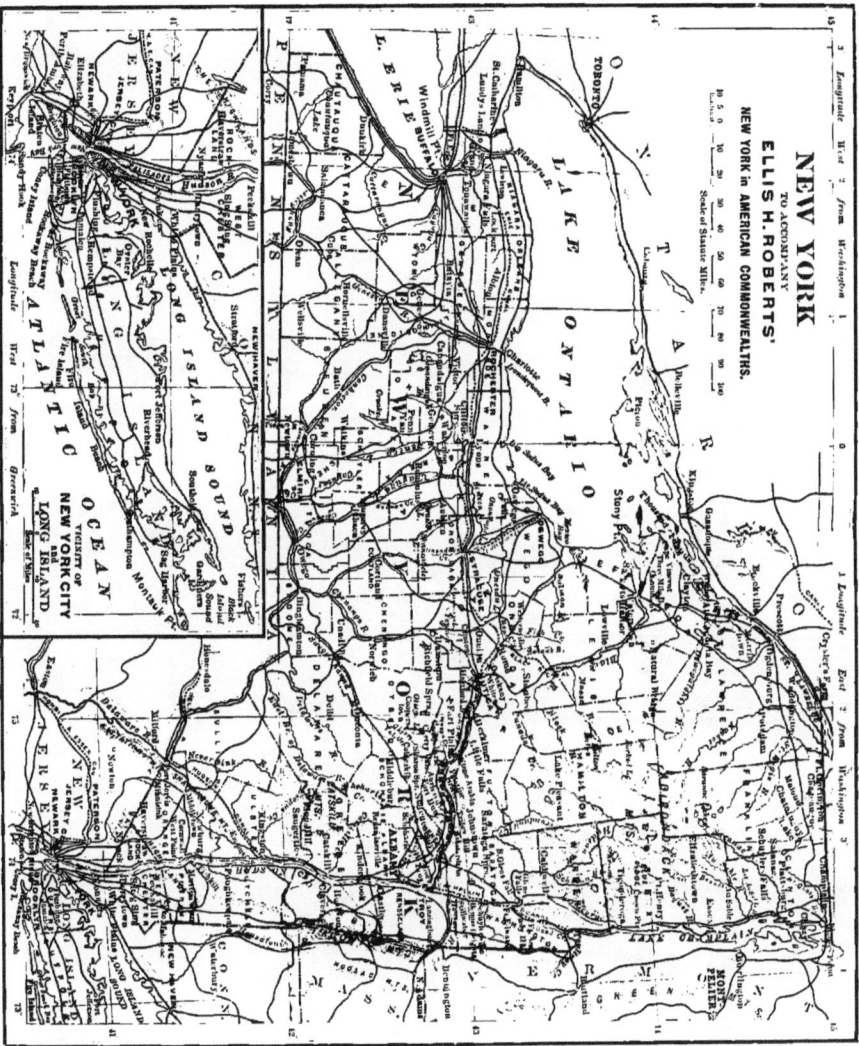

NEW YORK

TO ACCOMPANY

ELLIS H. ROBERTS'

NEW YORK in AMERICAN COMMONWEALTHS.

Scale of Statute Miles.

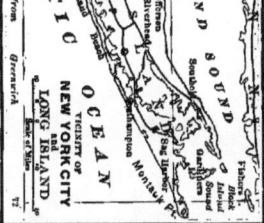

VICINITY OF
NEW YORK CITY
and
LONG ISLAND

𝕬merican Commonwealths

NEW YORK

THE PLANTING AND THE GROWTH OF
THE EMPIRE STATE

BY

ELLIS H. ROBERTS

IN TWO VOLUMES

VOL. I.

BOSTON AND NEW YORK
HOUGHTON, MIFFLIN AND COMPANY
The Riverside Press, Cambridge
1892

CONTENTS OF VOLUME I.

CHAPTER IV.

TRIALS OF THE DUTCH COLONY.

CHAPTER V.

CULMINATION OF THE DUTCH SWAY.

CHAPTER VI.

SURRENDER OF THE DUTCH.

CHAPTER VII.

THE ATTEMPT OF THE SWEDES.

CHAPTER VIII.

THE TOPOGRAPHY OF NEW YORK.

CHAPTER IX.

THE PEOPLE OF THE LONG HOUSE.

CHAPTER X.

FRENCH MISSIONARIES AND FRENCH ARMS.

CHAPTER XI.

THE EXPLOITS OF FRONTENAC.

II. A BRITISH COLONY.

CHAPTER XII.

BEGINNINGS OF ENGLISH RULE.

CHAPTER XVI.

STRUGGLES FOR POPULAR RIGHTS.

CHAPTER XVII.

THE PRESS MADE FREE.

CHAPTER XVIII.

COLLISIONS AND AFFLICTIONS.

CHAPTER XIX.

OPPOSITION ORGANIZED.

CHAPTER XX.

THE FRENCH WAR.

CHAPTER XXI.

PREPARATION. — FIRST STEP TOWARDS UNION.

NEW YORK.

I. BEFORE THE ADVENT OF THE ENGLISH.

CHAPTER I.

DISCOVERY BY THE FRENCH — THEIR INVA-
SION FAILS.

1524–1615.

SEBASTIAN CABOT'S map of his discoveries
on the Western Continent hung, in Queen Elizabeth's time, in the gallery at Whitehall. That
daring navigator had doubtless plainly marked
the point on the mainland which he had discovered on the 24th of June, 1497, when he
first penetrated the western seas, and had traced
the coast which in his two subsequent voyages
he had sailed along from the mouth of Hudson's
Bay to Cape Breton, and not to the Chesapeake,
as was once suggested. For while he reached
the parallel of 38°, it was doubtless on the high
seas, as he makes no mention of any of the
chief features of the shore south and west of
Cape Breton. No claim is urged in his behalf

that he entered the broad bay in latitude 44°
40' and longitude 74° 2', into which a great
river discharges its flood from the north, and
from which a sound trends eastward, separated
from the ocean by a low-lying island. Yet for
the domain adjacent to that bay, as well as for
other parts of the continent, the English title
begins with the discovery of Cabot, and the
possession of colonies to the eastward and southward. This title was the pretext for the seizure of the trading factories from the Dutch
by the English, and for the bestowal on that
colony, which has become the greatest of the
American commonwealths, of a name derived
from the Duke of York, the most bigoted of
the Stuarts.

The English were not, in fact, the discoverers
of any part of the land which has become New
York. A map was presented to Henry VIII.
of England by Giovanni da Verazzano, which
traced the sea-coast of the Western Continent
from Cape Breton to Florida; and a globe is
described in Queen Elizabeth's private gallery
in Westminster including the like details by
the same navigator. Verazzano was a Florentine
who entered the service of Francis I. of France,
and according to Hakluyt was thrice on the
American coast; first in 1508, a second time in
1524, and again two years later. On his first

voyage he sailed from Dieppe, in a vessel accompanied by another, commanded by Thomas Aubert, and they discovered and named the St. Lawrence River, which they first entered on the day of St. Lawrence. They carried to Europe some of the red men, as was the practice of the adventurers. Verazzano started on a second voyage in 1523, but his fleet was driven back by a severe storm. In the next year he sailed in La Dauphine, from Dieppe, and reaching the American coast at about 34°, after seeking a harbor southward for four degrees, surveyed the coast northward to 50°. He saw across the peninsula the Chesapeake Bay after passing its mouth. At the close of April, 1524, he arrived at a point which he called the Cape of St. Mary, now Sandy Hook, and cast anchor. The natives came in multitudes to the shores to look upon the strangers and their ship, as Verazzano sailed through the narrows into the bay, and into the stream which he styled "a very great river." His description of the bay, which he styles a "most beautiful lake," and of the "extent and attractiveness of the region," exists in a letter to Francis I., in a library in Florence. He found the adjacent country to be "thickly inhabited," and thirty boats appeared upon the bay. Verazzano continued his explorations on the coast to the east and north,

and he has left an interesting narrative, over
which critics have battled ; but the Maiollo map
in the Ambrosian library in Milan marks the
general line of his survey, and another map,
made in 1524, probably by Hieronimus da Verazzano, a brother, is preserved in the Borgian
Museum in Rome, and is further confirmation.[1]
Other maps of the sixteenth century sketch the
general features of this bay and river.   French
writers of that period speak of the region as
Norumberge or Norimbega, and the " great
river " is represented to a point where its chief
branch enters from the west, and the main
stream flows from the unknown north.   In a
manuscript in the National Library in Paris,
by Raulin Secalart and Jean Alphonse, the
writer, about 1545, describes the shallows,
" dangerous on account of rocks and swash-
ings," as Hell Gate has proved to be, and says
" the river is salt for more than forty leagues
up," as the Hudson River approximately is.   He
thinks " the river runs into the river of Canada, and into the sea of Saguenay," according
to the belief long received that the waters of
the St. Lawrence and this " great river " com-
mingled.   He describes " a town up the said
river fifteen leagues, called Norombeque."   In

[1] See the discussion over Verazzano in papers by J. Carson
Brevoort, H. C. Murphy, G. W. Greene, and B. F. De Costa.

it there was " a good people," and they had
" peltries of all kinds," and were " dressed in
skins, wearing mantles of martens." He sailed
up the river for many leagues.

On the map of Gerard Mercator, made in
1569, a fort is represented on the east side of
the " great river." The claim is urged that
the French navigators built some kind of works
near the mouth of the river, and the ruins on
" Castle Island " below Albany are supposed to
be those of the fort marked on his map by Mercator. Traditions claimed even an earlier date
for a part of these ruins, and attributed them
to Spanish adventurers. Certainly, the bull of
Pope Alexander VI. gave all America to the
Spaniards, and some wanderers from the followers of Menendez may have penetrated to
these lands.

Esteban Gomez was a Portuguese, who was a
mutineer in the fleet of that discoverer who
gave his name to the Straits of Magellan. In
1525, sailing under the flag of Charles V. of
Spain, he ran his ship, the San Antonio, into
the bay already visited by the French, and
doubtless ascended the river for a considerable
distance. He carried home with him a cargo
which included furs and red men for slaves.

Fortunately, Francis I. and Charles V. did
not find on these shores a field for their bloody

contests. France carried its discoveries farther
northward, and the Spaniards chose more sunny
climes for their colonies on the Western Continent. No Cortez here carried the cross at
the point of his sword. The civilization was
to be of another type. The Breton fishermen
sought profit on the Newfoundland banks, and
there trained mariners, who found their mission in seeking for a site for a new France,
and for religious conquests. Inspired by their
adventures, Jacques Cartier was the earliest to
organize an expedition. He sailed in 1534, under commission of Francis I., to explore the
western lands about which hung the mystery
of romance and the possibility of empire. On
the day of St. Lawrence, as Verazzano had done
before him, he entered the gulf to which his
piety again gave the name of the Saint. He
won favor with the aborigines in the bay of
Gaspé, and the chief permitted two of his sons
to make a visit to France, on a promise that
they should be brought back in the ensuing
year.

In 1535 Cartier, as commander and pilot, conducted a second expedition to the same waters,
and the chronicles describe in his company some
of the young nobility of the kingdom. During
this voyage he ascended the stream to a settlement of red men at Hochelaga, near the hill

which he called Mont Real. He extended his
discoveries to the rapids of the St. Lawrence
River, and looked wistfully to the southward.
The information which the red men gave him
of the country in that direction was not very
definite. They told him of a river running to
the southwest (the river of the Iroquois), and,
by following it, a moon's journey would bring
one to a land where there was never any ice or
snow, rich in oranges and almonds and nuts
and plums, but where continual wars were
waged. The people there were clothed in skins
like themselves. They reported that no gold
or copper was found in that land, which Cartier understood to be toward Florida. The
country nearest to the St. Lawrence southward
was known only as the seat of continual conflict.

The French immigrants, whether Huguenots
or Jesuits, whether authorized by Francis I. or
Henry IV., were fully occupied for two generations in caring for themselves at the village
which grew to be Montreal and the fort which
they built at Quebec. Wrangling and incom-
petency checked growth and delayed schemes
for advancing the lines of occupation. These
quarrels and weaknesses belong to the chronicles of Canada. They served to prevent the extension of the boundaries of New France south
of the St. Lawrence and the Lakes, at that crit-

ical era. Then the continent lay open, and the
French might have chosen the shores of the
Atlantic, and sought friendship with the Five
Nations instead of with the Hurons. If the
currents of their migration had flowed down the
Sorel and Lake Champlain, if their enterprise
had penetrated southward of the Adirondacks,
the French colonies which grew into perma-
nence along the Saguenay and the lower St.
Lawrence might well have been planted in the
country of the Oneidas, the Mohawks, the Onondagas, the Senecas, and the Cayugas. France
might have held the mouth of the Hudson and
the Chesapeake as well as of the St. Lawrence,
and even the fate of war in Europe might not
have checked the course of migration and settlement.

The French were the first Europeans to come
into contact with the Five Nations. The advance which, at an earlier day, might have
changed the course of history and the fate of
the Western Continent was providentially delayed until 1609. The wars of the red men
drew in the French adventurers. The opportunity was given to Samuel de Champlain to
carry his faith and his nationality to the natural seats of empire on this continent. He became a discoverer, and sought to be a conqueror.
He failed to be the architect of a grand com-

monwealth on the soil which he invaded. Yet
Champlain must be accepted as the original
European upon the domain which is now New
York, the first white actor on this broad stage.
He was worthy in many respects to be the
founder of a State. He was a favorite in the
court of the French king known to song and
story as Henry of Navarre. His family was
trained to the sea, and he was himself a captain and a quartermaster of cavalry. He was
a zealous Christian, and he declared the sal-
vation of one soul more important than the
founding of a new empire. Yet he strove with
all his energy to lay the foundations of New
France. He was chief in expeditions which
aimed at trade with the natives, but he never
engaged in traffic on his own account. He was
a soldier and a Frenchman, so it was easy for
him to listen to Huron appeals for alliance for
warlike enterprises. He did not come as the
Pilgrims came afterward to Plymouth, driven
by religious persecution, but he directed himself to carrying Christianity to the native people, and introduced to them the Recollets and
the Jesuits. His enterprise had nothing in common with the adventures soon to follow in
Virginia. No contrast can be stronger than
that between his advance up the Sorel and to
the lake which he discovered, and the peaceful

coming of William Penn to the commonwealth
which honors him. The French captain combined religious zeal with military and naval
accomplishments, with graces fostered at court,
and with a reputation as an author which his
works yet preserve. He was merciful if severe ;
he was self-restrained in the midst of speculation ; he commanded the confidence of successive holders of royal grants and of successive
ministers of state, and this confidence was justified by his discretion, his courage, and his
integrity. His persistence and the reliance
placed upon his sagacity and capacity by the
French authorities saved Canada from abandonment in the period between 1615 and 1632.
Under the Count de Soissons and the Prince of
Condé, he was lieutenant, and thus really the
first governor of New France. It was only as
an incident in his Canadian career that he became the earliest European figure in the history of New York.

Born in Saintonge in 1567, he sailed in 1599
for Mexico in the Spanish fleet, and reported
his voyage with charts of the western shores.
This service it was, doubtless, which led to his
designation to explore the territory in America
granted to De Chastes, governor of Dieppe,
and to found a colony on the St. Lawrence.
The commander of the fleet, which sailed March

15, 1603, was Pontgravé, but the task of exploration fell to Champlain, who ran in a light
boat up the river from the mouth of the dark
and deep Saguenay, to the St. Louis Rapids
above Montreal. De Monts, who succeeded to
the claims of De Chastes, sought to divert
Champlain to the coast of Nova Scotia or even
as far southwest as Cape Cod. After examination, however, choice was definitely made of
Quebec as the site of the colony. There, in
1608, he began to build homes and defenses,
and by putting the ringleader to death checked
a plot to end his career by assassination. The
French chieftain at once made friends with the
neighboring red men. He calls those whose
home was on the adjacent hills Montaignars,
and the name was extended to several friendly
tribes. In 1609 these tribes appealed to Champlain to help them in their strife with their enemies, the Iroquois, with whom they had waged
mortal war for a long time. On his maps the
French discoverer assigns to these warlike people the country south and west of Lake Champlain and of the St. Lawrence, and also west
as well as south of the Lake of the Iroquois,
now Lake Ontario. His red allies told him also
that east of the lake which he discovered as far
as mountains seeming to be covered with snow
in July (thus since known as White Mountains),

the Iroquois raised grain and fruit in beautiful
valleys. The Montaignars gathered their allies
before the French adventurer. Among them
were chiefs who knew the rivers and the lands
of the Iroquois. The red men told of the cruelties of the Iroquois, and of their own desire for
vengeance, and they pledged their readiness to
render him implicit obedience on the sole condition of his help in this war. Champlain listened to their plea, and promised to go with
them, not to trade, as he said enemies had
charged, but simply to fight for them. The
treaty was celebrated by the firing of muskets
and arquebuses "as a sign of great friendship
and rejoicing."

Champlain's narrative of the negotiation and
of the expedition is the first chapter in the
chronicles of European invasion of the land of
the Iroquois. The treaty was agreed upon
June 19, 1609, on the Isle of St. Esloy, really
a point lying east of the mouth of the Three
Rivers on the St. Lawrence.

Champlain was on his advance on the 2d of
July at the rapids of the River of the Iroquois,
connecting the St. Lawrence with the lake to
which he was to give his name. This point
is now known as the Chambly Rapids. The
force consisted of twenty-four canoes and sixty
men. On the 29th of July, at night, a war

party of the Iroquois was encountered on the
west side of the lake. The Iroquois hewed
trees and set up barricades. The Montaignars
lay in their canoes tied to poles. After parley,
battle was postponed until morning. The night
was spent in song and dance and in repartee
between the hostile parties. At daybreak the
Iroquois, to the number of three hundred, left
their barricades, led on by three chiefs who
wore lofty plumes. The forces marched "slowly
with gravity and assurance" toward each other.
The Iroquois halted and stood firm; the Montaignars "ran about two hundred paces toward
their enemies." Here Europe appears on the
scene. Champlain in quaint words outlines
the tragedy: "Our savages commenced calling
me in a loud voice, and making way opened
ranks and placed me at their head, marching
about twenty paces in advance until I was
within thirty paces of the enemy. The moment
they saw me they halted, gazing at me and I
at them. When I saw them preparing to shoot
at us I raised my arquebus and aimed directly
at one of the three chiefs. Two of them fell
to the ground by this shot, and one of their
companions received a wound of which he died
afterwards. I had put four balls in my arquebus. Our savages on witnessing a shot so favorable for them set up such tremendous shouts

that thunder could not have been heard; and yet there was no lack of arrows on one side or the other." Another Frenchman fired from ambush and added to the astonishment of the Iroquois, who soon fled. In pursuit some were killed, and ten or twelve were taken prisoners. The spoils of battle were Indian corn and meal and arms thrown away in flight.

This is the beginning of European invasion in this domain. Champlain carefully locates it "in forty-three degrees some minutes latitude." The place is between Lake George and Crown Point, in Ticonderoga, Essex County. The battle prompted the commander to name the water by which he had come Lake Champlain.

Rarely does history possess so complete a record of an event marking an era as it enjoys of this achievement. Champlain has told his own story with charming detail. He has also perpetuated it by art. In the original edition of his voyages, printed at Paris in 1613, is a bold engraving of this struggle. The canoes of both parties lie on the shore of the lake. On the right are the pickets of the Iroquois, and before them their warriors armed with bows. On the left are the Montaignars and their allies with like weapons. A forest forms the background, and on its edge are two Frenchmen, each armed with an arquebus. In the centre, nearly midway between the hostile forces, while arrows are showered about him, stands Champlain, with helmet and plume, with corselet and sword, and with arquebus blazing with the discharge of its four balls. Opposite him, prostrate at the feet of their followers, lie three plumed Iroquois chiefs. So France began its career south of the St. Lawrence.

This first act of French invasion was a blunder. It arrayed the great confederacy of the Long House against the authorities at Quebec. It rendered difficult any negotiations, and finally cast the masters of Lake Ontario, the Mohawk, and the Hudson into close alliance with the English. Champlain's advent was picturesque and chivalrous. The echo of his arquebus rang long in Indian wars, and was heard in the fall of French power in America on the Plains of Abraham. He was to continue his fighting with the Iroquois. After a visit to France he returned, and in 1610 had an encounter with them on the river then called by their name, now the Richelieu or Sorel. He claims a victory over them, and describes in detail their defeat.

Champlain kept close relations with the French court by visits home, and pressed discoveries to the north and west. In September, 1615, he discovered Lake Huron, *La Mer*

Douce, and on his return joined the Huron tribe in a movement against the Iroquois. He came from the west overland, and crossed Lake Ontario at its outlet into the St. Lawrence, and advanced into the land of the Iroquois for fourteen leagues along the eastern shore of the lake. He concealed the canoes of his force on the banks near what is now Henderson, Jefferson County. The hostile march extended to an outlet of Oneida Lake, which Champlain describes. Here eleven Iroquois, four of them squaws, were captured by the invaders. The men were tortured to death by the red allies, but the women were spared on the appeal of the commander.

On the 10th of October Champlain and his little army found the foe at a point which, not without controversy, has been fixed south of Oneida Lake, in Fenner, Madison County. The Iroquois occupied a fort which he pictures as a square of wooden pickets, and a village "inclosed with strong quadruple palisades of large timber, thirty feet high, interlocked the one with the other, with an interval of not more than half a foot between them. Galleries in the form of parapets were defended with double pieces of timber, proof against our arquebuses, and on one side they had a pond with a never failing supply of water, from which proceeded a number of gutters, which they had laid along the intermediate space, throwing the water without, and rendering it effectual inside for the purpose of extinguishing fire." Champlain tried to set fire to these works, and he built a tower of timber from which "four or five arquebuses might fire over the palisades and galleries." Even from the French narrative it is easy to see that this movement was a failure. Champlain himself "received two wounds from arrows, one in the leg and the other in the knee, which sorely incommoded" him. He expected reinforcements from the Hurons or their allies, but they did not come. Several skirmishes occurred, and safety was secured only by the arquebus. On the 16th of October, and as soon as he could bear his weight on his wounded leg, Champlain retreated "out of this prison, or, to speak more plainly, out of hell." The Iroquois pursued "about the distance of half a league," but he found his way to the lake where his canoes had been concealed, and they bore him away. The defeat had made it certain that this daring and able French adventurer was not to build walls for New France in the land of the Iroquois.

In 1612 Champlain was appointed lieutenant to the Count de Soissons, governor of New France, and was kept in place by the Prince

of Condé, who succeeded as governor, as he
was also by the Duke de Montmorency and
the Duke de Ventadour. He was in command
in Quebec in 1629, when an English fleet compelled him to surrender. When Canada was
restored to France by treaty in 1632, Champlain again became governor. He devoted himself to strengthening and extending the colonies
on and near the St. Lawrence, but died Christmas, 1635, in the scene of his labors. He is the
European pioneer in the land of the Iroquois.
We owe to his policy that French settlement
was directed north of the St. Lawrence and
Lake Ontario and to the west.

CHAPTER II.

THE French under Champlain penetrated to Lake Champlain July 30, 1609. In September of the same year the Half Moon, a Dutch vessel, sailed up the River of the Mountains, and the name of the discoverer, Hudson, was given to the stream. Henry Hudson was an Englishman, who, after trying twice to find the passage to Cathay under the English flag, transferred his services to the Dutch East India Company, and received the command of a vessel of eighty tons burden, with twenty sailors, some Dutch and some English, with instructions to seek China by the northeast or northwest. This company was the earliest organization for discovery and trade in that era when adventure became a passion, and trading companies were soon multiplied as its instrument. The States General of the Netherlands were intent on a full share in the commercial enterprise of the age. The far East and not

the New World was the destination of the
Half Moon, as of so many of its predecessors.
Hudson was driven by ice from an attempt to
pierce to the northeast. He turned to seek
China by the westward. He ran along the
banks of Newfoundland and the coast of Nova
Scotia, and after looking upon Cape Cod sailed
southward as far as the mouth of the Chesapeake Bay. He then turned northward and
came to anchor in Delaware Bay. Those waters
did not attract him, and he put out to sea and
again took a course to the northward. September 3, he rounded Sandy Hook, and the Half
Moon was anchored in the lower bay. John
Smith of Virginia had told him of the great
river in these latitudes, and the maps doubtless
accessible to him marked their general features.

The Dutch sailors went ashore and found
the land "pleasant with grass and flowers and
as goodly trees as ever they had seen, and very
sweet smells came from them." The Indians
were friendly. They returned the visit, and
curiosity ran high on both sides. The white
men were as strange to the red men as the red
men were to the sailors who came in their
white-winged ship. The weapons and ornaments and attire of Europe were as novel a
sight on the one hand as were, on the other
hand, the mantles of feathers and robes of fur

and copper necklaces of America. For three days the sailors went and came in peace. September 6, as a boat engaged in exploration was returning to the ship, savages in two canoes attacked it, and John Colman, an English sailor, was shot to death with an arrow in his throat. The cause of the attack is not stated by Hudson. If the Indians had received no provocation their guilt would have been charged. Colman was buried on Sandy Hook, the first European to die on these waters. After his death the Indians were not permitted to come on board the vessel, but two were taken captive, and red coats were put on them.

September 11, the Half Moon "went into the river," — the River of the Mountains, — and drifting with the incoming tide, the vessel advanced for three days. Then with favoring winds Hudson sailed beside the palisades and in sight of the mountains. Near the site of the present village of Catskill natives with friendly signs — "loving people" the old narrative styles them — brought ears of Indian corn and pumpkins and tobacco, and exchanged them for the trifles of the sailors. In latitude 43° 18', near Castleton, September 18, Hudson went ashore in a canoe with an old chief, and visited his tribe and home. The next day the Half Moon anchored near where now

stands the city of Albany. Here the Indians
in numbers came on board with grapes and
pumpkins and beaver and otter skins, and sold
them for beads and knives and hatchets. Here
occurred an incident prophetic of evils for the
red men. Hudson and his mate were suspicious
of the purposes of the Indians, and "determined
to try some of the chief men of the country
whether they had any treachery in them."
They therefore took them into the cabin of the
Half Moon, and "gave them so much wine
and *aqua vitæ* that they were all merry." The
Iroquois long retained a tradition of the first
meeting of the Europeans with their chiefs and
of the effects of the fire-water. On the day
succeeding the revel one of the chiefs "made
an oration" to Hudson, and "showed him all
of the country round about."

In the hope of finding an open channel to the
northward, Hudson sent a boat's crew eight or
nine leagues further up the river, where they
came to "but seven feet of water and in constant soundings," and the report was brought
back that the crew "found it to be at an end
for shipping to go in."

For eleven days Hudson had been occupied in
the ascent of the river; he now turned the prow
of the Half Moon to the southward, and sailed
toward the sea. The Indians came on board

wherever he cast anchor. Near Stony Point one of them was detected in stealing through the cabin-window, and he was shot down by the mate. This was the first Indian blood shed through the act of Europeans on this river. The natives were frightened at the killing of their associate, and another life was lost in their hasty flight.

When the Half Moon descended the river to the head of Manhattan Island, two canoes full of fighting-men approached the vessel, and as they were not allowed to come on board, they sent a flight of arrows into it. The party was led by one of the captives who had been clothed in a red coat, and had escaped to his people. The assailants were met by musket-shots, and two or three were killed. Near the point where is now Fort Washington, the Indians attacked the Half Moon as it passed. Two were killed by a shot from the large gun, and the rest fled into the woods; another canoe bore a company for assault, but the bark was shattered by a ball, and the red men retired, after losing in all nine warriors. These first collisions on the Hudson occurred October 2.

That night the Half Moon was anchored in the bay where " one side of the river was called Manna-hatta," and lay there for a day. October 4, the navigator ran out of the " great mouth of the great river " which preserves the memory of his voyage in its name, the Hudson.

Fearing his crew, who began to " threaten him savagely," Hudson determined to cross the Atlantic, anxious to return to Holland, but finally seeking port in Dartmouth, England. He sent a report of his discoveries to the Dutch East India Company, with a proposal to renew the search for the northwest passage. He was summoned to Amsterdam, but the English authorities forbade his departure, and kept him at Dartmouth for several months. He reëntered the English service the next year, and sailing in the Discovery penetrated to that great bay in the far north, where, amid fields of ice, he was abandoned by his crew, and left to die alone. Hudson's Bay was the scene of his death, as it was the limit at once of his discoveries and of his adventures.

Holland merchants engaged in the fur trade sent a second vessel to the River of the Mountains, in the summer of 1610. The crew included several sailors who had returned in the Half Moon, and it is surmised that the mate of that vessel was the commander on this second voyage to Manhattan. The records are scant, but tradition tells that when the whites met the Indians on this occasion " they were much rejoiced at seeing each other."

The Dutch were looking to the country on the Hudson River with growing interest. They called it the Mauritius, after the Stadtholder, Prince Maurice. Hendrick Christiaensen of Cleves contributed to the new ventures. He had been on a voyage to the West Indies before he joined Adriaen Block in excursions to the American coast, in 1611, when they visited Manhattan, and carried back two sons of an Indian chief, who were named Orson and Valentine. These savages had the attraction of novelty, and were taken as representatives of a numerous population in the western land. The merchants of the United Provinces were prompted to seek trade with the continent along the routes which their vessels had traversed; and a memorial on the subject was addressed to the chief cities of Holland.

Hans Hongers, Paulus Pelgrom, and Lambrecht van Tweenhuysen, three merchants of Amsterdam, were the pioneers in Dutch commerce with Manhattan. They equipped in 1612 two vessels, the Fortune and the Tiger, under the command respectively of Christiaensen and Block, to seek trade along the Hudson River. The next year the Little Fox and the Nightingale were also sent out from Amsterdam, and the Fortune sailed from Hoorn. The Tiger was accidentally burned at Manhat

tan, and Block built a vessel to take its place
in the winter of 1613–14. At the same time
a few huts were built near the southern point
of the island, and for two winters the Indians
supplied the Dutch with food and necessaries.
The beginning of shipbuilding was dependent
upon Indian friendship and supplies. The new
vessel was called the Restless, and with it
Block explored the waters east of the mouth
of the Hudson.

In the same year, if not before, Christiaensen built a strong house on Castle or Patroon's
Island, on the west bank of the Hudson, a little
below the site of Albany, and called it Fort
Nassau. The dimensions of this structure de-
serve to be recorded. It was thirty-six feet by
twenty-six feet, and had a stockade fifty-eight
feet square with a moat eighteen feet wide. The
armament was two large guns and eleven swiv-
els, and the garrison numbered ten or twelve.
Christiaensen was the first commander, and his
second was Jacob Eelkens, who had been a
clerk for a merchant in Amsterdam. Orson,
one of the Indians who had been taken to Holland, proved to be " an exceedingly malignant
wretch and was the cause of Hendrick Christiaensen's death." The cause of the tragedy is
not related, but those were days of prompt vengeance, and Orson " was repaid with a bullet

as his reward." The incident does not seem
to have had any effect on the relations of the
Dutch with the red men. To Fort Nassau the
buyers who went out among the Mohawks returned with their purchases, and the Indians
soon learned to repair thither for traffic and
adventure. It was so badly damaged by a
freshet in the spring of 1617, that it was suffered to go to decay. These Mohawks told the
Dutch that the French came to the upper part
of their country in shallops to trade with them
there. Competition between nations had already begun in American commerce.

The States General of Holland granted a
charter, October 11, 1614, to a company of Amsterdam merchants, "exclusively to visit and
navigate to the newly discovered lands lying in
America, between New France and Virginia,
now named New Netherland, for four voyages
commencing on the 1st of January, 1615, or
sooner." Block, who had returned to Holland,
was active in securing this grant, which organized Dutch trade in New Netherland. This
company sent traders into the interior. Three
who followed the Delaware southward were
taken prisoners, and were recovered by the
payment of ransoms.

This Dutch company has the distinction of
framing the first treaty with the red men.

After the abandonment of Fort Nassau the Dutch, under the command of Eelkens, in 1617 erected a new fortified trading-house at the mouth of the Tawasentha, or Norman's Kill, two miles below the present site of Albany. There the Mohawks gathered representatives not only of the Iroquois, but of the Mohicans, the Mingoes, the Minnisincks, and the Lenni-Lenapees, in a council of peace. An alliance was formed between the Dutch on the one hand and the Iroquois as chief negotiators on the other hand, with the other tribes as subordinates. They held the belt of peace as a sign of union ; they smoked the calumet, and they buried the tomahawk at a spot where the Dutch promised to build a church to cover it so that it could not be dug up. This was the beginning of the friendly relations which the Dutch carefully maintained with the red men. The treaty of Tawasentha stood unchanged for twenty-eight years, and was renewed in 1645, and then was continued during the entire period of Dutch possession.

This treaty was the practical act, on the part of the Dutch, of men who sought trade and profit, and favored peace as a means to that end. They had no dreams of conquest, they were fired by no religious zeal. They recognized the Indians as persons whose rights were to be respected, and whose lives were not to be sacrificed; as parties to a treaty standing on the same plane with themselves, with ideas of natural justice and due sense of obligation and of honor. In the time of its framing, in the participants, in its scope, in its bearing on the commonwealth, the treaty of Tawasentha was of the utmost significance. It arrayed the Iroquois as a barrier against French invasion, it enabled the Dutch to get a solid foothold on the Hudson and its western branches, and went far to determine that the country of the Five Nations should not be governed from Versailles.

A company of English people sought freedom of religion in Holland, in 1608, the year when Champlain was busy advancing up the St. Lawrence and its tributaries, and twelve months before the French discoverer found the lake, and Henry Hudson the river, which are chief features in the topography of New York. These Englishmen caught eagerly at the stories of a new land beyond the sea, and were zealous to establish there the faith to which they were devoted. Dissatisfied with their refuge in Holland, they weighed the attractions of several colonies then newly founded. Robinson, their pastor, in 1620 applied for permission to remove to New Netherland, and promised to take with him four hundred fami-

lies, on condition that the Dutch government
would protect them from the assaults of any
other power. He wanted to plant in New
Netherland "the true and pure Christian religion," and "to colonize and establish a new
empire there," under the States General. The
Amsterdam merchants trading to the New
World submitted a memorial approving the
application of the "English preacher at Leyden," especially as a means to secure the colony to the Dutch. The States General, April
11, 1620, refused to grant permission to Robinson and his associates to colonize in New Netherland. The Englishmen therefore concluded
to sail under arrangements, not wholly satisfactory, previously proposed by the Virginia Company, and they laid the foundations of another
colony the history of which runs in broad, distinct channels of its own. Some lessons they
had learned in twelve years of banishment in
Leyden, lessons of toleration, of the union of
provinces, of the intellectual activity of a people rising out of conflict to primacy in many
branches of civilization. The colony on the
Hudson lost all that this zealous company might
have brought to it. That colony continued for
forty-four years under Dutch control, separate
from English influence, and working out a development peculiar and unique on this continent.

That development entered upon a new stage when, in 1621, the Dutch West India Company was chartered. The charter of the New Netherland Company had expired three years before, and the States General refused to grant a renewal; but a license was granted to Hendrick Eelkens and his associates who had been members, to send a ship to Manhattan to trade. Controversy arose concerning discoveries between him and Cornelis Jacobsen May, who had come over in the Fortune, and in 1620 made a second voyage, now in the Glad Tidings, and sailed southward of Manhattan, giving his name to a cape to-day fashionable as a watering-place. The controversy helped to direct attention to the American coast, and both claimants were repulsed while vast privileges were conceded to the West India Company.

The powers granted to this new organization were monstrous even in that age when European states gave away the control of immense regions in the New World. The company was clothed, in fact, with exclusive rights in the domains of the Dutch between the tropic of Cancer and the Cape of Good Hope, in the West Indies, and on the coasts of America between Newfoundland and the Straits of Magellan. It might make treaties and maintain courts of justice, and employ soldiers in the name of the States General. Oaths of allegiance ran both to the home government and to the company. The company was to be ruled by chambers divided into nine parts, of which Amsterdam possessed four, and other Dutch provinces five, parts. Nineteen delegates exercised its executive power, and the States General were represented by one of them, while eighteen were distributed among the home cities and provinces. Governors were to be appointed and their instructions ratified by the States General. This body gave a million guilders to the company, and pledged to defend it, and in case of war to furnish sixteen ships of three hundred tons each, and four yachts of eighty tons each, to be maintained by the company and be commanded by an admiral appointed by the " high mightinesses " in Holland.

The purpose of the Dutch West India Company was first commercial, but its charter expressly provided that it was " to advance the peopling of the fruitful and unsettled parts " of the wide domain intrusted to it, and to " do all that the service of those countries and the profit and increase of trade shall require."

With all these advantages the promoters of the company occupied two years in perfecting its organization, and they did not secure the approval of the States General until June 21,

1623. Under a provision continuing the license previously accorded to traders to sell goods shipped to the colony and to make return voyages, private merchants kept up active traffic, and several vessels were dispatched to Manhattan and other points on the coast.

When active operations began, the affairs of New Netherland were consigned to the chamber of Amsterdam. The members most prominent were Jonas Witsen, who since 1614 had been interested in trade with the Mauritius, Hendrick Hamel, Samuel Godyn, Samuel Blommaert, John de Laet, noted as a historian, Kiliaen van Rensselaer, to become the first of the patroons, Michael Pauw, who also became a patroon, and Peter Evertsen Hulft, who shipped the first cattle to the colony.

Before the formal organization the company took measures to secure its possessions in New Netherland, and in 1622 sent out the yacht Mackerel for that purpose. The yacht arrived in December of that year and went up the Hudson River to trade with the Indians, and its return was fortunately timed so that it was in the bay when the first colony sent out by the Dutch West India Company came into those waters.

3

CHAPTER III.

DUTCH COLONIZATION.

1622–1637.

THE first colony to New Netherland under the auspices of the Dutch West India Company consisted in largest part of Walloons, persons of French blood resident in the southern provinces of Holland. They had been refused the privilege of immigrating to Virginia on terms satisfactory to them, and were welcomed as passengers in the New Netherland, a ship of two hundred and sixty tons, which sailed in March, 1623, under the superintendence of Cornelis Jacobsen May, and after a voyage of two months arrived at the mouth of the Hudson.

Here was found a French vessel, and its captain insisted on taking possession of the country for the king of France. The Mackerel was able by the display of cannon to convince the French captain that his claims could not be enforced. The passengers by the New Netherland were distributed over the territory which the Dutch West India Company sought to possess. Eight men were deemed sufficient for Manhattan, several families were sent to the South River, now the Delaware, and two families and six men to the Fresh River, now the Connecticut, while another party settled on the west shore of Long Island.

The vessel proceeded up the Hudson River. The larger part of the immigrants landed on the west bank of the river, where Fort Orange had been laid out the preceding year. Adriaen Joris, who was director under May, went with eighteen families, who found a home here. The fort was soon completed, and the settlers devoted themselves with energy to tilling the earth, to building huts of bark, and to trading for fur with the Indians. These included the Mohicans and the several tribes of the Iroquois. They all made covenants of friendship, and brought furs with hearty good will. This was the beginning of Albany, the capital of New York.

In 1623 Fort Nassau was built on the South River, but was soon deserted. No marked success followed efforts to extend Dutch occupation so far southward until 1631. In that year a colony built a brick house for a fort and a residence, and named it Swaanendael. Gillis Hossett, who had come out as Van Rensselaer's agent on the Hudson, was in charge, and the sprout there planted has grown into the State of Delaware.

Of the colonists generally Joris was able to report at the end of their first year, in 1624, that they were "getting bravely along." He took to Holland with him a cargo of furs, which gave over twenty - eight thousand guilders to the treasury of the company, as material proof of the success of the enterprise.

In Dutch literature New Netherland became a prominent feature. The "Historical Relation of Wassenaer," begun in 1621 and continued for twelve years, recorded all the information which could be gathered from the Western Continent. John de Laet, one of the directors of the West India Company, published at Leyden, in 1625, from "various manuscript journals of different captains and pilots," including Henry Hudson, a rich and full volume entitled "The New World, or Description of the West Indies." These works stirred the hearts and hopes of the adventurous to engage in trade or colonization in the broad new fields.

Peter Eversen Hulft, of Amsterdam, deserves the credit of shipping, in 1625, in three vessels, at his own risk, horses, cattle, swine, and sheep, with seeds, plows, and other implements for farming. When May handed over the direction of the colony to William Verhulst, in 1625, the population was two hundred souls.

In 1626 Peter Minuit came out as director general of New Netherland, and the government of the province became more formal and definite. A council of five assisted the director, and they together possessed all authority, subject to the company in Holland. Gage de Rasieres, the first "koopman," served as secretary of the province, and Jan Lampo, the first "schout," performed the duties of procurator, sheriff, and supervisor of customs.

Minuit's administration was distinguished by the purchase from the Indians of the entire island of Manhattan for sixty guilders or about twenty-four dollars. The transaction to the honest Dutch traders was so simple and proper that no glamour was thrown about it, and it was only one of the series of transactions by which, during their whole occupation, the Dutch held the red men in amity and peace. Two "consolers of the sick" followed the new director in the same year, Sebastian Jansen Krol and Jan Huyck by name, and they, on Sundays, read texts out of the Scripture and the creeds to such as would attend. An upper room in a horse-mill served for the congregation, and a tower with Spanish bells, captured at Porto Rico, marked its religious character.

Fort Amsterdam was built on the southern
point of Manhattan Island, and the original
battery, which has become a historical feature,
was begun.

Fort Orange suffered in this year from one
of the few wrongs perpetrated upon the red
men by the Dutch.   The Mohicans from a
village on the east side of the river crossed the
stream to attack the Mohawks, and induced
Krieckebeeck, the commissary of the fort, to
join in the expedition with six men.   The
Dutch leader soon paid the penalty of his
blunder, for the Mohawks did not wait to be
attacked, but fell upon the invaders, killed the
commissary and three of his men, and put the
rest of the force to flight.   Tymen Bouwensen,
one of the killed, the Dutch averred, "was eaten
by the savages after he had been well roasted."
The Mohawks displayed in their wigwams an
arm and a leg of their victims as proof of their
victory.   When inquiry was made of the cause
of the trouble the Mohawks pleaded that they
had done nothing against the whites, and had
acted simply in self-defense.   In consequence
of the fight the families at Fort Orange were
removed to Manhattan, and a garrison of sixteen men, without any women, was left in
charge, under Krol, who had just arrived as
one of the " consolers of the sick."   For two

years the dread of Indian hostilities hung over
Fort Orange, and kept settlers away. In 1628
the Mohawks drove the Mohicans from the
banks of the Hudson and conquered a peace.

Krol continued to hold the garrison, and sent
such reports of the soil and the climate and the
advantages of trade, that Kiliaen van Rensselaer, a director of the West India Company in
Amsterdam, who had grown rich by polishing
pearls and diamonds, chose that site for invest-
ment. Van Rensselaer instructed Krol to buy
for him from the red men a tract of land on
the west side of the river. This purchase was
made in 1630 under a charter of privileges and
exemptions creating patroons, a system which
had a marked effect on the tenure of land in
New York. Krol bought a tract extending
northward from Barren Island to Smack's Island, and "stretching two days' journey into
the interior." This was called Rensselaerwyck,
and colonists were sent out in 1630, well provided with cattle and implements. With them
came Wolfert Gerritsen as overseer of farms,
and Gillis Hossett as special agent for the
proprietor. Hossett was so well pleased with
the prospect that he arranged for the purchase
of additional land on both sides of the Hudson
River, and both north and south of Fort
Orange. The fort itself remained in possession

of the West India Company, but the new patroon became with these and later purchases the owner of a great part of the land now constituting the counties of Albany, Rensselaer, and Columbia.

Michael Pauw was, like Van Rensselaer, a shrewd and adventurous director, who took advantage of the charter for patroons. He bought from the red men the whole of Staten Island and the land now occupied by Jersey City. Minuit, as director general, approved of the contract for Staten Island July 15, 1631. The consideration for the land was "certain parcels of goods."

The bargains may have been sharp on the part of the Dutch, but the red men were voluntary actors, and the title to New Netherland was not tainted by blood or violence. Minuit bought Manhattan for the company, and Van Rensselaer and Pauw bought their tracts as other directors secured land on the outer limits of the province, in free and peaceful trade. The record is creditable to the humanity of the promoters of the colony, and it established precedents, so that purchase and not conquest became the rule for the acquisition of land from the red men in all parts of the colony. The original patroons were charged with greed in grasping for such vast tracts of the most

eligible land. To assuage the jealousy they
divided their purchases with fellow-directors.

ˌ Eastward on the Fresh River the West India
Company claimed possession in 1623, but in
1627 its representatives informed the Puritans
at Plymouth of the river "now known by the
name of the Conighticute River, which they
often commended to them for a fine place both
for plantation and trade, and wished them to
make use of it." In 1633, however, a new
policy was set on foot. Jacob van Curler was
sent to build a fort, " Good Hope," and to buy
from the red men a large tract of land. He
succeeded in both tasks, and secured title from
the Pequods, who were the conquering tribe.
They, in the succeeding year, murdered an
English captain who came to trade at the fort,
and Van Curler executed some Indians in return. War followed, and the Pequods sought
help from the English, and by treaty transferred all their rights on the Connecticut to
them. An English colony had been planted at
Windsor, and held the place against Dutch
protests. Emigration from several points in
Massachusetts was organized, and in 1635 colonists in considerable numbers sailed from England to Boston on their way to Connecticut.
They grew strong enough to repulse a display
of force by the Dutch. From this time the

Fresh River cannot be claimed as a part of
New Netherland, but controversy over the possession of it lasted for many years.

Manhattan, with occasional rivalry from Fort
Orange, became the chief market and settlement of New Netherland. It was the natural
seat of authority for a government deriving its
authority from beyond the sea. It was the
port through which exports and imports must
pass. Already, in 1629 and 1630, Manhattan
exchanged with Amsterdam one hundred and
thirty thousand guilders' worth of commodities,
with a balance in favor of the colony of seventeen thousand guilders. In 1631 a ship called
after the province and after the vessel which
brought over the first colony of the West India
Company, was built at Manhattan. It was
from six hundred to eight hundred tons burden, and carried thirty guns, and was one of
the largest merchant vessels then afloat. Such
an enterprise proves the prosperity of the province and the broad and far-reaching hopes of
its managers.

With prosperity came collisions. The patroons had interests apart from the company.
They sought a share in the fur trade, at least
at points where the company did not maintain
stations. Their rivalry brought the recall of
Minuit, the director-general of the province, in

1631, and the struggle over the appointment of his successor kept the place vacant and administered by subordinates for two years. The company having the power insisted on its monopoly in trade.

In 1633 Wouter van Twiller was appointed director general. He was a clerk for the company in Amsterdam, had married a niece of Van Rensselaer, and had attended to some of the colonial interests of his uncle. He sailed in the Soutberg, bearing twenty guns and a hundred and four soldiers, and the vessel captured and brought into Manhattan a Spanish caravel. Among his companions were Everardus Bogardus, the first clergyman, and Adam Roelandsen, the first schoolmaster, who came to the province. Among the changes at the beginning of his administration was the substitution at Fort Orange of Hans Jorissen Houten, who was familiar with trade on the river, for Krol, who had been in command since Krieckebeeck was killed in his foolish raid on the Mohawks.

In the administration of Van Twiller Washington Irving finds the beginning of that historical *opera bouffe* in which he has celebrated the Dutch rule in New Netherland. The burlesque has taken its place in our literature, and has colored the estimate of events in that pe-

riqd. With much that is quaint, and with
figures which it is possible to regard as very
comical, the Dutch, from the coming of Van
Twiller to the surrender of Stuyvesant, did a
great deal of practical work in organizing and
settling the province, and in establishing, by
friendly treatment and fair trade, cordial relations with the red men.

The colony was under a trading company,
but it had its sources in that reorganized nation whose struggle with Spain had ended in
the very year of Hudson's voyage hither. The
religious activity of the Netherlands was exhibited in the synod of Dort, and in the leadership which it held in the movement for release
from the shackles of priestcraft and superstition. During the period of the growth of New
Netherland the mother country was one of the
foremost powers of the world. For thirteen
years Van Tromp carried its victorious flag
over all seas, and in 1652 bore his defiant
broom at the masthead through the English
Channel. France and England were glad to
take the States General into alliance as an
equal. The treachery of Charles Stuart broke
the relations with Holland, but only to produce that situation which trained William of
Orange to become king of England, and to
impress his policy as a permanent system on

the diplomacy and the conduct of his adopted country. The intellectual and literary life of the Netherlands was at this period not inferior to that of any part of Europe. The University of Leyden challenged all rivals. The city of Amsterdam was so far a leader that its style in art gave name to a school. In mechanism, and especially the skilled branches, which are akin to art, the Dutch were masters. Their towns were little republics, which educated citizens and developed men. For culture, for political and religious freedom, for varied development in literature and art, the Netherlands of William the Silent and Prince Maurice, of Barneveld and Grotius and John DeWitt, were not second to any other nation in that age. The commercial enterprise of the Dutch was a natural growth of the broad and generous life of their republic.

New Netherland received the adventurous spirits of such a country. While they came for traffic primarily, they brought the clergyman and the schoolmaster with them. While the directors were clothed with vast powers, the settlers insisted on applying the principles of self-government which they had learned in their native towns. Because it was the earliest, the influence of the Dutch upon the commonwealth has been radical and enduring.

The language of the early settlers has given
way to a tongue which is conquering in trade
and in literature. The mother country has
fallen behind in the race of nations, and has
lost many of its historic provinces. But no
colony can wholly outgrow the impress given
to it in the first generations of its existence,
and it is certain that New Netherland has not
done so.

While the early settlers tried to support
themselves, in part at least, from the soil, they
did not attempt in any large degree to raise
agricultural products for export. They made
experiments with tobacco and gradually extended their crops of grain, so that after a
while wheat was shipped to Boston, and in due
time became a factor in trade with the Old
World. At the outset the source of profit was
in furs, and the general policy was determined
by this fact. The devotion of New England
to the fisheries, and of Virginia to raising tobacco, gave to the Dutch colony the control if
not the monopoly of the fur traffic. The climate of New Netherland, its wealth in certain
animals, and its ease of communication with
Canada, determined the policy of the West
India Company. The zeal to get furs gave
tone to the treatment of the red men. Peace
with them was the sure way of securing the

rich peltries which they hunted for in the distant forests and on the streams which they alone knew. The cheap trifles of the Dutch markets afforded a more profitable means of capturing beaver and otter, and fox, and deer and bear skins than arms and strife could offer. The obvious and immediate interests of the colonists accorded with their humane desires and Christian purposes, and rendered their relations with the Indians during the Dutch occupation as a rule friendly and peaceful, to a degree beyond the experience of their neighbors.

The large profits of the fur trade, and the restricted field within which it was pursued, led to suspicion and watchfulness by the Dutch Company. The directors from first to last found this one of their chief tasks. Van Twiller did not shrink from it whether foreigners or fellow-countrymen crossed his path.

The first English vessel to visit Sandy Hook came in 1619, under command of Thomas Dermer, but the only result was a report which Purchas published in his " Pilgrims." In 1633, a London vessel, the William, came to Manhattan to trade upon the Hudson River. Jacob Eelkens, who had been commissary at Fort Orange, directed the enterprise for English capitalists. With display of the Dutch and English flags and a salute on both sides,

the William defiantly sailed up the river.
Eelkens established a trading tent a mile below Fort Orange, and for a fortnight held his
ground ; but Van Twiller gathered a fleet of
three vessels, seized the goods of the intruder
and put them on the William, turned the vessel about, and took it out to sea under convoy
of the little Dutch fleet.   Eelkens did mischief
by exciting the red men against the Dutch,
but he failed to establish English trade on the
Hudson River at that time.

Van Twiller had that virtue in a ruler which
consists of faith in his country.   He devised
large things for Manhattan : the repair of Fort
Amsterdam, new windmills, houses of brick
and frame, a brewery, and other structures.
A plain wooden church was built to take the
place of the loft used for religious services, and
a dwelling-house was provided for the "domine," as the preacher was called.   Elsewhere
in the province also improvements were made:
on the South River, and at Pavonia, the station of Patroon Michael Pauw, while Fort
Orange rejoiced in an " elegant large house,
with balustrades and eight small dwellings for
the people."   The director - general and his
friends secured large tracts of land from the
red men.   The rights of Patroon Pauw to Pavonia and Staten Island were transferred to the

West India Company. Trade with New England and with the West Indies was extended. The Dutch gave sympathy to the English in their war of extermination against the Pequods in Connecticut. The signs of activity and growth were many.

But Van Twiller had made enemies. David Pietersen de Vries of Hoorn tried to sail with a French commission to trade in furs on the American coast, in 1624, but was prevented by the West India Company. In 1630, he secured an interest on South River as a patroon. Two years later he came out just in time to see the ruins of Swaanendael, the station on that river. He succeeded in securing peace with the red men who had caused the destruction, and then made an excursion to Virginia. Returning to Manhattan in time to greet Van Twiller on his arrival, he witnessed the conduct of the director general in the affair of the William, and deemed it too slow and weak. In 1633, he had a controversy with Van Twiller, who proposed to search his vessel as he was starting for Holland, for articles subject to tax to the company. He arranged to establish a colony on Staten Island. He was in Holland when Van Dincklagen, who had been schout-fiscal, and removed by Van Twiller, appeared with charges against his former chief. De

Vries intimated that the director general, who seems to have been a plodding, self-seeking official, "acted farces" in the province. Domine Bogardus had more than once quarreled with Van Twiller. On one occasion he described the director as a "child of the devil," and threatened him with "such a shake from the pulpit as would make him shudder." Van Dincklagen aimed his censures at the domine as well as the director, but no change was made in the ecclesiastical control. Van Twiller was removed under charges in 1637. He retired with a large estate. He appeared later as one of the executors of the Patroon Van Rensselaer, and in 1650 he was a leading opponent of the administration of Stuyvesant. The company charged him with aiming to "appoint himself as the only commander of the North River," and with threatening "to repel with force every one who with a commercial view shall come there or to Rensselaerwyck." He was appointed governor to sustain the monopoly of the company against the patroons. His last appearance is as the champion of the chief patroon against the company.

In his career the spirit of the colony at this period was embodied. The company was vigorous in the assertion of its claims, and the director general gave exhibition of personal traits in the exercise of arbitrary powers. Protest was not infrequent against the claims of the company and the domination of the director. The growing power of the patroons was making trouble. There were scattered farms, but in the main the life of the settlers was concentrated about the trading-posts and two or three villages. These, however, were yet weak, and the rate of growth was not rapid.

CHAPTER IV.

TRIALS OF THE DUTCH COLONY.

1637–1647.

THE decade in which William Kieft held the place of director general was marked by an aggressive policy toward the red men, exceptional in Dutch history, by an exaggeration of difficulties incident to the relations of the two races, and by consequent dangers and collisions. These gave the occasion for the bold assertion by the settlers of a right to share in the government, which was thereafter steadily maintained. Kieft came out as director in 1637, but the reason for his selection is not easy to find. He had no previous connection with colonial affairs, and was charged with appropriating money given to him to ransom Christian prisoners in Turkey. He had failed in business as a merchant in Rochelle, and for that offense his portrait had been affixed to the gallows. He was as active as Van Twiller was slow, and was no less greedy of gain. He was equally self-willed, as he showed at once on arriving in the province by organizing the council so as to retain the entire control. He made haste to testify that his predecessor left affairs in a very bad condition. The company's farms were not tenanted; its cattle had been sold; its buildings were out of repair; and the fort was in ruins and its guns dismounted. Six years before Van Twiller had been censured for extravagance in building and repairing the fort, so that some allowance must be made for the dark colors in this picture. Kieft himself, among his first acts, rented one of the company's farms to Van Twiller, and the rent was two hundred and fifty guilders a year and one sixth of the produce.

The new director general, like his predecessor, began with strengthening the monopoly of the company in trade. He put an end to operations in that line by employees. He enacted stringent police regulations, restricting the sale of liquor and imposing an excise on tobacco, while passports were required from persons wishing to leave Manhattan. He bought additional lands for the company from the red men as opportunity arose, and sold parcels to individuals who made eligible offers.

In the first year of his administration the States General investigated the management of the company in New Netherland, and inquired into the policy of assuming immediate control. The affair was complicated by demands on the part of the patroons for additional privileges. The era was stormy on all sides for the province. One result of the discussion was a concession on the part of the company by which any person could trade "in the company's ships" to the province subject to ten per cent. duty on shipments from New Netherland in addition to the charges of transportation. Immigrants were to receive as much land as they could cultivate, paying one tenth of the produce as quit-rent. De Vries returned with a colony to Staten Island. In this year also came Joachem Pietersen Kuyter of Darmstadt and Cornelis Melyn, who took, at a later day, a prominent part in affairs. Immigrants from Virginia and New England joined in increasing the population. Fresh impulse was given to agriculture and especially to the cultivation of tobacco. Captain John Underhill, who had won a name in the Pequod war, brought several families from Connecticut, and cast his lot in New Netherland. Anthony Jansen, a French Huguenot, was one of the immigrants in 1639, when also Thomas Belcher took up a tract upon the site of the present city of Brooklyn. The foreigners were welcomed on equal terms with Dutchmen, and the chronicles certify that the English settlers were prompt to promise by oath " to follow the director or any one of the council wherever he may lead," and to support the province against all enemies.

Kieft's great blunder was committed in 1639, and was due to mingled greed and ignorance. He demanded tribute from the red men in maize, furs, or service, on the plea that the Dutch had defended them against their enemies. This demand was connected with an effort to prevent the sale of guns or ammunition to the red men. Relations between the races had grown familiar. The red men made frequent visits to the houses of the Dutch, and some were employed as servants. The Iroquois at first feared a gun, and styled it the " devil," from its satanic power, but they soon learned to use it with skill, and found traders willing to furnish weapons at a round price in furs. Possession of firearms enabled them to assert domination over other tribes.

The director general tried his scheme of collecting tribute first on the Raritan Indians, with whom trouble had previously occurred. They refused to pay, whereupon several Indians were killed and corn crops were destroyed. To the claim that the tribute was in return for defense, the red men on the banks of the Hudson pleaded that they had not only looked out

for themselves, but had for two winters supplied food and other necessaries to the Dutch
when long ago they were building a ship, and
had always paid for everything they had received. The Raritans took quick revenge for
the assault upon them by sweeping out of
existence by murder and fire the colony of De
Vries on Staten Island. Kieft responded by a
proclamation offering ten fathoms of wampum
for the head of every Raritan, and twice as
much for that of one of the murderers. The
bounties enlisted some red men on the side of
the whites. Twenty years before an Indian
who had come with his nephew to Fort Amsterdam to sell furs was killed without provocation. At this time of disturbed relations
between the races the nephew sought revenge
by killing an inoffending blacksmith named
Claes Smits. The tribe protected him for the
act, and the director did not venture on his
own authority to arrest him. The incident is
notable because it was the occasion for the first
exercise of popular rights in the colony. Kieft
was so much alarmed by the course of events
that he summoned all the masters and heads of
families in and near Manhattan to meet at
Fort Amsterdam. To this popular assemblage
he submitted the question whether the murder
of Claes Smits should not be punished, and in

case the tribe would not surrender the culprit
if it would not be just to destroy the village to
which he belonged. Twelve selectmen were
chosen to consider the matter. They were all
Hollanders, and De Vries was named as president of the Twelve. The advice of the Twelve
was to ask for the surrender of the murderer,
and in the mean time to procure coats of mail
for the soldiers, and to await the hunting season before offensive operations.

Kieft was intent on war, but it was six
months before he could secure the assent of the
Twelve for an expedition. In January, 1642,
they assented to an expedition under the personal command of the director, and with ammunition and supplies furnished by the company.
As the price of such concessions the Twelve
demanded from the director a reconstruction
of the council, with a fair representation of
the people. They insisted also that the militia should be organized and armed, and that
judicial proceedings should be before the full
council. They asked besides for the removal
of restrictions on trade for themselves, for the
exclusion of cows and sheep brought from New
England because they interfered with those
brought from Holland, and for an increase in
the value of the currency. The director un-
graciously gave promise to admit popular rep-

resentatives to the council, to exclude New England cows and sheep, and to amend the currency. But the Twelve men, he declared, had been chosen only to advise relative to the murder of Claes Smits, and as that duty was finished he dismissed them and forbade any meetings of the people without his order, as they "tend to dangerous consequences." The chapter reads much like the experience of other peoples in other lands, where arbitrary power has been forced by necessity to appeal for the help of those who can bear arms and furnish supplies. The parallel is complete also in that the director never carried out his pledges. He, however, began his operations against the red men. An expedition was sent out, which, without bloodshed, secured a treaty for the delivery of the murderer, but he was never given up, and Director Kieft learned little from the experience.

While these events were in progress the religious controversies in New England, with the greater freedom of traffic in New Netherland, turned a strong tide of migration to the latter province. Several notable persons removed to Manhattan. Francis Doughty came for "freedom of conscience, which he missed in New England." John Throgmorton located on the East River with thirty-five English families "for the free exercise of their religion," driven out by the stern orthodoxy of Hugh Peters. The noted Anne Hutchinson was foremost among the religious immigrants of 1642, who, from persecution in Massachusetts and Connecticut, fled to find spiritual peace in New Netherland, and finally, with her family, to be butchered by the red men. The influx of English people at this period prompted the appointment of an English secretary as an officer of the province.

The director general was busy with many things besides the administration of the colony. He set up a distillery and buckskin factory on Staten Island. At the charge of the company he built a stone hotel to entertain travelers near the fort. A new church, also of stone, with oak shingles, was erected, and it is narrated that at a wedding feast, "after the fourth or fifth round of drinking," subscriptions were completed for the purpose. The coming of Domine Johannes Megapolensis to Rensselaerwyck, the first clergyman for the interior of the province, gave a prudent counselor in secular affairs as well as a faithful religious teacher.

In 1643, a serious Indian outbreak occurred. The immediate occasion was the stealing of a beaver-skin coat from a red man at Hackensack, where he had been drinking. He gath-

ered some of his tribe and killed a colonist,
Van Voorst, who was quietly at work. The
Indians at once offered to pay an atonement of
two hundred fathoms of wampum, and protested
against the sale of liquor to their young men.
The director general would listen to nothing
but the giving up of the murderer. At the
same time, the Mohawks, in collecting tribute
from the tribes on the lower Hudson, enforced
their power by killing and capture, so that their
tributaries fled before them, and sought shelter
with the Dutch in Westchester. Kieft took
advantage of this circumstance to wreak vengeance for the murder of Smits and Van Voorst.
At Pavonia, the Dutch fell upon the Indians as
they slept, and slew men, women, and children
to the number of eighty persons. At Corlaer's
Hook, forty persons were butchered with like
circumstances of atrocity. The result was to
drive the river tribes into a union, and eleven
of them combined to carry terror to the Dutch.
Kieft made a general levy for two months, and
the colonists hastened to Fort Amsterdam and
other strong places. The property of the Dutch
was ravaged, and destruction threatened the
province. Adriaensen, who led the slaughter at
Corlaer's Hook, was one of the chief losers. He
became so excited as to try to assassinate the
director general, and was arrested and sent to

Holland for trial. Kieft proclaimed a day of fasting and prayer, while the colonists held him responsible and talked about sending him for trial to Amsterdam. The Indians of Long Island, however, soon made advances for peace, and a treaty was framed with them and soon after with the river tribes. But the pacification was outward, and left rankling sores on the part of the red men. The director general found it necessary to forbid the sale of liquor to any of the tribes.

Peace was not long maintained. Attacks were made by the red men on boats coming down the Hudson River from Fort Orange, their furs were seized, and some of the crews slain. Once the red men were beaten back with loss of their warriors. Colonists were killed, too, often by red men who approached as friends. The situation grew very serious, and a second time the director general appealed to the people " to elect five or six persons from among themselves " to consider the emergency. Eight men were chosen, and they agreed upon preparations for war against the river tribes, while peace was to be kept up with the Long Island Indians. Among the soldiers enrolled were fifty Englishmen, who came from New England, and who were placed under the command of John Underhill, who had kept his fame as a fighter. The red men were more prompt than the Dutch. They swept with fire and slaughter in every direction, and the colonists who could escape fled to Manhattan. The destruction was relieved by the gallant defense made by Lady Deborah Moody, who had been dealt with by the church at Salem for denying baptism to infants, and now at Gravesend, with forty supporters, repelled the savage attack, and held her position. This was almosɩ the sole oasis in the red desert of carnage. Only under the shelter of Fort Amsterdam was security felt. An officer relieving guard even here was shot in the arm.

In his extremity the director general sent delegates to Connecticut to ask for help; but it was refused. Fortunately, a hundred and thirty Dutch soldiers arrived in the nick of time, from Curaçoa, in the West Indies, sent by Peter Stuyvesant, director there. This relief may have decided the struggle which threatened to turn against the colony. De Vries, who had been a friend of peace and was trusted by the Indians, having been ruined by the war, left the colony to return home, and his parting with Kieft was like that of a Hebrew prophet: "The murders in which you have shed so much innocent blood will yet be avenged on your own head."

The Eight resolved to appeal to the fatherland. They sent an address to the West India Company, full of plaintive recital of their troubles. Famine was now threatening them, for they could not till the land by reason of the war. They also submitted to the States General a statement of their suffering and weakness, and of the strength which the savage foe possessed from the familiarity which he now had with firearms. At the same time they urged the importance of " the sea-coast, bays, and large rivers" to Dutch commerce. The Eight charged the director general with bringing on hostilities with the Indians without sufficient cause, and with making misrepresentations concerning the resources and growth of the colony. He had especially offended by imposing taxes upon his own authority, to the great indignation of the people. The removal of Kieft was demanded with a new system and policy.

Both the West India Company and the States General were stirred by these appeals to consider the affairs of New Netherland. The company was bankrupt, chiefly through its operations in Brazil. It had lost five hundred and fifty thousand guilders, above all receipts, in New Netherland. A report to the States General recommended the recall of Kieft, the abandonment of his warlike policy towards the Indians, the adjustment of the boundaries with the English, and the settlement of towns rather than scattered farms. It was proposed to reconstruct the council, so that it should consist of the director, a vice-director, and fiscal, and this council was to exercise wide authority. Provision was made for delegates from the commonalty to meet every six months at Manhattan "for the common advancement of the welfare of the inhabitants." The introduction of negroes from Brazil was recommended, and general trade was allowed with that country. No firearms were to be sold to the Indians, and charges upon exports and imports were to be relied upon for revenue.

The Indian war was prosecuted with the usual incidents of such struggles until 1645. Kieft had learned by the condemnation in Holland and the odium in the colony that his conduct towards the red men had been a blunder, and he sought diligently to secure peace. He framed treaties with some of the minor tribes, and for the first time visited the Mohawks, for whose friendship he was anxious. With them a treaty was signed at Fort Orange, and a general peace followed. This was confirmed by a treaty at Fort Amsterdam, where the Mohawks appeared for the Five Nations as arbitrators.

The 6th of September was appointed as a day of thanksgiving "to proclaim the good tidings."

The chronicles narrate that sixteen hundred red men were killed during the two years of hostilities. The scattered settlements were almost obliterated. Manhattan could count only about a hundred men besides the traders. Rensselaerwyck and the colony on the South River had been exempt from the carnage.

The company in Holland decided to remove Kieft, and the decision did not improve his relations with the colonists. They talked freely, and he imposed fines and banishment, refusing appeal to the home authorities. Domine Bogardus, from his pulpit, said, " What are the great men of the country but vessels of wrath and fountains of woe and trouble? They think of nothing but to plunder the property of others, to dismiss, to banish, to transport to Holland." Kieft retorted by charging the domine with drunkenness, and emphasized his retort by staying away from church services, and having drums beat and cannon fired to interrupt them.

In spite of all strife the settlements expanded as soon as the Indian hostilities ceased. Brooklyn set up a municipal government in 1646. Mines of valuable ore, quicksilver and gold, were reported on Staten Island and towards the South River. Barytes supposed to be gold

was found in the Catskills, and dreams of fortune intoxicated many persons. Long Island
was accounted prosperous, as was Rensselaerwyck. The boweries or farms, besides, were
about fifty. The whole province, it was estimated, could furnish not more than three hundred fighting-men, and its entire population
must, therefore, have been less than fifteen
hundred or at most two thousand souls.

Kieft closed his administration in unpopular-
ity, and at the inauguration of his successor a
vote of thanks was refused to him. Kuyter
and Melyn led the hostile party, and petitioned
for an investigation of his conduct. Their
complaints were dismissed, and they were subjected to counter-charges. They were formally
indicted, Melyn for rebellion, and Kuyter for
counseling treachery toward the red men. The
new director took strong grounds against them,
and refused to allow them to appeal to Holland
when they were sentenced. Melyn's sentence
was seven years' banishment and a fine of three
hundred guilders, with forfeiture of all benefits
derived from the company. Kuyter was to suffer three years' banishment, and to pay a fine
of one hundred and fifty guilders. Kieft sailed
for Holland on the ship Princess, carrying with
him a fortune of four hundred thousand guil
ders. His two accusers were also among the

passengers, with Domine Bogardus and other persons of note. The vessel was wrecked in Bristol Channel. Kieft, in the danger, addressed his accusers: "Friends, I have been unjust toward you; can you forgive me?" He with eighty other persons, including Domine Bogardus, was drowned. Kuyter and Melyn were saved, went to Holland, and afterwards returned to Manhattan. They were uneasy spirits to the end.

The verdict of history must be that Kieft wrought great mischief by his rage against the red men and his lack of administrative wisdom. His greed and his violence were not offset by any important services rendered to the colony. The redeeming traits in his administration are the advent of the Twelve and the Eight as representatives of the people in the government.

CHAPTER V.

CULMINATION OF THE DUTCH SWAY.

1647–1663.

THE successor of Kieft as director general was Peter Stuyvesant, who had already rendered the colony important service by sending military help, during the Indian war, from Curaçoa. He had held the like position there, and had, by an attack on the Portuguese island of St. Martin, won praise for courage and censure for misjudgment. He was the son of a clergyman in Friesland, had received considerable education, and was now forty-five years of age. Ill health had taken him to Holland from his post in the West Indies, at the time of the controversies between the Eight men and Director Kieft, and the company naturally turned to him on account of his experience and character, as a desirable person for the more difficult and influential station at Manhattan. Van Dincklagen, whose quarrrel with Van Twiller has made him known to us, had received a provisional appointment for the chief place, but before he sailed was named as vice-director under Stuyvesant.

Great joy was manifested in Manhattan when Stuyvesant and his party landed there, May 27, 1647. He had been long expected, for he had been appointed nearly two years before. He put on airs on his arrival, strutted " like a peacock," and " as if he were the Czar of Muscovy," say the chroniclers. He was a notable figure. He had lost a leg in the attack on St. Martin's, and had supplied its place with one, called silver by one writer, and wooden by others, and in fact doubtless of wood with silver bands. He was autocratic in manner, decided in speech, and prompt in action. He was a devoted churchman, was diligent in his duties, and devoted to the interests of the company and the colony, as he understood them. His arbitrary conduct continued the struggle between the settlers and the ruler, so flagrant under his predecessor. The new code of instructions which he brought with him required him to guard against encroachments on the boundaries of the colony, to preserve peace with the Indians, and to encourage the settlement of the colonists in villages. Delegates were to be invited from the outlying hamlets to the council in Manhattan, and some mitigation was ordered in the severe restrictions on trade. The home company had learned that consideration must be extended to the settlers, but necessity was more imperative than the instructions and extended further. Fort Amsterdam needed repairs, and the cost of general administration must be met. The director must have money, and he could get it only from the people. Accordingly, by the advice of his council he ordered an election at which the settlers in Manhattan, Brooklyn, Amersfoort, and Pavonia were to designate eighteen persons from whom the director and council should select nine, " as good and faithful interlocutors and trustees of the commonalty," to confer with the director " on all means to promote the welfare of the commonalty and the country." Three were to sit in council in rotation to judge civil cases, and in each year six of the nine were to retire, but to be eligible for reëlection. This representation was a concession in return for taxation.

The director immediately asked for money for schools and for finishing the church, and a tax was voted for that purpose. The Nine refused to provide means for repairing the fort, on the ground that the company had agreed to maintain the defenses. They endeavored to encourage permanent settlers by concentrating trade in their hands. As a means not only for raising money, but for insuring safety, efforts were made to regulate the sale of liquor, especially to the red men, for "almost one full fourth part of the town of New Amsterdam" was devoted to "houses for the sale of brandy, tobacco, and beer." The sale of arms to the red men also caused trouble, and yet persons in official station, and even one of the Nine, were engaged in it. The director in his efforts to check this traffic made his first visit to Fort Orange in 1648, where Brandt van Slechtenhorst, a new agent of the patroon, claimed the right to sell arms and generally to act on his own discretion. Stuyvesant had to send troops to enforce the authority of the company, but finally set free from the patroon's title much of the land on which the city of Albany now stands.

Stuyvesant acted vigorously, even aggressively, for the company against all rivals. His troubles arose from his zeal in this direction, and not primarily from personal quarrels. Patroon, colonists, or even the States General, met in him a sturdy champion of the company which he served. His first controversy began, as was inevitable, over the finances. The Nine protested against the director's management. He insisted on the payment to the company of what was due to it, while he was lax in settling such claims as it owed. They complained also of the heavy charges levied upon trade. They proposed to send a delegation to Holland, and as the grievances ran on, the proposal was renewed. Stuyvesant was unwilling to have any appeal made to the home authorities except through him. In 1649 he suggested to the Nine to inquire " what approbation the commonalty would give to the business, and how the expenses should be defrayed." He would not permit the people to assemble, and the Nine sought counsel from house to house. The director was displeased at this course, and summoned delegates from the militia and the burghers, to consider the subject of a delegation. The Nine, finding events to be growing exciting, ordered a journal to be kept by Adriaen van der Donck, one of their number. The director seized the papers, arrested the writer, and put him in prison on the charge of libeling the government, and demanded that he should either retract or be excluded from the Nine and the council. This behest was ratified and the author of the journal was unseated, but the popular sympathy was strong in his favor.

Stuyvesant failed to obstruct the appeal to Holland. The Nine sent a petition to the States General, accompanied by an elaborate

" remonstrance " against the management of
the West India Company in the province, and
a detailed statement of grievances and of measures for relief. The first demand was for abdi-
cation of power by the company in favor of the
States General. The second was for a public
school with at least two good masters. The
third was for " godly, honorable, and intelligent rulers," because " a covetous governor
makes poor subjects," and " the mode in which
the country was then governed was intolerable." With public colonization New Netherland would on these conditions " in a few years
be a brave place, and be able to do service to
the Netherland nation, to pay richly the cost,
and to thank its benefactors."

Both sides sent representatives to Holland.
For the people, Van der Donck and two others
of the Nine appeared, with Domine Backerus,
who had served as the successor of Domine
Bogardus at New Amsterdam, and who now
returned, leaving Megapolensis as the only
clergyman in the province. On behalf of the
director, Cornelis van Tienhoven, his secretary,
was the delegate. By the Nine sixty-eight
specifications were submitted to the States·
General of " excessive and most prejudicial
neglect " on the part of the company, resulting
in making the condition of New Netherland far

inferior to that of New England. A committee
of the States General reported to that body in
1650 a "provisional order" for the settlement
of the controversy. In that document we can
discern the extent of the evils which really
existed, and the remedies which far-sighted
statesmen proposed. It condemned Kieft for
bringing on the Indian war, and forbade hostilities against "the aborigines or neighbors"
without action of the States General. It required that the sale of arms and ammunition to
the red men should be prevented, and the inhabitants enrolled as militia. Three clergymen were to be provided for the province, and
the youth were to be instructed by good schoolmasters. The commonalty was to be convoked
and was to choose two members of the council,
and the "collection, administration, and payment" of taxes were to be "placed on such
footing as their constituents should order."
The courts should be reorganized, and burgher
government was conceded in the "City of New
Amsterdam." Stuyvesant was to be called to
Holland to report, and a suitable person, "ex-
perienced in matters relating to agriculture,"
was to be dispatched to "take charge of the
country lying on both sides of the great North
River, extending south to the South River, and
north to the Fresh River."

The Amsterdam chamber criticised and opposed this provisional order. The contest was waged in the province and in Holland. The English in the province took the side of the director, while the Dutch were more and more arrayed against him, and the Nine renewed and expanded their complaints in additional papers forwarded to the States General. In Holland the "remonstrance" had been published, and was answered by a "brief statement" by the secretary, Van Tienhoven. Stuyvesant afforded fresh grounds for criticism by his operations against the Swedes on the South River, and by a treaty which he negotiated at Hartford concerning affairs and boundaries on the Fresh River. Dissensions arose between the various chambers of the West India Company, and the greed and control of the Amsterdam chamber were resented. In 1652 the Amsterdam chamber yielded, and removed the export duty on tobacco which had been collected in the province, permitted the importation of slaves from Africa, and reduced the charges for passage of emigrants. Burgher government was conceded to New Amsterdam with the condition that the schout or sheriff should maintain the privileges of the West India Company.

Stuyvesant was far enough away from Holland to exercise his own will with little let or

hindrance. He paid scant heed to the orders
of the States General in behalf of Kuyter and
Melyn against his sentence. While he tried
to prevent the sale of arms by others to the
Indians, he imported a case of guns himself to
sell to them, and the Amsterdam chamber censured him for the act and for the purchase of
lands on Manhattan Island for private purposes.
Patroon Van Rensselaer, in 1649, bought from
the red men tracts at Catskill and Claverack,
and to check such purchases the director secured for the company the Indian title to what
is now the chief part of Westchester County.
He refused to recognize the " provisional order "
of the States General. He prevented the mus-
tering of the burgher guard, and deprived the
Nine of the pew in the church which the con-
sistory had assigned to them. He neglected to
send to the authorities in Holland any copy of
the treaty which he negotiated at Hartford.
He set up a -body guard of four soldiers, who
attended him whenever he went abroad. In
his hate of Melyn he seized a ship in which
the latter had returned from Europe, and on a
technicality confiscated vessel and cargo, for
which, after a long suit, the West India Company was compelled to make restitution. Stuyvesant went even further. He sent soldiers to
arrest the vice-director, Van Dincklagen, and

held him a prisoner in a guard-room for several days. Dirck van Schelluyne, a notary public, who had come out in 1650 to practice his profession, had given the vice-director professional aid, and was forbidden to practice further. The schout-fiscal, Van Dyck, was excluded from the council. With such a high hand Stuyvesant bore sway, and, like other arbitrary rulers, fell into the practice of mingling his resentments with his assertion of authority. Like his predecessor, he taught the colonists to consult for their own rights and interests.

Under the Dutch sway religion and education received early and constant attention. In 1650 William Vestens was sent from Amsterdam as schoolmaster and consoler of the sick. A common school was maintained at the time with a succession of teachers. In 1652 Domine Samuel Drisius, who could preach in Dutch, French, and English, was sent as colleague for Megapolensis, at a salary of fourteen hundred and fifty guilders, and Domine Gideon Schaats, at a salary of eight hundred guilders, came out to Rensselaerwyck as preacher and schoolmaster. Four years later Domine Johannes Theodorus Polhemus, who had been in Brazil, arrived and was made pastor of the church at Flatbush. Brooklyn had no separate pastor until 1660, when Domine Henry Selyns came from Holland to occupy that position. In 1654 the Lutherans asked permission to erect a church in New Amsterdam, but the director refused to permit them to do so, and an appeal to the West India Company brought the answer that no other doctrine should be encouraged in the province than "the true reformed." The classis of Amsterdam in Holland claimed spiritual jurisdiction over the province. Domine Megapolensis, zealous in seeking to instruct the red men, was no less intent on enforcing the teachings of the Synod of Dort. In the English settlements these teachings were not accepted as binding, and there were Lutherans among the Dutch. On the appeal of the reformed clergymen Director Stuyvesant, in 1656, issued a proclamation forbidding preachers not called by ecclesiastical or temporal authority to hold meetings, under a penalty of a hundred pounds; and any person attending assemblages addressed by such preachers was to be fined twenty-five pounds. The prohibition was vigorously enforced until the West India Company rebuked the director, and declared its purpose to let the Lutherans and logically others outside of the reformed communion "enjoy all calmness and tranquillity." In the succeeding year, however, John Ernestus Goetwater, a Lutheran clergyman who had been sent out to

preach, was notified that "he might have freedom within his own dwelling," but could not
organize a church, and he was silenced. Two
Quaker women, Dorothy Waugh and Mary
Witherhead, banished from Boston, were imprisoned for preaching in the streets, but were
discharged after a few days. Robert Hodgson,
a Quaker, fared worse for preaching in Flushing. He was taken to the dungeon of Fort
Amsterdam, was fined and set to work, and
failing in his task was beaten with a tarred
rope until he fell. He was finally released and
compelled to leave the province. In Jamaica
and Flushing and Heemstede, also, severe measures were taken against Quaker teachers and
such as listened to them, and fines and imprisonment were imposed on many persons. So
abominable was the heresy regarded, and so
dangerous, that Stuyvesant and his council proclaimed a fast day to check its progress. The
authorities in Holland found it necessary to
warn the clergymen of New Amsterdam against
"overbearing preciseness," and to counsel them
to try, by adhering to old forms rather than
new, to keep the Lutherans within the fold.

The States General in 1661 sought to tempt
immigrants by inviting "Christian people of
tender conscience, in England or elsewhere oppressed," to make homes within the jurisdiction

of Stuyvesant. He, however, kept up his persecutions of the Quakers until he banished John Bowne for holding meetings of the sect in his own house. The martyr proceeded to Amsterdam, and the directors of the West India Company, after listening to his plea, rebuked Stuyvesant and announced to him this rule of religious freedom: "Let every one remain free as long as he is modest, moderate, his political conduct irreproachable, and as long as he does not offend others or oppose the government. This maxim of moderation has always been the guide of our magistrates in this city, and the consequence has been that people have flocked from every land to this asylum. Tread thus in their steps and we doubt not you will be blessed."

February 2, 1653, Stuyvesant issued his proclamation to set in motion the burgher government conceded to the city of New Amsterdam. He assumed the authority to name the burgomasters, the schepens, and the fiscal. One of the first tasks of the new government was to provide for the defense of the city, for war had broken out between England and Holland. The New England colonies were also ready for attack, excited by a charge that the Dutch governor had tried to hire the Indians to kill all the English. The people set to work on the defenses, provided for money by loan and then by tax, and a ditch and palisades twelve feet high with a breastwork were constructed inclosing the city from the East to the North River. Fort Orange was also prepared for defense. Stuyvesant undertook to adjust the difficulties with New England, and invited commissioners to come to New Amsterdam for the purpose. Their visit produced no direct result other than to incite Captain John Underhill to hoist the colors of the English parliament at Heemstede and Flushing, and to seek to stir up armed revolt. He was banished from the colony and fled to Rhode Island, where a commission was given to him and to others to prey on Dutch commerce. The attempt to organize war between the colonies failed for the time, although by excluding Dutch vessels from New England harbors and renewing and publishing the charges of inciting the Indians to slaughter, the eastern colonists kept alive the embers of strife.

Under this stress and a movement from the colonists on Long Island, delegates convened to consult for the welfare of the country. A preliminary gathering arranged for a popular convention at New Amsterdam, December 10, 1653. The delegates came from New Amsterdam, Brooklyn, Flushing, Middleburg, Heemstede,

3092

Amersfoort, Flatbush, and Gravesend. Four Dutch and four English towns were represented by ten persons of Dutch nativity and nine of English nativity. This convention unanimously adopted a remonstrance to the States General protesting against the course of the director and council in enacting laws and appointing officers without the consent of the people, and against the granting of large tracts of land to favored individuals. Stuyvesant prepared a formal answer to this document. The remonstrance is a singularly clear declaration of popular rights combined with loyalty to the States General. The answer is a spiteful arraignment of the delegates and a bold denial of the wisdom of elections, where "each would vote for one of his own stamp, the thief for a thief, the rogue, the tippler, and the smuggler for his brother in iniquity, so that he may enjoy more latitude in vice and fraud." To a rejoinder the director responded with an order to the delegates to disperse, with his declaration: "We derive our authority from God and the company, not from a few ignorant subjects, and we alone can call the inhabitants together."

The burgomasters and schepens appealed to the West India Company for fuller powers for the municipal government, like those of the home city, especially for the election of the fiscal and complete control of the whole excise, and power to levy new taxes and to farm out the ferry between New Amsterdam and Brooklyn. The magistrates of Gravesend, by letter, renewed their allegiance to the States General and the company, while reciting certain grievances, and François le Bleeuw, an advocate, went as agent to Holland to plead the popular cause.

Such events did not tend to reduce the friction in the province, where the English began to show sympathy with the eastern colonists just at the time that Connecticut seized on the Fort of Good Hope at Hartford, and news came that Cromwell had sent four ships of war to help in the capture of "the Manhattoes" and any place held by the Dutch on the Hudson River. New England was ready for active hostilities, when information was received of the ratification of the treaty of peace between England and Holland, April 15, 1654, and the threatened collision was postponed. Stuyvesant showed zeal, courage, and capacity in his preparations for defense, and he granted some privileges to the Dutch towns which took part with him in the work.

Bleeuw, the agent of the burghers, was not received with favor by the Amsterdam chamber. On the contrary, the members declared

that Stuyvesant should have acted with more
vigor, and commanded him to punish the com-
plainants so that others might be deterred from
following their example. They charged the
burgomasters and schepens to "submit to the
government placed over them," and "in nowise
to hold particular convention with the English
or others on affairs of state which do not per-
tain to you, and what is yet worse, attempt an
alteration in the state and its government."
The director soon resumed the control of the
excise, which he farmed out. He found people
at Beaverwyck and on the lands of the patroon
about Fort Orange unwilling to pay taxes to
the company. Trouble befell him also from
the affairs on the South River, for at this time
Fort Casimir was surprised, and he secured only
partial satisfaction by seizing a Swedish ship,
the Shark, which by mistake entered Manhattan Bay. The purchase by English colonists of
land in what is now Westchester County and
at Oyster Bay called out protests from the director, but they proved of no effect. The English at Gravesend had hoisted a British flag
and given signs of sedition.

Yet Stuyvesant must have regarded affairs
as in the main satisfactory, for in December,
1654, he took a trip to the West Indies to establish trade with those islands. The vessels

he took were seized by British commissioners, who enforced a rigid embargo. As soon as he returned the recovery of Fort Casimir demanded his attention. He was absent on the South River when New Amsterdam and its vicinity were startled by a demonstration by Indians in force. Van Dyck, who had been schout-fiscal, had killed a squaw for stealing peaches from his garden, and bands of the river tribes, said to number nineteen hundred, appeared in canoes before the city, in the early morning, September 15, 1655. They killed Van Dyck with an arrow and another burgher with an axe, before they were driven back to their canoes. They turned their weapons against Hoboken, Pavonia, and Staten Island, and in three days a hundred Dutch settlers were killed, a hundred and fifty taken prisoners, and the damages were estimated at two hundred thousand guilders. Some of the prisoners were ransomed, and Stuyvesant entered into treaties with the red men on Long Island and renewed intimate alliance with the Mohawks. Help was asked from the authorities in Holland, block-houses were erected at exposed points, the settlers were enjoined to form villages for self-defense, and after a while arms were furnished to some of the inhabitants with which to protect themselves. For three years peace was preserved.

Esopus then became the seat of new troubles. The settlers there insisted on living at a distance from the centre and each other, and since they had found liquor the readiest means of buying furs from the red men they paid them in the desired commodity. Quarrels were the natural result, and persons were killed and houses burned. Stuyvesant visited the place, conferred with the red men, promised them presents, and found it necessary to guard the settlers by soldiers. Some of these became excited at seeing the red men in a drunken carouse and fired on them. This slaughter was revenged by the seizure of Dutch prisoners, eight of whom were burned at the stake, and by the destruction of buildings and crops. A truce was secured through the mediation of the Mohawks, with whom the Dutch, with much formality, had framed fresh treaties. But hostilities were revived; the soldiers attacked the red men, and took prisoners, most of whom were sent to the West Indies, but one of the oldest chiefs was, after capture, killed with his own tomahawk. Not until 1660 was a treaty of peace framed, when a Mohawk and a Minqua sachem acted as arbitrators, and enjoined upon both parties to live in amity.

In 1656 Stuyvesant conceded to the burgo-masters and schepens of New Amsterdam the right to nominate their successors, subject to his approval. After some friction the privileges of Westchester were enlarged and a village was set up, now known as Jamaica. In 1658 a petition was submitted to the Amsterdam chamber for a master for a Latin school, and the next year Alexander Carolus Curtius, a professor in Lithuania, came out in that capacity, but he gave way in 1661 to Domine Aegidius Luyck, whose reputation drew pupils from families as far away as Virginia and the Carolinas.

The province was growing in these years, notwithstanding Indian troubles and religious controversies. New Harlaem secured a village charter. A municipal court was established at Esopus, under the name of Wiltwyck, the first in the present county of Ulster. Settlers were planting homes north and west of Fort Orange, and, in 1661, Arendt van Curler, for love and trust for whom the white governors were long known to the red men by the name by which they called him, " Corlaer, " was authorized to buy the " Great Flats " where Schenectady now stands. In 1642 he was the first from the south and east to penetrate the Mohawk country, visiting the castles, and seeking to mitigate the condition of Father Jogues and other French prisoners. He not only reported the lands "the most beautiful that eye ever saw," but established with the red men a friendship both romantic and beneficent. Bergen received name and local magistrates, and marked the beginning of municipal administration in the present State of New Jersey. The West India Company secured all the patroon titles on Staten Island, and gave grants of land there to Waldenses and Huguenots. An association of Mennonists was assisted to locate south of the city.

Esopus was again to be the centre of strife and carnage. In 1663 the continued sale of liquor and fire-arms to the red men threatened trouble; but the settlers permitted themselves to be surprised, when the village of Wiltwyck was nearly destroyed, with the loss of twenty-one lives, and forty-five, chiefly women and children, carried into captivity. Expeditions were sent from New Amsterdam, so that the red men were punished, and the settlements at this point were strengthened.

CHAPTER VI.

ON various occasions the English settlers, especially on Long Island, had given signs that they were a distinct body from the Dutch inhabitants. They had acted together for or against Director Stuyvesant as they had seen fit. In the appeals to Holland against him they had joined in declarations of hearty loyalty to the fatherland. In 1663 several of them residing in Jamaica, Middleburg, and Heemstede sent a petition to Hartford asking Connecticut to cast " the skirts of its government" over them to protect them from their " bondage," and suggesting also the seizure of the Dutch towns on Long Island. The general assembly of Connecticut challenged the authority of the West India Company except as a trading corporation, and the English settlers on Long Island seemed intent on actual revolution. To meet the emergency Stuyvesant called a convention of delegates at New Amsterdam. Eight towns were

represented, while those on the upper Hudson
sent no delegates. The remedy for the evils
was, as so often before, an appeal to Holland,
now especially for formal proclamation of the
rights of the West India Company, in a form to
restrain the English and to confirm the loyalty
of the Dutch settlers. In the mean time Stuyvesant agreed to a proposition from Connecticut
to forbear the exercise of jurisdiction by either
claimant in Westchester and on Long Island.

The signs of English aggression multiplied.
John Scott, who had brought out stringent
orders for the enforcement of the British navigation laws in the colonies, and who claimed
that Long Island belonged to the Duke of York,
was designated a commissioner by Connecticut,
and he organized a combination of the English
towns on Long Island. He was chosen president of the combination, which was to last
until the English king or the Duke of York
should establish a government over the town.
He tried to draw the Dutch towns on the island
into the combination, but they refused to join
in it. In 1664 Stuyvesant and Scott made an
arrangement by which the question of jurisdiction should be referred to England and Holland for adjustment. In the mean time the
English towns were for twelve months to be
under the English crown, and the Dutch towns

under the States General, but the latter were to pay royalties to the English king.

The Dutch authorities determined to fortify New Amsterdam and to increase its military force, so as to maintain two hundred militiamen and a hundred and sixty regular soldiers. Another popular convention was held in 1664, and twelve towns sent delegates. The first demand was for the provincial government to protect the people against the savages and " the malignant English." The convention wanted the States General or the company to meet the expense. Director Stuyvesant responded that the company had spent on the province twelve hundred thousand guilders more than it had received. The convention received from the States General answers to the appeals of the preceding year. The authority of the West India Company was ratified and proclaimed, and the provincial government was ordered to exterminate the Indians about Esopus, to check the English, and to subject the revolted settlers to allegiance. To help in these tasks sixty additional soldiers were sent out. The Esopus war was ended by a treaty of peace, which was celebrated by a day of thanksgiving. The revolt on Long Island and the aggressions of the English from without, the convention pronounced beyond its power to meet. The let-

ters of the States General were indeed laughed
to scorn in the English towns, and Governor
Winthrop formally repudiated the temporary
arrangement for jurisdiction and asserted the
absolute title of the English king.

Vessels were already at sea, sent by the Duke
of York, as Lord High Admiral of England, to
enforce his claims not only to Long Island, but
to the whole of New Netherland. Rumors of
the expedition had reached Director Stuyvesant, but a dispatch from the Amsterdam chamber announced that the purpose of the Duke
of York was to establish Episcopacy in the
English colonies and to look after their affairs.
The English squadron, however, after rendez-
vousing at Gardiner's Island, summoned help
from Massachusetts and Connecticut, and came
to anchor off Coney Island. It blockaded the
river and the bay, seized several vessels, and
August 29, 1664, the commander, Colonel Richard Nicolls, demanded the surrender of the
" towns situated on the island commonly known
by the name of Manhattoes, with all the forts
thereunto belonging."

The town was in no condition for defense.
The fort had been pronounced untenable. The
burghers had long been impressed with the neglect of the Dutch authorities at home. Stuyvesant was plucky and loyal and wanted to

resist, but he notified the Amsterdam chamber that " Long Island was gone and lost," and New Amsterdam " could not hold out much longer." Nicolls, the English commander, adroitly promised to hold the place subject to negotiations between the home governments, and to extend to the Dutch equal privileges with the English in case the surrender should be made. In vain Stuyvesant stood on one of the angles of the fort, ready to fire on the fleet, for the domines in behalf of the people begged him to desist. Placing himself at the head of his little garrison, he then proposed to resist the landing of the English, when petitions of men, women, and children came to him to surrender, and he sadly answered, " I would much rather be carried out dead." A formal remonstrance against further opposition was signed by most of the officers and many principal inhabitants, and the brave director was compelled to yield. Security of property, liberty of conscience, and of church discipline, and the maintenance of existing customs of inheritance, were guaranteed to the Dutch settlers, and military pride was flattered by allowing the garrison to " march out with their arms, drums beating and colors flying and lighted matches." The surrender was made September 3, but was not formally completed until September 8.

The treachery of James Stuart, Duke of York, thus broke the Dutch domination in New Netherland, and foreshadowed its end. The Dutch rule had lacked system, vigor, constructive and generative force. The divided authority in Holland had rendered it weak in matters of vast moment, and negligent of provision for large growth and permanent prosperity. The personal power confided to the director general encouraged him in an arbitrary policy, and the temper of the incumbents of that office did not tend to diminish the evil inherent in the system. Those very evils developed here, as such causes elsewhere have done, resistance to oppression and the assertion of popular rights. The intellectual and religious activity and freedom which illuminated the home country at that epoch were transferred to New Netherland, and while something of the intolerance which in that age was so general stained its records, this colony beyond any other, except that founded by Roger Williams, was the refuge of the persecuted of every sect. One of the last acts of Stuyvesant was to welcome a company of French Huguenots, and in spite of his own previous attitude, one of his last communications to his directors proclaimed that it " would be highly desirable that the yet waste lands which might feed a hundred thousand in-

habitants, should be settled and cultivated by
the oppressed; on the one side by the Roman
Catholics in France, Savoy, Piedmont, and elsewhere, and on the other by the Turks in Hungary and upon the confines of Germany." This
was a vision of cosmopolitan growth not common in those days. But New Netherland had
even then a population more diversified than
any other American colony. Stuyvesant estimated it at full ten thousand in number, but
others placed it at six thousand. Perhaps eight
thousand is a liberal estimate. Agriculture was
prospering ; the trade inland with the red men
was profitable and was extending. The Amsterdam chamber declared, when its population
and navigation " should become permanently
established, when the ships of New Netherland
ride on every part of the ocean, then numbers,
now looking to that coast with eager eyes, will
be allured to embark for your island." Stuyvesant labored to extend the foreign trade of
the province, but he was met on every hand by
British restriction, by the severe enforcement
of the navigation laws, and by a jealousy which
was argus-eyed, and a rivalry which brooked
no competition.

His surrender galled his proud spirit, but it
was unavoidable. He was summoned to Holland to give account of his conduct, and bore

with him warm testimonials of the burgomasters, and was in the end sustained by the government, although the West India Company
blamed him for the consequences of its own
neglect. When by the Treaty of Breda the
Dutch finally conceded the American colony to
the English, Stuyvesant set about increasing
its commerce by securing concessions to Dutch
vessels. Returning to New York, he made his
farm, the Bowery, a feature in the town, and
died at the age of eighty. His monument may
still be seen by the studious visitor.

The Dutch soldiers were sent aboard ship,
destined for Holland, as Nicolls, the English
commander, at the head of his infantry, took
possession of Fort Amsterdam. The Long
Island and New England auxiliaries were not
allowed to enter the town, and were soon dismissed to their homes. The city was at once
officially named New York and the fort was
called Fort James. The English governor surrounded himself with English counselors and
an English secretary, occasionally summoning
one or two of the former Dutch counselors for
advice. The religious situation remained as it
had been except that services after the Episcopal order were established in addition to those
previously held.

Fort Orange accepted the terms of capitulation and was christened Albany, and an English garrison was placed there under command of Captain Manning. An oath of allegiance to Great Britain was required of the settlers while they lived in its territories, and it was freely taken as it included no renunciation in terms of the Dutch government.

The boundaries of the colony called for early attention. Commissioners awarded Long Island, then styled Yorkshire, to New York, and refused to it the land claimed in its behalf on the Connecticut River, and adjudged for an eastern limit a line running from the head of Mamaroneck Creek to the north - northwest, "about twenty miles from any part of the Hudson River." This line, it was charged, was the result of a trick on the part of the Connecticut delegates, — one of the earliest "Yankee tricks."

Governor Nicolls was the personal representative of the Duke of York, whose patent authorized him to make all laws and to carry on the government. In no other colony was arbitrary power so distinctly recognized. It was a formality, therefore, in which the governor indulged, when he summoned a meeting of two delegates from each town to consider a code proposed by him. The meeting assembled at Hempstead (for English forms were now adopted for the old Dutch names) February 28, 1665, and thirty-four delegates appeared. They asked for the privilege of electing their own officers, but this was contrary to the duke's commission and was not granted. Since they were not permitted to do anything else they thankfully accepted the code as prepared, and it was promulgated as " The Duke's Laws." It was systematic and elaborate, establishing courts, town offices, and certain rates. It required a church to be built in every parish, and no minister was allowed to officiate without testimonials of ordination. It provided that "no persons should be molested, fined, or imprisoned for differing in matters of religion who profess Christianity." The code was only gradually applied in practice, and the prejudices of the Dutch were regarded. The task was to bring the Dutch, who were a large majority, under English laws and English rule, and in the main Governor Nicolls showed moderation and discretion.

The municipal government of the city which had become New York was at that early day, as so often since, the cause of trouble. The Dutch system was set aside, and the English plan of mayor and aldermen was established by the governor, with Captain Thomas Willett as the first mayor. At Albany, where he licensed "the only English schoolmaster," the governor found that the Mohawks and the Mohicans had quarreled and some Dutch persons were killed. The murderers were detected, and one Indian was hanged and another was sent in chains to Fort James. At Esopus the military rule was strengthened with an injunction to the commander to maintain peaceful relations with the burghers. The forethought of the governor did not prevent a riot, which it required all his sagacity finally to adjust. By purchase from the Indians the domain of the Duke of York in this vicinity was extended, and especial effort was made to attract settlers.

In 1665 Ralph Hall and his wife, Mary, were brought up for trial for witchcraft and sorcery, but the jury, in spite of "some suspicions," found "nothing considerable" against them. They were, however, put under bonds, which Governor Nicolls, at the end of three years, ordered canceled. The treatment of the charge affords notable contrast to the action taken elsewhere under the dictates of superstition and cruelty.

As war progressed between England and the Dutch republic, Governor Nicolls enforced a policy of confiscation of the property of such Dutch people as had not taken the oath of allegiance. When the Dutch power was restored vengeance was taken in turn.

Interruption of trade with Holland caused serious disaster to the colony, and relations with England were not yet sufficient to make up the deficiency. Of revenue the collections were inadequate to meet the charges upon it, and the private fortune of Governor Nicolls was exhausted in supporting the government. He sought to make up his losses by methods not above criticism. On Long Island discontent was general, in large part on account of " The Duke's Laws," and the Court of Assizes issued a decree against sedition, under which several persons were punished by fines and the stocks.

The Duke of York, without consulting the governor, gave away to Lord Berkeley and Sir George Carteret a vast tract of land to be called New Jersey. On the other hand Governor Nicolls claimed for the duke all the islands from Cape Cod to Cape May, and sent a commission to Martha's Vineyard, where he collected customs. Staten Island he confiscated to the duke as the property of the West India Company.

In 1668 Governor Nicolls gave up his position and returned to personal service with the Duke of York. He was killed on board the flag-ship of the duke in the naval fight in Solebay, in 1672, and thus the seizure of New

Netherland was avenged. He bore on his departure from the colony the good-will of the people and won the approval of the ducal proprietor. His rule of four years was one of difficulties, for the colony was poor. The wars in Europe kept settlers away, while the French overran the northeastern part of New York. His position was trying, but he met his duties bravely. He sent out a privateer in 1667 against the French and the Dutch, and its captain, Exton, burned two forts in Acadia and captured as "many guns and other plunder" as his vessel could carry. Nicolls asserted all the prerogatives of his patron, but he maintained liberty of conscience, and when he went away the testimony was given that "the several nations of Indians were never brought into such a peaceable posture and fair correspondence as by his means they now are."

The new governor was a court favorite, Francis Lovelace. His task, like that of Nicolls, was to bring the Dutch quietly under English authority. He fostered social relations between the Dutch and English settlers, and he was personally interested in building two ships. The prosperity of New York city was measured by the possession of four hundred houses. Some movement of migration toward the colony was indicated. He encouraged the

Lutherans to bring a minister from Holland, and sustained him against opposition, while the Reformed Church was protected in all its privileges, and the Presbyterians had a strong footing, particularly on Long Island. Religious freedom was thus fairly illustrated.

In 1667 petitions were presented to the governor from a number of towns asking for a legislature chosen by the freeholders, but answer was not given until the coming of Lovelace, who responded that he had no power to grant their request, and "nothing was required of them but obedience and submission to the laws of the government, as appears by his highness' commission." Three years later, when Governor Lovelace wanted a levy through the Court of Assizes for the repair of Fort James, several towns objected by petition and protest, declining to aid unless they should have the right of representation. He and his council ordered the papers to be publicly burned as " scandalous and seditious." Appeal was made by some Long Island towns to the king, and when war became flagrant between England and Holland a " benevolence " was asked instead of a tax.

In 1671 efforts were made to promote migration from New York to the Carolinas. Governor Lovelace sought to check it by requiring passports for departure, but the number of emigrants did not prove to be large.

Lovelace continued the policy of buying lands from the red men. A question which arose over the title to Staten Island was ended by him in favor of the Duke of York by a deed obtained by the payment of certain wampum and wares.

The establishment of post messengers between New York and Boston is to be credited to Governor Lovelace, and it is a sign of the growing intimacy between the colonies.

The Dutch navy had for many months been sweeping the seas in victory, and a fleet under Cornelis Evertsen and Jacob Binckes had been busy on the coast of America capturing and burning the tobacco ships of Virginia in spite of their armed convoys. Among the vessels captured was one bearing Captain James Carteret and his bride from New York to Virginia, and with them as a passenger was Samuel Hopkins. While the master of the ship represented New York to be strong in its armament and defenses, Hopkins reported truly that the garrison consisted of only sixty or eighty men, and that the fort was defended by only thirty to thirty-six cannon, that it would be difficult to raise more than three or four hundred men against a sudden assault, and that since Governor Love-

lace was absent, delay would occur in any defensive movement.

The opportunity was welcomed by the Dutch
commodores. They gathered their fleet off
Sandy Hook, and August 7, 1673, anchored opposite Staten Island. With seven ships of war,
they had sixteen prize vessels, and these bore
sixteen hundred men. The Dutch inhabitants
were gladdened at the sight, and many visited
the fleet, bearing information as well as con-
gratulations. The next day the fleet moved
within the Narrows, and anchored in sight of
the city.

Captain Manning, who had once been in command at Albany, and since Nicolls' coming prominent in the government, was, in the absence
of Governor Lovelace, in control at Fort James,
with Captain Carr, who had been in command
on the Delaware, as his chief counselor. He appealed for volunteers, seized provisions, and tried
to put the fort in condition for defense. Instead of giving help, the inhabitants spiked the
guns at the city hall, and left the garrison to its
fate. The Dutch commodores were nevertheless challenged to answer why they "had come
in such a hostile manner to disturb his majesty's subjects in this place?" and their answer
was, that the place "was their own, and their
own they would have," and they demanded the

surrender of the fort. The fleet was already
within musket-shot of the fort, and when Manning asked for delay until the next morning to
consult the mayor and aldermen, he was allowed
only half an hour. The Dutch commodores
promised " to all men their estates and liberties," and promptly at the time named opened
their broadsides on the fort, and killed and
wounded some of the garrison. The fort returned the fire, and "shot the general's ship
thro' and thro'." The Dutch landed six hundred men at the point where Wall Street now
reaches the East River, and these were joined
by four hundred of the burghers, and the latter urged an immediate advance to storm the
fort.

Such an attack was barely avoided. Manning asked for a parley and showed a flag of
truce, but Carr at the same time struck the
royal flag. The latter, when charged to convey
to the fort the conditions of surrender fixed by
the Dutch, fled instead of delivering the message. The army therefore began its march
down Broadway. Fortunately Captain Anthony Colve, the commander, received on the
way a proposal from Manning to surrender the
fort and garrison with the honors of war, and
promptly accepted it. The gates of the fort
were opened to him, the surrender was made

with colors flying and drums beating, a Dutch garrison was placed within the walls, and the ensign of the Dutch Republic was restored to the flagstaff, to float over New Netherland recovered by open assault in time of war.

The capture of New York was made by the Dutch fleet and forces without direct orders. The attack was a surprise to the local authorities, although warning had been received to put the fort in condition for defense. But with three fourths of the people Dutch in sympathy as well as in fact, defense was impracticable. The show of force might have been greater if proper preparations had been taken. The Dutch, however, came in numbers and might sufficient to make the conquest against all that the English authorities could have done. They yielded to a power too great for them.

New Netherland was once more the name of the colony, while the city became New Orange and the fort on the bay was called William Henry. The Dutch commodores summoned a council of war, and designated Captain Colve as governor general. Six burghers were invited to advise for the restoration of municipal government. The commodores issued a decree of confiscation of all English and French property. Vessels were sent up the river and reduced Esopus and Albany without resistance.

Most of the Long Island towns accepted the Dutch rule without delay. In New Jersey the conquest was at once recognized.

Governor Lovelace received word at New Haven of the capture of Fort James, and hurried to Long Island to defend his colony. He talked a little but did nothing, and soon accepted an invitation to visit the fort, where he was arrested for debt, his property fell under confiscation, and he was taken to Europe in one of the Dutch vessels. He was charged with being in debt to the Duke of York, and on the return of the English his estate was seized to make the account good. He died in disgrace a few years afterwards.

When the commodores sailed away they bore an address from the government which they had set up in New Orange, to the States General, magnifying the attractions of the colony. Three cities and thirty villages were prospering. With a larger farming population, grain and many necessaries could be produced for Holland, and peltries would furnish a profitable trade. Especially was the port of value as a naval station to guard against English aggression. For all of these reasons reinforcements were solicited for the Dutch inhabitants, who now numbered six or seven thousand. The address took no account of the inhabitants of

English and other nationalities, at this time probably from three to five thousand in various parts of the colony. The States General received the communication after the decision had been reached to abandon the cities and villages and farms and naval station to the English rival.

Governor Colve returned to the policy of Stuyvesant in the provisional instructions which he issued to the towns. In the eastern part of Long Island his authority was not accepted, and Connecticut sent agents to stir up the disaffected. Massachusetts seized a Dutch vessel; reprisals followed by the Dutch. War between the colonies seemed imminent. Colve ordered all strangers away and forbade the entrance of any person not bearing a passport. To strengthen the fortification he levied a tax on the estates of all residents worth over a thousand guilders, and the list showed more than five hundred and twenty thousand guilders. A part of the tax was demanded in advance by way of loan. He put the fort into good repair and mounted on it a hundred and twenty guns. He was busy with a soldier's care of the colony, until October 15, 1674, when orders came to him to surrender New Netherland to the King of Great Britain.

The seizure of the colony by the Duke of

York had been one of the incidents in the policy which arrayed England and Holland in deadly strife. For two years the demand for its recovery had been pressed by the colonists upon the Dutch government and was urged by the latter in negotiations with England. The reconquest by the Dutch was one of the series of victories which in those years gave glory to the States General. The necessities of Holland forced upon her unwelcome action. Great Britain and France had formed an alliance, and Holland had been driven to rely on her old enemy, Spain, and on Germany. In her stress Holland offered to yield New Netherland to Britain. The States General were not informed of the reconquest of the colony when pledge was given to recognize the British title. William of Orange was directing the negotiations which resulted in such aggrandizement of the realm of which he was within a few years to become king. The Treaty of Westminster was signed February 19, 1674, and all lands captured during the war were restored. Dutch rule on the continent of America was ended.

New York as it was finally transferred to British authority did not contain twelve thousand white persons. The population reached as far north as the vicinity of Albany, and Schenectady was the remotest settlement on the Mohawk. Settlers nestled about the Hudson. The French had missionary stations at various points among the red men. The population was already varied in its elements. Swedes and Finns in New Jersey reached over nearly to the chief seaport. Waldenses and Huguenots had been from the first welcome settlers. English had come from home directly and through the colonies to Long Island and the eastern banks of the Hudson. In the list still preserved of immigrants are found names of persons from various parts of France, from Prussia, Germany, Switzerland, Norway, Denmark, and Bohemia. The prophecy of a cosmopolitan population was already apparent.

The Reformed Church had official recognition during Dutch rule. The Lutherans were subject to occasional annoyances, but in the main were free to worship in their own way. The Presbyterians secured a strong footing, and with the advent of the new English governor the Episcopal Church was planted. Roman Catholics had at this time no settled pastors within the recognized limits of the Dutch colony, but received occasional visits from their missionaries among the Indians, who were treated with marked courtesy by the governor. The visit of Father Le Moyne, in 1658, led to arrangements for trade with Canada as well as to favorable feelings toward the French missionaries among the Iroquois. Jews were not allowed to serve as soldiers even under a pressing exigency, but no other disability seems to have been imposed upon them. Charges of witchcraft were treated without passion, and no life was sacrificed to the superstition. If religious freedom was not perfectly asserted it would be hard to find in that age any other land in which closer approach was intelligently made to that result.

The dominant influence except in certain towns, chiefly on Long Island, was that of the Dutch. They brought with them the controversies between Calvinism and Arminianism, and the forms and practices of the home country. The colonists took pains to establish schools and they maintained them in a modest way. Unless Stuyvesant is a slanderer, fully one fourth of the houses in New Amsterdam was devoted to the sale of brandy, tobacco, and beer, and the regulation of them was a source of trouble. Their existence tells the story of the habits of the people. The chief city was followed in this respect by the villages and the country. Hard drinking was not unusual. The taverns were the places of constant resort, and firewater was one of the easy instruments of trade with the red men. Withal the piety of

rulers and people was pronounced. Governor
Colve only illustrated the spirit of the colony
when he appointed the first Wednesday of every
month as a universal day of thanksgiving and
prayer. In spite of personal blunders and
crimes the Dutch fostered humane and honest
relations with the Indians, and established a
friendship with the Iroquois which, inherited by
the English, became a safeguard against French
invasions.

The fur trade brought red men and white
men into more close intercourse than was common in the other colonies. It tended somewhat
to turn attention from immigration. For while
company and governor and patroon and merchant sought profit from that source, numbers
were less required than when energies were
turned chiefly to the culture of the soil. For a
like reason, what was wealth for those days was
represented by a considerable body of capitalists,
and society had its full share of display. The
silver ornaments on the wooden leg of Governor
Stuyvesant, and the " coach and three " which
Governor Colve felt called upon to set up, not
only reflect the character of the men, but their
estimate of the taste of the inhabitants. But
the governor's carriage was alone in its glory
for no little time.

The struggle for a share in the government

by the settlers began early, and was kept up during the whole period of Dutch rule. The West India Company could arrogate no claim of divine right, for all men knew it was a simple organization for making money. It commanded no veneration, and the governors were regarded as mere individuals, often not so wise or so brave as the settlers. The home government was a republic during its whole control of New Netherland.

The Dutch settlers brought with them manners, style of dress, furniture, habits of life. In a colony so remote, manners and habits were somewhat relaxed. Dress and furniture were in large part free from the raids of fashion. In an engraving in the "Description of New Netherland" by Arnoldus Montanus, of the date of 1671, New Amsterdam appears with its fort and its church, not far from the bay. The houses stand with their sharp gables to the street; not a few of them have two stories besides the angle close to the roof. Some of only one story are situated below the fort. The town runs off from the river upon the creeks and ponds which were then frequent on the lower part of the island. The cold climate called into requisition whatever clothing one possessed, and the manifold petticoats and trousers which have aroused ridicule contributed to comfort during the long winters. The taverns added the attractions of the American weed, tobacco, to the liquor and beer familiar at home, and the pipe adapted itself to the phlegmatic nature of the Dutchmen. Market days were a convenience for a population widely scattered. The Kermess, a sort of fair, brought this population together for a succession of holidays. Church festivals were observed with zeal and with peculiar practices, as memories of Paas and Pinxter and the jollities of Christmas testify, and St. Nicholas, the Santa Claus of the children, has come down to us as the patron saint of the colony. The new year was celebrated by social calls on neighbors, a sign of comity and good will, which, while sometimes abused, has spread into other parts of the country. The commonwealth retains the impress of many of the peculiarities of its early settlers. If it has shown less state pride than some of its sisters, the reason may be found in part in the passing away of the language used during the first sixty years of its life, and in the diverse elements which from the beginning entered into its composition.

CHAPTER VII.

THE ATTEMPT OF THE SWEDES.

1626-1656.

THE Dutch claimed all the territory south as well as east of New Amsterdam. and the South River as well as the Fresh River are accounted in the early annals as no less included in New Netherland than the Hudson River. These claims were challenged at an early day by the English on pretense of earlier discovery, and by the Swedes because the land was open and unoccupied. Gustavus Adolphus of Sweden was led in 1626 to organize a company for trade and emigration to this coast, but his death prevented the impress of his genius and energy upon the enterprise. Queen Christina and her great minister Oxenstiern took up the project twelve years later. The matter was brought to the attention of the Swedish government by Usselinx, the projector of the Dutch West India Company, who had become dissatisfied with the people of Holland; and it was Peter Minuit, the dismissed director of New Netherland, who led the movement for New Sweden. In 1638 a man-of-war and a tender were placed at his service, and with about fifty Swedes, mostly convicts, he sailed, and landed at James- town, Virginia. In April he took up a posi- tion on the South River, now the Delaware, and began to trade for furs with the Indians. Di- rector Kieft served a protest on the part of the Dutch, but it was disregarded, and Swedish ves- sels sailed with cargoes of tobacco, while a gar- rison was established in a fort called Fort Chris- tina. The Swedes from this point entered into competition for furs in trade with the red men. They were not prosperous and were ready to abandon the post, when accessions came in 1640 from the home country, with fresh supplies, and as deputy governor, Peter Hollandaer. Thus strengthened, they bought lands of the Indians, and asserted a claim to a tract extend- ing thirty German miles along the sea, and in- land " as much of the country as they chose to take." The colony grew to such importance that John Printz, a lieutenant-colonel of cav- alry, was sent out in 1642 as governor, with orders for developing industry and trade. He took pains to command the mouth of the river, although the Dutch had established Fort Nas- sau on its eastern bank, and the Swedish settle- ments were on the western bank exclusively.

Collisions arose between the Dutch and the Swedes, and when the former put up the arms of the States General on the completion of a purchase of lands from the Indians, Printz in a passion ordered them to be torn down. The Swedes gained in strength while the Dutch lost ground in the vicinity.

In 1646 the Dutch attempted to build a trading post on the Schuylkill, when they were repulsed by force by the Swedes. Individuals seeking to erect houses were treated in the same way. The Swedes in turn set up a stockade on the disputed ground.

Director Stuyvesant found it necessary in 1651 to go to confer with Printz with a view to holding the country against the aggressive English. The Indians were called into council and confirmed the Dutch title, allowing the Swedes little more than the site of Fort Christina. Fort Casimir was erected lower down the river, to protect Dutch interests. The two rulers agreed to be friends and allies, and so continued for three years.

The distress of the Swedish colony led to appeals for aid from the home country whither Governor Printz had returned. In 1654 help was given, and a new governor, John Claude Rysingh, marked his coming by the capture of Fort Casimir, pretending that the Dutch

West India Company authorized the act. The only revenge the Dutch could take was the seizure of a Swedish vessel which by mistake ran into Manhattan Bay. But the next year orders came from Holland exposing the fraud of Rysingh and directing the expulsion of the Swedes from the South River. A fleet was organized and Director Stuyvesant recovered Fort Casimir without firing a gun. After some parley Fort Christina was also surrendered. Such Swedes as would not take the oath of allegiance to the Dutch authorities were sent to the home country. Only twenty persons accepted the oath, and of three clergymen two were expelled, and the third escaped like treatment by the sudden outbreak of Indian troubles.

In 1656 the States General and Sweden made these transactions matter of international discussion. The Swedes presented a protest against the action of the Dutch, and it was talked over, but the matter was finally dropped. In the same year the West India Company sold its interests on the South River to the city of Amsterdam, and the colony of New Amstel was erected, so that the authority of New Netherland was extinguished.

After New Amsterdam was seized by the Duke of York an expedition was sent under Robert Carr to reduce the settlements on the

Delaware. The Swedes welcomed his arrival. The Dutch resisted ; but while three of their garrison were killed and ten wounded, the assailants suffered no injury. John Carr, a lieutenant, and son of the commander, seized the captured property, sent the Dutch soldiers to Virginia to be sold as slaves, and set himself up as governor. He was after a while forced to recognize Governor Nicolls as superior, but he was left in command.

The Duke of York's concessions to Berkeley and Carteret led to a separate government. On the conquest of New York by the Dutch, the original claims of New Netherland to the southward were again asserted, and were not contested. A government was established on the Delaware with Schout Alrichs as its head, reporting to Governor Colve.

The surrender of New Netherland carried with it the settlements down to Cape Henlopen. But the Duke of York's gift to Berkeley and Carteret reduced the fair proportions of the province which bore his name, and established its boundaries upon the Lower Hudson and the waters of the Delaware.

CHAPTER VIII.

THE English conquest brought a new name
to the colony, and the Duke of York by giving
away New Jersey marked out its bounds on
the south. The defeat of the French in Canada
and the treaty with Great Britain after the
Revolution were required to fix the limits on
the north. The domain when the French first
came in was the seat of a powerful confederacy.
Champlain's first chart, edition of 1613, marks
the St. Lawrence, with Quebec and Montreal
the seats of his authority, and locates the lake
to which he gave his name in fair relations to
them. The Lake of the Iroquois is not identical in form or situation with Lake Ontario, but
stands for it. North and west of that lake is a
great body of water, unnamed, which he describes as measured by fifteen days' travel of the
canoes of the savages. The whole domain surrounding Lake Champlain, except on the northeast, and all south of the St. Lawrence and
these lakes, indefinitely westward, he defines as

the country of the Yrocois. The orthography later became Iroquois.

Champlain's map of 1632 is more full and more extended. Its features for the domain which has become New York are the St. Lawrence, Lake Champlain, with a trend too much to the southwest, Lake St. Louis, where now is Lake Ontario, extending westward into narrower proportions, and northwestward a *Mer Douce* and a *Grand Lac.* He locates a very high waterfall at the west of Lake Ontario. The Hirocois occupy the centre of the domain, the Antouoronons (the Senecas) are south of the western limit of the Ontario, and west of them he places the " neutral nation." The only French sign is Saintonge, the name of his birthplace, which he gives to the site of his first battle with the Iroquois, but he is careful to mark no settlement. The Hudson, Long Island and its sound are sketched but not named. Southward and inland he locates Virginia.

Its natural features helped in great measure to separate the domain west of the Hudson and south of the lakes from the Plymouth colony on the east and Virginia on the south. By the charters of both they had a claim to all this territory. Nature had foreordained that its history should be distinct and different. By the formation of its soil, the trend of its mountains, by its relation to the ocean, and by its lakes and the course of its rivers, its people must have peculiar tasks. For they were to stand at the gateway of empire on this continent, and were to control its earliest paths. Here were to be the battlefields on which were to be determined the type of the civilization to become dominant and the political control of the chief part of the New World.

The lines of discovery were prophetic. The French entered from Lake Champlain. The Dutch came up the Hudson. The Swedes challenged the southern border. The English crowded in from the east and south. The choice of Fort Orange as the original settlement and the early advances along the Mohawk touched the heart of the continent. The red men knew, the white men soon learned, that from the centre of the land of the Iroquois, the rivers flow to all points of the compass. The head waters of the Mohawk, which pass through the Hudson to the Atlantic, interlace with streams which sweep northward and join the majestic St. Lawrence. Waters which a stone's throw separate start some for the Mohawk, and others, by the Susquehanna, to the far distant Chesapeake. Within the land of the Iroquois Champlain might have found streams to conduct him before Joliet or La Salle, by way of the Ohio, down the controlling current of the Mississippi.

This watershed marks also the mountains which are the ribs of the continent. Across from the north of Lake Champlain the Adirondack Mountains run southward, sinking their summits to the Catskills, and extending then to the hills which join the Alleghanies. These elevations are a part of that continental system of mountains. The Hudson cleaves them. The Mohawk divides the hills which open to make a gateway for its waters. Minor rivers seek final outlet by the St. Lawrence at the north or by the Hudson at the south. The Delaware, the Chenango and the Susquehanna, and the Chemung flow southward, and the Alleghany to the southwest. The interior lakes all discharge across the lines of latitude.

This conformation affords natural channels for advance north toward the lake and the St. Lawrence and southward almost indefinitely. The earliest and most inviting gateway westward has proved to be by the Mohawk valley. The earlier French governors saw in this domain the seat of empire. Baron D'Avaugour wrote in 1663 to the minister Colbert, "The St. Lawrence is the entrance to what may be made the greatest State in the world," and he urged the erection of a strong fort where Albany now stands. Talon, a few years later, recommended the purchase or seizure of New York with a view to the control of the continent. These designs inspired the contests of the French against the Iroquois which followed these natural lines and led to the counter-assaults carried seven times to the gates of Montreal. The British advanced by the same paths to conquer Canada. The royal attempts to check the revolution of the colonies chose the Champlain and the Hudson and the Mohawk for some of the decisive demonstrations. Washington, in his visit in 1783, to the Mohawk, Oneida Lake, and the sources of the Susquehanna, was impressed with the "immense diffusion" of inland waters and the facilities for making intimate connections with other parts of the country. In 1812 British arms again sought to penetrate the United States by the water-routes leading from Canada southward. A leader in the rebellion of 1861 alleged that one chief cause of the failure of the Confederacy was due to the flow of the rivers and to their open valleys leading from New York to the heart of Virginia. General Scott, standing on the field of the battle of Bemus Heights, declared this Commonwealth to hold the military key of the continent east of the Mississippi, and on the same spot General Grant confirmed the judgment.

In 1721 the Lords Commissioners of Plantations proposed to the British crown to place a captain general in this province on account of its commanding position, and to " render the several provinces from Nova Scotia to South Carolina" subject to his orders. The suggestion was due not to the population of the province, for it was smaller than that of others, but solely to the natural relations of New York to the British possessions. It was an official recognition of the geographical situation.

To these natural features must be assigned the current of migration, of trade, of growth, of wealth, and of power, which has passed through the valley of the Mohawk, from the Old World and the eastern part of the continent, first to western New York, and in due order to Ohio, to the Northwest, beyond the Mississippi, to the Pacific, and finally to Oregon and the Columbia. Settlers in the early days went west by the flatboats on the Mohawk, and up the Delaware and Susquehanna, before artificial channels multiplied the facilities of the pathways marked out by nature.

We shall describe the domain which has become New York, in a general way, if at the mouth of the Hudson we draw a right-angled triangle. The perpendicular will follow the Hudson and Lake Champlain, and our territory will extend eastward beyond the river so as to control both of its banks. The base of this triangle from the Hudson will follow mountains to the eastern bend of the Delaware and along that river to the forty-third parallel, thence along that parallel west to a line bounding Pennsylvania and running to the middle of Lake Erie. The hypothenuse Lake Ontario and the St. Lawrence supply. A like triangle was cut off between the head waters of Lake Champlain and the St. Lawrence by the Treaty of Ghent, which drew a line westward from the sources of the Connecticut on the forty-fifth parallel. New York, besides its outlying islands, is such a truncated triangle, with the Hudson extending from its main angle down to the sea. A more homely resemblance is found in the form of a shoe with a long heel resting at the seaport, broad toes touching Lake Erie, and a large ankle spreading along the St. Lawrence. The area is 47,620 square miles, if we measure to the centre of the lakes and rivers which make part of its boundaries, and the extreme measurements are 311⅔ miles from north to south, and 412 miles from west to east, including Long Island. At the main angle of our triangle spreads the bay which commerce has chosen for its chief seat, and which receives and distributes its treasures in large part along the paths that nature has provided through the domain which has become the Empire State.

This domain could not well be an attachment to any other colony. It must be itself the source of development, the centre of growth. Settlement was checked during the struggles of France and England, and the battles of the Revolution, and the movements of troops kept the increase below the rate of other colonies. These were consequences due to the position and topography of New York. As soon as continental strife ceased, natural advantages drew settlers and developed resources, and gave the reins to commerce. The map of the State, and especially its lakes, the course of its rivers and the trend of its mountains, are the key to its history.

CHAPTER IX.

THE PEOPLE OF THE LONG HOUSE.

THE title of the Empire State is a modern invention. Yet at the time the white men came into New York, a confederacy, which boasted that it had already existed six generations, occupied the chief part of this territory and wielded a power imperial in its extent and exercise. The aborigines on the lower Hudson and the seacoast consisted of several tribes who gave no particular direction to the current of events. From the mouth of the Mohawk northward and westward dwelt a people known as the Five Nations, allied in a union which with their genius for control, made them masters over a large part of the continent. They had at one time held full sway on the north shores of the St. Lawrence. In Cartier's time one of their tribes occupied the site of Quebec. Champlain found them on the west shores of the lake which bears his name, and the terror of their arms introduced French warriors and French missionaries to far western lakes and rivers.

They at once became the masters of the
trade in beaver skins, and were not second to
any tribes in hunting and fishing. They were
hardly less noted for the culture of the soil and
for the building of cabins and defensive works
than for military prowess. The first white
visitor found frame cabins, and fields of corn
and beans, and tobacco, pumpkins, and small
fruit; and thrift as well as industry were proved
by the preservation of crops, which were buried
in the winter. The Iroquois had stone axes,
and chisels, and knives, before the whites gave
them metal implements. They produced pot-
tery, and the specimens preserved in graves
show a rude skill and some merit in design.
They fashioned moccasins of deer skins and
shoes of the hide of the elk. They tanned
leather, they made needles of bones; from bark
they wrought rope, baskets, and barrels, and
graceful and useful canoes. From wood they
devised many implements which they carved
elaborately. They used armor of twigs and
hides, and their fortifications had a certain military strength even against French arms. Their
speech was direct and vigorous and effective,
and proves, as Max Müller declares, that they
were powerful reasoners and accurate classi-
fiers. By a very full and rich pictorial language, abounding in compounds, they recorded

on skins remarkable achievements, and sometimes so conveyed messages. Their money
was wampum or seawant, strips of leather
adorned with shells from the lakes, and afterwards with beads. The pipe of peace they
used as a sedative and a symbol.

They styled themselves *Ongwe-Honwe*, men
surpassing all others, when they yielded to
their swelling oratory. They were also " The
People of the Long House," priding themselves on the domain they occupied, or quite as
likely on the form of the cabins they built, and
probably the phrase had reference to both.
Their orators were wont to speak of the eastern valley of the Mohawk as the entrance of
the mansion which extended to the falls of
Niagara, where was the western door. Here
were their castles and their home, however far
they ranged in hunting or in war. The French
called them Iroquois, the "men who say *Iro*,"
or "I have said *Koue*," a word of approval, as
it is the habit to explain the derivation. It is,
however, noteworthy that one of the earliest
chiefs whom Champlain met was called Iroquois, although not of this confederacy, and the
inference is fair that the personal name existed
in other tribes, and was transferred by the
French to the united Five Nations, or, indeed,
was applied by the red men themselves.

These tribes derived their origin from a divine source. Their traditions were various and were enriched by noble conceptions. According to one of them the first of the nation was a celestial being, Atotarho, or To-do-da-ho, whose hair was serpents, and whose name was retained for the chief of the Onondagas. Hiawatha, also divine, is reputed to be the architect of the confederacy, transformed by modern criticism into a "lawgiver of the stone age." The contest between these two persons affords wide scope for myths. Hiawatha, although an Onondaga, found the first response to his plans for union from the Mohawks, and the support of other tribes was won by concessions in rank and power. Another tradition is that Ataentsic, a goddess, accidentally fell from heaven, or was excluded for a human amour. She bore two children, the sun and the moon, and, although a Huron, became the mother of these tribes, and with some qualities of a universal mother on earth. The higher version recognizes the "holder of the heavens" as the master of life, and in a peculiar sense the god of the Iroquois.

The names of tribes as we know them in English are formed from those of the people themselves, except the Senecas and the Mohawks, who were probably so styled by epithets

of dislike. The title Mohawk was a term of
terror and of hate first applied to the tribe by
the eastern Indians, and to the French it was
a note of alarm while they held sway in Montreal and Quebec.

The Mohawks lived in the eastern part of
the valley which still bears their name, the
Oneidas next west in the vicinity of Oneida
Lake, the Onondagas in the region of the Salt
Springs, the Cayugas reaching to the shores of
Lake Ontario, and the Senecas spreading to the
south and west. The Tuscaroras, defeated in
North Carolina, joined the union in 1715 as a
sixth nation, and received from the Oneidas
lands between the latter and the Onondagas.
The Senecas were the most numerous, with
as many as twelve hundred fighting men,
while the other four tribes could together mus-
ter hardly so many. The total population of
the confederacy after white men came to know
them did not exceed twelve thousand souls.
One of the remarkable facts of history is, that,
scattered as they have been, with all the vicis-
situdes of exclusion and the flood of a new civilization, an equal number of representatives of
these tribes exists to-day. The records of the
Interior Department in Washington contain
the demonstration.

American research among the traditions of

our original tribes does not discover, the annals
of mankind do not afford on the same grade of
general civilization, any parallel to the political
system which existed among the Iroquois as a
confederacy, or among the tribes composing it.
Within the tribes were clans, sometimes seven
or eight, distinguished by names of animals, as
the Tortoise, the Bear, and the Wolf, and organization was close and complete. These people
lived in castles which were towns, with homes
and their appendages. Fifty sachems were apportioned, not according to population, but by
arbitrary rule: nine each to the Mohawks and
Oneidas, fourteen to the Onondagas, ten to the
Cayugas, and eight to the Senecas. These constituted the national council, and the succession was by inheritance on the female side,
with apparently a right of choice by the women among their heirs. The name descended
with the office. Next to the sachems were
chiefs, elected by their tribes, and distinguished
achievements at once gave access to this rank.
All old men and all warriors exercised an advi-
sory part in affairs, and the women held meetings in which their will found utterance and
it was formally communicated to the chiefs and
sachems. In matters of property and especially
of land their voice was potent.

It would appear thus that councils were held

of various grades, rising by degrees to those of
the sachems. They were all conducted with
dignity and decorum. The resemblance to
town meetings and to modern legislatures is not
a mere fancy. These councils were held in the
several tribes, and when exigency arose, a congress of the union was summoned by runners
bearing belts of wampum. All decisions required a unanimous vote. Deliberation and
debate were employed to secure this result. If
at last all did not approve, the project proposed
was abandoned.

Such institutions were the school of freedom
and of loyalty. They developed intellectual
activity and force, and created a confederacy
remarkable in its elements and notable for its
duration. It stood the strain of contact with
the invading whites, and fostered a military
prowess of which the proofs are simply wonder-
ful. The supremacy of the Iroquois was recognized by the red men of New England. They
collected taxes from those who lived on Long
Island. In 1608 John Smith met a war party
of them on the Chesapeake. In 1663, Sir
Thomas Temple, governor of Nova Scotia, sent
a remonstrance to Fort Orange, to ask that the
Mohawks might be restrained from waging
war on the Indians within his jurisdiction.
The fear of the Iroquois rested on the tribes

about Montreal and north of the St. Lawrence, and they roamed in battle to the far south and west. When they bought arms of the Dutch and French, in exchange for peltries, they carried terror before them. The upper lakes were the scene of their conquests. They drove the Hurons and the Ottawas to the head-waters of the Mississippi. They became masters along the Illinois, the lower Ohio, and to the mouth of the Mississippi. Champlain suffered defeat at their hands. Tracy exhausted his resources in an invasion of their domain in which they foreshadowed the tactics of the Russians before Napoleon. They held their territory against French power, and became the shield of English civilization on this continent.

Peter Schuyler in 1710 took five of their sachems to England with him, with a view to impress Queen Anne and her ministers with the importance of their alliance. Great show was made of them, and an address was presented by them urging the conquest of Canada, because they had been a "strong wall" against the French, and now the reduction of that power was "of great weight to their free hunting." The "Tatler" and the "Spectator" spoke of these visitors as "Indian kings," and the sparkling essayists adorned their productions with references to the "Emperor of the Mohocks."

The "kings" were accepted as typical of the most formidable of the red men of America.

Gouverneur Morris was wont to relate an incident received by him from an eye-witness, illustrating the estimate which that statesman had formed of the red men, whom he knew well. The Long Island Indians, according to the narrative, had neglected to pay tribute to the Iroquois for several years, about 1760, and had sold some land without their leave. One evening a Mohawk warrior in full dress appeared on Long Island, and stated that he had a message from the Six Nations to present to the tribe at a council in the morning. At the council, standing alone, he asked why the tribute had not been paid, why the land had been sold, and who first signed the deed. An old chief confessed that he was the first signer. As the words passed his lips the Mohawk split his head with a tomahawk. Then without let or hindrance he left the paralyzed council and went safely home. Such audacity and such sovereignty by a single chief, in a hostile tribe, a hundred and fifty miles from his castle, epitomize the power and eminence of the Iroquois.

They believed in a great spirit and in immortality in happy hunting grounds. In their "keepers of the faith," a priestly order may be discerned, and in their festivals and form of burial are ceremonies not without sacrificial and spiritual significance. Their religion lifts them above brute barbarism to a semi-civilization which separates them from the tribes surrounding them. They respected woman and honored matrimony, and inheritance was from the female. Chivalry did not accord her so much as did these red men, for they gave her a part in their councils and their governments, and made her voice potent in the choice of chiefs. The family was a sacred institution, and children were carefully trained. For the aged high regard was exhibited, and the rites of hospitality were honored with chivalric strictness. In the passions of war the Iroquois tortured prisoners at the stake with terrible inhumanity. They were sometimes cannibals, but they often spared their captives and adopted them into the families of their chiefs, with a method of generous naturalization. They even merged tribes defeated in battle into their own system, and thus, as the Romans were wont to do, extended their sway and strengthened their force for future warfare.

They were natural diplomatists. The Dutch, in 1617, established a firm and lasting treaty with them, and relied upon the Mohawks, as the readiest agents for adjusting difficulties arising with the tribes on the islands and the lower

Hudson.   The French found the Five Nations
all adepts in negotiation.   Neither by arms nor
by treaty could the successive governors secure
a permanent foothold in the country of the
Iroquois.   These red men regarded ambassadors as peculiarly entitled to honor and protection, and to compacts once formed they
were quite as faithful as modern nations are
wont to be.

The chronicles of French intercourse with
the Iroquois exhibit in strong light the courage, the audacity, the independence and patriotism of these red men.   They never ceased
to defy and challenge French power, however
they might at intervals seek to gain time and
advantage by negotiation; and when Canada
fell into British hands the result was due in no
small degree to the checks put by Iroquois
arms on the broad and aggressive policy of the
governors sent out from Paris, and of the ministers and sovereigns who directed them.

The French writers learned to know the
character of these heroes of the forest.   Charlevoix saw them as early as 1706, and testifies
" these Americans are perfectly convinced that
man is born free, and that no power on earth
has any right to restrict his liberty, while nothing can make up for its loss."   La Potherie
declares in his book, published in 1722, that

"their union worked like a clock" from the marvelous adjustment of its parts. The Jesuit Lafitau represents their "senate" — a title perhaps too formal — as "discussing affairs of state with as much coolness and gravity as the Spanish junta or the grand council of Venice." The Dutch always found them good neighbors and trustworthy friends.

Oratory bore an important part in the life of the Iroquois. In their councils they practiced it, drawing figures from the phenomena of nature, and retaining after long intercourse with the whites a rhetoric original and unique. In negotiations the oration was a leading feature. Charlevoix testifies that Joncaire, a Seneca, "spoke with all the vivacity of a Frenchman and the sublime eloquence of an Iroquois." Jefferson "challenged the whole orations of Demosthenes and Cicero and of any more eminent orator of Europe, if Europe has furnished more eminent, to produce a single passage superior to the speech of Logan," who was descended from the Cayugas. De Witt Clinton declares it to be "impossible to find in all the effusions of ancient or modern oratory a speech more appropriate and convincing" than an argument made by Garangula, a chief of the Onondagas. Living men testify to the marvelous eloquence of the Seneca, Red Jacket, who died in 1830.

By such qualities the Iroquois not only won but held supremacy over the red men of the continent. Not a tribe could successfully dispute their might in battle. The settlers in Maryland framed a treaty with them for the protection of their own borders. The governors of Virginia, beginning in 1679, more than once deemed it vital to enter into negotiations with them. In 1689 Massachusetts found it necessary to frame a treaty with these redoubtable tribes, and both that colony and Connecticut appealed to them for aid in their expedition against Canada. In 1753 the governor of South Carolina besought Governor Clinton of New York to make peace between the Iroquois and the Creeks, to check French schemes in the southern colony.

From Hudson's Bay and Lake Superior to the mouth of the Chesapeake, from the Penobscot to the Kentucky and Savannah rivers, and one author says even to the Isthmus of Darien, at the close of the seventeenth century, the Indian nations recognized the domination of the Iroquois. The French failing to conquer them vied with the British in seeking their alliance. They supported the British government in general policy, and gave it strong help in the Revolution. At Fort Duquesne Washington appealed to the Six Nations because he was fighting for their rights to territory. Britain always recognized their title to the domain south of the St. Lawrence. In 1755 the Lords Commissioners of Trade and Plantations authorized a map of the colonies in America, by Mitchell, and it fixes the extent of the Iroquois dominion at that day, as claimed by the English, and practically recognized by the French, in their negotiations with each other. The southern boundary runs from the Atlantic through the middle of North Carolina to the Mississippi, up that stream to the Illinois, thence through Lake Michigan to the north of the Straits of Mackinaw, and eastward to the Ottawa River, and thence to Montreal, the Sorel, and the Hudson. The map states that the southern portion of this domain was yielded to the crown in 1729.

In the controversy which arose between the British and French over the territory along the Ohio and southward, the British claim always rested on the title derived from the Six Nations. To a memorial in behalf of France, made by the Duke de Mirepoix, May 14, 1755, response was published in the French language on the part of the British ministry, and prominence is given to a memorial of the Earl of Albemarle, of March 7, 1752, in which he declared that " the court of Great Britain asserts and insists that the five Iroquois nations, acknowledged by France to be the subjects of Great Britain, are either originally or by conquest the lawful proprietors of the territory of Ohio."

Virginia by treaty defined its boundaries with the Iroquois, and Pennsylvania secured a cession of its soil from them, while Connecticut people bought of them large tracts on the Susquehanna River. To all that remained New York attained by purchase and fair negotiation the right of eminent domain.

In the Iroquois confederacy the Mohawks were the " true heads," as they were recognized by the treaty of 1768 at Fort Stanwix. Their castles were nearest to the whites, and they became first known and bore the brunt of the earliest fighting. The Oneidas were inclined to moderate counsels, the conservatives of the union. The Onondagas became the most affected by French influences. The Senecas probably were most apt in tilling the soil. The Six Nations, except a share of the Oneidas, were led by Sir William Johnson to the British side in the Revolution, fighting at Oriskany and under Burgoyne, and harassing the settlers until cruelly crushed in the Sullivan campaign of 1779. Some of them appeared under the British flag in 1812 during the operations in New York.

The domination of the Iroquois over the red men was due in part to the natural avenues which they possessed for making swift inroads in every direction, assured to them by the topography of their country. Their imperial domain helped to make them what they were. They had qualities of sagacity, courage, organization, eloquence, which were not elsewhere found when Europeans entered the continent. They had farms and homes and towns and a political system. They had medicine men and a sort of religion with sacrifices. Without courts, justice was regarded, and the chiefs and councils supervised the exercise of personal adjustment and vengeance. Their character and their military strength were important elements in determining the settlement and development of the commonwealth which grew up in their Long House.

CHAPTER X.

1640–1671.

FRENCH rights derived from the discoveries of Champlain extended to the sources of the waters tributary to the St. Lawrence. They covered, therefore, all of northern New York. No effort was made by the French to occupy this domain, until the attacks of the Iroquois compelled retaliation. The forethought of missionaries and adventurers reached further west. Even religious zeal was directed into the country south of the St. Lawrence and Lake Ontario chiefly by the fate of war.

The French used those waters as a pathway to the West. As early as 1640 fierce enemies were threatening them. Montmagny, governor of Canada, to hold the Iroquois in check, built a fort at the mouth of the Sorel River. It was part of a broad policy conceived by one whose name translated— *Onontio*, Big Mountain — the red men applied to his successors, and indeed to the French power. His establishment of such an advanced post was none too soon.

Two Frenchmen captured by the Iroquois in 1641 were taken as interpreters to Montmagny, by a large company of the red men asking for a treaty. The French commander haughtily rejected the proffered terms, which excluded the Indian allies of France, and the captives, instead of heralds of peace, became the ministers of intensifying relations already hostile. They notified the French that the Five Nations would soon be on the war-path, and would especially seek to destroy the other tribes and put an end to French alliance and intercourse with them.

Twelve canoes were on the Lake of St. Peter in the St. Lawrence, August 3, 1642, on their return to the Hurons. The company consisted of Huron boatmen and converts, with three Frenchmen engaged in missionary work. Two were lay assistants, René Goupil and Guillaume Couture. The third was Isaac Jogues, a Jesuit, an accomplished scholar, an adventurous traveler devoted to French interests, but above all, a zealous apostle of Christ. Upon this peaceful fleet suddenly dashed a force of Iroquois in canoes, and bearing arms. The show of defense was brief, and was followed by a panic. Jogues escaped for the moment, but speedily returned to his captured companions. Couture in fleeing was caught, but killed a pursuer. A Huron maiden, Teresa

Oiouhaton, was among the prisoners, and becoming the wife of a Mohawk, long preserved
the reputation of saintly virtues. The three
Frenchmen were beaten, their finger-nails were
torn off by the teeth of their captors. The
conquerors led their victims away by the Sorel
River and Lake Champlain. Near the south
end of that lake, a band of Iroquois warriors
was met advancing for fight in Canada. The
captives were compelled to run the gauntlet
between two rows of savages beating and bruis-
ing them, and Jogues received the decoration
of the worst treatment. Proceeding to the
south and west, in thirteen days from the St.
Lawrence the company reached a palisaded
town on the banks of the Mohawk River. On
their arrival here the captives were driven between a double line of the people, who beat
them with rods, amid wild yells and screeches.
Jogues was knocked down, but arose and stag-
gered on; his thumb and that of Goupil were
cut off. At night they were bound to stakes,
and the children cast live coal and hot ashes
upon their naked bodies. They were led for
seven days to the second and third Mohawk
towns, and back and forth, and the tortures
were repeated. Goupil was struck in the head
with a tomahawk and released from his sufferings, September 29, and the dogs feasted on

his body. Couture for his bravery in defending himself was adopted into the tribe. Jogues was compelled to serve the Indians, and sought to teach them the Gospel. In the forest he repeated his prayers and carved the cross and the name of Jesus on the bark of the trees. He saw Huron captives brought in by war parties, and burned, and their flesh eaten by the conquerors. The next year he accompanied a party to Fort Orange, and made an effort to escape. His effort was a failure, but he was befriended by Rev. Johannes Megapolensis, the Dutch minister, and finally ransomed by his Dutch benefactors, and was invited to Manhattan, where Governor Kieft welcomed him, and enabled him to return to Europe. The Pope by special dispensation restored to him, crippled by his sufferings, the privilege of saying mass, forbidden to any person having physical deformity. He returned to Canada in 1644, and in May, 1646, he was sent to the Mohawks where Couture was residing, on a mission of peace, and carried back to Quebec responses fairly satisfactory. September 27, he set out on his final tour to the tribe to found the " Mission of the Martyrs." On his previous visit he had left a box, which the red men were induced to believe contained a sorcerer's evil charms. On that suspicion a war

party met the brave priest, who had a single
French companion. The warriors seized them,
and cut strips of flesh from the back of Jogues,
taunting him with threats of death on the
morrow. Invited to a feast on that day, he
was struck with a hatchet and fell dead. His
companion was also killed, and the bodies of
both were thrown into the Mohawk, and their
heads placed on palisades. The date of their
martyrdom was October 18, 1646, and the scene
has been definitely located near the present village of Auriesville. His murderer was identified among prisoners taken by the French, and
he was burned to death at the Sillery Mission.
This was the manner of the advent of the first
missionary among the Iroquois, and he proved
that he had many of the virtues of a true
martyr.

Joseph Bressani, also a Jesuit, was the second missionary, and his experience of captivity
was not dissimilar. He was captured April 29,
1644, by one of the many war parties of Iroquois then ravaging the country down the St.
Lawrence. He was on his way as a missionary
to the Hurons, and his party in three canoes
was captured on the river. The captives were
taken by the route of Lake Champlain to the
upper Hudson. There was a camp of four hundred Iroquois, and Bressani was given over to

torture by the children, after the men were
weary. He was stripped naked, his nails and
the joints of his fingers were burned off one by
one; he was hung in chains by the feet, and the
dogs were set to lacerate him. In June he was
sent to Fort Orange, to be sold to the Dutch,
who in their humanity ransomed him, and he
was enabled to go to Europe. He returned
and afterwards labored with zeal among the
Hurons.

Father Joseph Poucet repeated the same
experience of captivity. In August, 1653, he
was seized at Three Rivers and by the same
route taken a captive to the Mohawk castles.
Threatened with torture he was saved by adoption into an Indian family. He was taken to
Fort Orange and his wounds healed. After
administering religious rites to two Catholics
resident there, he returned to the Mohawks,
who gave him up to the French authorities in
November of the same year.

These three missionaries brought by force
into the land of the Iroquois took back, and
Jogues sent back in writing, information concerning the red men, their surroundings, and
their plans. The Iroquois had for years har-
ried the French in Canada, and fear of them
was on priest and soldier. Father Vimont at
the beginning of their many victorious raids

declared: "I had as lief be beset by goblins as by the Iroquois. The one is about as invisible as the other. Our people on the Richelieu and at Montreal are kept by them in a closer confinement than were ever monks or nuns in our smallest convents in France." The Mohawks were the leaders in the assaults on the French, often the only members of the war parties which tinged the St. Lawrence with blood. In 1653, a peace was made by the French with them, and the recovery of Father Poucet was made a condition by De Lauzon, the French commander.

In response to a request from the Onondagas for a Jesuit father to live with them, and for help to build a fort, Simon Le Moyne was sent in July, 1653, as a missionary with the deputation that presented the invitation. He was first of white men to observe the Salt Springs which to this day have been a source of wealth to the Onondaga country. The Indians had told the French of these springs, but they attracted no notice until Le Moyne tested them and made them known. The Mohawks were only a few months later than the Onondagas in asking for a missionary, and were annoyed that a rival tribe had been first in the matter, but they were promised a share in the labors of Le Moyne. He was with the Onondagas when in 1655 the Iroquois engaged in the war with the Erie tribe which resulted in its practical annihilation. In the autumn of that year two other Jesuit missionaries came to the Onondagas by the way of Lake Ontario. They were Joseph Chaumonot and Claude Dablon. The preaching of the former roused the red men to shout under the lead of their chief: " Glad tidings! Glad tidings! " A chapel of bark was built in a single day, and a site for a permanent French settlement was chosen at the Salt Springs. In 1656, Father Le Mercier brought a colony of fifty Frenchmen and five additional missionaries. Under the lead of Sieur Dupuys they reached their destination July 12, and five pieces of cannon announced their arrival. A redoubt was built on an eminence overlooking the lake, then called Genentaha, and cabins soon provided shelter. The Mohawks disliked the lead taken by the Onondagas, but the other tribes of the great confederacy welcomed the missionaries who went forth to give instruction in the faith.

Alarms came quick and fast upon the adventurous French colonists. The Iroquois prepared for war parties. Dupuys heard of plots for exterminating his little company. He arranged a feast for the Onondagas, and in the midst of their revelry he led his fellow-colonists through the floating ice of March, and took them safely back to Canada. The abandonment was complete. In 1661, Father Le Moyne returned to the scene, and sought to reëstablish a mission. The Mohawks did not forget the repulse which they had received years before, but Senecas and Cayugas joined with the Onondagas to greet the missionary. The winter did not bring sufficient promise of encouragement, and Father Le Moyne gave up the field in the succeeding spring, taking with him to Canada prisoners released by the three western tribes of the confederacy.

The Oneidas and Mohawks kept up their forays even to the gates of Montreal. In 1663, the French governor, D'Avaugour, asked the home authorities for three thousand troops to destroy the Iroquois, and urged the building of forts on the Sorel and upper Hudson to keep open communication by that route. The Jesuit missionaries pleaded that the sale of liquor to the red men was one cause of their violence. Quarrels arose between successive governors and the priests over the proper policy to be pursued with the red men. In 1665, the French king gave instructions to treat the Five Nations as "perpetual and irreconcilable enemies," and to carry war "even to their firesides in order totally to exterminate them." A thousand French

veterans of the Carignan regiment were transferred from fighting Turks in Hungary to per-
form this task of extermination, and with them
came large accessions to the Canadian colony.
The Marquis de Tracy entered upon his duties
as viceroy by rebuilding a fort at the mouth
of the Sorel, and by erecting Fort Chambly
on the rapids of that name, and Fort Ste.
Therese, still nearer to Lake Champlain, and
soon after Fort La Motte, on an island in the
lake. These demonstrations and the persua-
sions of the Onondagas, led by their chief, Garakontie, brought all the Iroquois, except the
Mohawks, to Quebec, to frame a treaty by
which the French king was recognized as their
protector, and the tribes were styled his vassals
and allies. The French were to be welcomed
into the land of the Iroquois, and immigrants
from the red men were to have farms assigned
to them in Canada. The Mohawks who had
no part in the treaty were to be dealt with by
force. General Courcelles, in January, 1666,
led an expedition of five hundred men by way
of Lake Champlain, and came near Schenectady, February 19. By an ambuscade several
were killed and wounded by the Mohawks, who
bore the heads of four Frenchmen as trophies.
Courcelles soon heard from Albany that he was
invading a colony no longer Dutch, but now

under English rule, and he hastened to retrace his steps. The Mohawks annoyed him on his retreat, and picked off prisoners from his discouraged column. The authorities at Albany gave tender care to wounded Frenchmen left with them, and so wrought upon the Mohawks that messages were sent to Quebec that this fierce tribe desired peace. Steps were taken for negotiating a treaty, by which missionaries were to be sent to them. The peace was interrupted by one of those incidents which sometimes turn the course of history. The Mohawks fell upon a French hunting party from Fort La Motte, slew Sieur de Chazy, a nephew of the viceroy, and took several captives. To avenge the outrage, Sorel, the commander of the fort, started with three hundred men towards the Mohawk country. The red men went out to meet him with their captives and new promises of peace. The prisoners were sent on to Quebec, where soon appeared Agariata, a Mohawk chief, to help frame a treaty. This chief boasted that his was the arm that broke the head of Chazy. Viceroy Tracy ordered him hanged at once, and a half-breed who was of his party was put in prison. It became certain the Mohawks could never be allies of France.

The other tribes of the Iroquois kept up a close intimacy by embassies to Quebec. Jesuit fathers continued to go to them at their request. Tracy proposed to wreak terrible vengeance on the Mohawks. An expedition of six hundred men from the Carignan regiment, a like number of militia, and a hundred Hurons and Algonquins advanced, September, 1666, by way of Lake Champlain. It was a formidable force with its abundant small arms and two pieces of artillery. Tracy himself was the commander, and was accompanied by Courcelles. The cunning Mohawks withdrew before the invaders. The latter had expected to get abundant corn, but for a while they were compelled to be content with the ripening chestnuts. On further advance corn was discovered buried in the earth. At the fourth village the Mohawks delivered a heavy fire before they dispersed into the forests. The French captured only one man and two women, too infirm to be moved, and found the remains of some prisoners. Tracy took formal possession of the country in the name of the King of France. The wealth of the tribe is indicated by the boast of the French that they destroyed on the expedition grain enough to sustain their whole colony for two years.

This destruction was the real result of so great an expedition led by the two chief officers of New France. The Mohawks were sheltered by the forests, as the French army withdrew before the severities of October. In the next year, as Tracy was ordered to report for service in France, Courcelles became governor general, and received instructions from the minister, Colbert, in Paris, to march again against the Mohawks, " for the purpose of utterly destroying them if possible." That tribe was inclined to temporize, and accepted a treaty of peace. Missionaries were assigned to the Mohawks, as well as to the other tribes, and among the six who started in July, 1667, was Father Jacques Bruyas, whose fame as a scholar is only second to that of his zeal as a teacher among the Oneidas. They took the route now so familiar to the French, over Lake Champlain. They were well received at Caughnawaga, where Jogues had suffered, at Kanagaro, and at the Mohawk capital, Tionnontoguen, where they were received with a fusillade of joy. With impressive religious solemnities, Father Fremin, September 14, 1667, confirmed peace between the tribe and the French, and established the " Mission of St. Mary of the Mohawks," on the site of the " Mission of the Martyrs." Father Bruyas went westward to set up a mission among the Oneidas, — that of St. Francis Xavier. The work of the Church was extended among the Onondagas, the Cayugas, and the Senecas, and a colony of the Cayugas on the Bay of Quinté in Canada. When the Mohawks went out to battle with the Mohicans, a priest accompanied the war-party to invoke the divine blessing on each step of the bloody enterprise.

The era of marvelous activity on the part of the Catholic missionaries, who combined the work of explorers with their religious tasks, was well begun. Stations were occupied among the Iroquois tribes by priests devoted to their faith and to French aggrandizement. Their ranks were now recruited by one of the most far-sighted and daring of them all, who combined with the old dreams of discovering a waterway to China a grand grasp of the possibilities of the West and Southwest. René Robert Cavelier La Salle was a Jesuit, with rare capacity for affairs, with unswerving courage, and peculiar gifts for dealing with the red men, who gave up all to become an enthusiast in exploration. He was destined to perish miserably by the hands of his companions in the far Southwest, after a career which has left its marks on the heart of the continent. His connection with the interior of New York was incidental to his plans for his advance over the continent toward the far distant East. He came from France in 1667, and devoted himself for two years to study and preparation, and his zeal for the plans which he was developing has left the name of La Chine at the spot where he dwelt. In 1669 he took with him certain fathers from the Quinté missions, and started westward by water. He sought among the Senecas for a guide to lead him in his explorations. They did not tell him of the route by the way of the Ohio to the Southwest, which they well knew. If he had then learned of the flow of the rivers and the easy passage to the Mississippi, it is conceivable that the French power might have been seated there too securely for easy interruption, and a movement by that flank might have shut in the Iroquois to its control. But he was sent by the Senecas to the north by the Falls of Niagara. La Salle took possession for King Louis of the country to the south as well as the north and west of Lake Ontario and Lake Erie.

Louis XIV. was looking not only wistfully but hopefully to all this domain. The missionaries were sending encouraging reports from the field of their labors among the Iroquois. The signs of change among the Mohawks might well arouse the hopes of the devoted missionaries. The Oneidas did not come so readily under religious influences. The work among the Onondagas received an impetus by the baptism of the chief, Garakontie, who took the name of Daniel. The mingling of political with reli-

gious purposes is expressed by the eulogy upon
this convert, that he was "the protector of the
French crown in this country."

In France the suggestion was considered, of
attempting to secure from England and Holland
the cession of the whole of New Netherland.
Talon, the intendant of Canada, urged that thus
the French would have two entrances to their
American possessions, and would control in
trade all the peltries of the North. More than
once, also, the Canadian authorities entertained
the purpose of seizing Fort Orange, and afterwards Manhattan. An expedition made by
Governor Courcelles in 1671 up the St. Lawrence, at great cost and with much display,
alarmed the English at New York quite as much
as the Iroquois, for effect upon whom it was
designed. But Charles II. threw himself into
an alliance with France, and the form of the
danger was changed.

CHAPTER XI.

1672–1698.

THE new danger was embodied in the person and the plans of Count Frontenac, who in 1672 became governor of Canada, in many respects the foremost of all the French representatives that colony ever received. He brought with him a reputation earned on Italian battlefields, and the honor of a designation by the great Turenne to lead the Venetian armies in Candia. He was fifty-two years of age, and had exhausted his fortune and his credit, and he, or, as the chronicles show, his wife, had wrecked his domestic relations. His plans for the government of Canada were broad and liberal, and his schemes for the extension of his jurisdiction to the southward were large and statesmanlike. He found in La Salle a co-laborer ready to suggest ideas and to carry out comprehensive plans. His first step was an expedition to Lake Ontario, and the construction on the north side, where Kingston now stands, of a fort, to which

he gave his own name. This fort was meant
to serve as a centre of operations against the
Iroquois, but no less of trade with them. La
Salle was placed in charge, and it was alleged
that the governor and his ally were seeking
personal profit quite as much as the building
up of New France. But the visit of Frontenac
and the erection of the fort and the influences
which emanated from it were followed by ten
years of greater quiet than the French were
accustomed to enjoy with the red men. Frontenac won favor with the Iroquois in an assembly which he invited when he was beginning his
enterprise, where he addressed them as " children," and therefore entitled to help, instead of
" brothers," as the practice had prevailed before
his time. It may have been only the expression
of his own personal arrogance, but the red men
liked the phrase and adopted its author as a
favorite. He was less fortunate in maintaining
harmony with the Jesuits and the official circle
in Montreal and Quebec. He charged the Jesuits with " thinking more of beaver skins than
of souls," and denounced their missions as
" mockeries." In return they alleged that he
was making profit out of his governorship, and
sought to hold a monopoly of trade in his hands.
To secular eyes, it must be confessed, the competition in trade between the Jesuits on the one

hand with their allies, and Frontenac and La Salle on the other, was very sharp. The Jesuits, in addition, charged the governor with debauching the red men by the sale of liquors.

The quarrel resulted in the recall of Frontenac to France in 1682. He impressed his views relative to Canadian affairs on the French court, but was left in poverty in Paris for seven years, when the exigencies of the colony summoned him again to Quebec. But those seven years had proved fatal to French control among the Iroquois. Some new characters had appeared on the scene. Father Louis Hennepin, a Recollet friar, afterwards noted as an author on American topics, made a winter excursion overland from Lake Ontario to the land of the Onondagas, Oneidas, and Mohawks in 1677, and in the succeeding year he, with Father La Motte, was for a while among the Senecas. La Salle built a fort at Niagara, and in his labors there and on the western borders, he was aided by Henri de Tonty, an Italian of courage and the sort of skill necessary in a wild country. At Cayuga Creek, on the south side of Niagara River just above the falls, they built a vessel for use in their western explorations. It was called the Griffin, and was lost in Lake Michigan with a cargo of furs on a return voyage.

Since they had obtained fire-arms the Iro-

quois had been pressing hard upon their neighbors. They had in 1680 crushed out the tribe
adjacent to them on the south, the Andastes,
as they had before made an end of the Eries,
who lived just west of them. The profits of
the fur trade induced them to extend their
forays farther and farther, and this reason is
alone sufficient to explain their appearance
among the Illinois and the Hurons, without
accepting the French stories that they were
urged to this course by the English and Dutch
traders. That charge has no more truth than
the other, that the Jesuits incited the Iroquois
to make forays on the settlements in Maryland
and Virginia.

Governor De La Barre, who came in when
Frontenac was displaced, found that the Iroquois were threatening the Illinois with destruction, but as La Salle controlled the French
interest among the latter, the governor left them
to the tender mercies of their foes. When
he sent a band out to the Illinois country
for his own purposes, it was attacked by the
Iroquois, and he began in earnest preparations
for an expedition which he had long boasted
over. He gave notice of his purpose to Governor Dongan of New York, who was not slow
in letting the red men have the information.
La Barre's own intendant wrote to the minis-

try at home that he was entering upon the
war for personal gain. The French governor
pressed forward with his expedition, and gathered his forces at Fort Frontenac. Disease
fell upon them, but they crossed the lake to
the mouth of the Salmon River, where the
name of La Famine serves to tell of the evil
which came to aggravate their fever. This
was in September, 1684. Through the efforts
of the Jesuits a council was arranged with the
Onondagas. La Barre told the Indian deputies that he came to smoke the calumet of
peace, if all the Five Nations would give indemnity for past wrongs and pledges of good behavior. Garangula responded with audacious
eloquence: "We are born free; we depend
neither upon Onontio nor Corlaer," — neither
on the French nor the English. La Barre
was glad to make the best peace he could.
The expedition had proved an utter failure,
and King Louis, when he heard of the treaty
agreed upon, pronounced it disgraceful to the
French. It was time for La Barre to yield
place to a successor. He came in the person
of the Marquis Denonville, who was not quite
so bombastic, but was little more successful
than his predecessor. He charged the English
with furnishing arms to the Iroquois, and felt
justified in resorting to all sorts of intrigues to

counteract such influence. Sharp correspondence arose between him and the governor of
New York over Fort Niagara, the sale of liquor
to the Indians, and over the attempt on both
sides to control trade at the West. Governor
Dongan urged the first claim of entire mastery
of the country south of Lake Ontario, June 20,
1687, saying: "I hope your Excellency will be
so kind as not to desire or seek any correspondence with our Indians on this side of the Great
Lake; if they do amiss to any of your government, and you make it known to me, you shall
have all justice done." The Iroquois, for the
first time, began to style the governor of New
York "Father Corlaer" instead of Brother
Corlaer, thus recognizing English protection.

Denonville felt that French power was destroyed in the Iroquois country unless a demonstration could be made to restore lost prestige.
With a barbarity which no savages could sur-
pass, as soon as he reached Fort Frontenac on
his advance, he bound a number of Iroquois to
posts for torture, and then sent fifty to France
as prisoners, according to special orders from
King Louis. These were in part peaceable
members of colonies on the north side of the
lake, and had been entrapped on pretense of a
feast, and they were in part ambassadors from
the tribes to treat for peace. This was the

first use Denonville made of his force of two
thousand men, which included regulars of the
army of France. The Onondagas received word
of this treatment of their brethren, and the
missionary Lamberville, who was living among
them, expected to suffer in retaliation. The
chiefs, however, sent him to the French, under
an escort to guard him from possible assault.

So French missions among the Iroquois were
finally closed, through cruel treachery on the
side of the Canadian governor and with a sublime act of humanity on the side of the Onondagas.

Denonville moved forward to Irondequoit
Bay on the south side of the lake. There he
was met by a thousand allies from the western
tribes, led by Tonty and by La Durantaye, who
brought with them two trading parties of English, Dutch, and Indians captured on the upper
lakes. The Senecas, from their village near the
present site of Victor, drew the French advance
into an ambuscade, and threw it into disor-
der. They supposed it was the main body
of invaders, and they in turn suffered bloody
punishment. The panic into which the French
were thrown at the outset was checked, and
the Senecas resorted to the usual tactics of
the red men of retiring into the forests. They
took their wounded and most of their dead with

them. The French loss was reported at five or six killed and about twenty wounded, while the Senecas, it was claimed, lost forty killed and sixty wounded. The villages and provisions of the Senecas were destroyed, but Denonville retired to Irondequoit. These events occupied twelve days, from July 12 to July 24, 1687. The achievement was not one of which such an army could be proud. The record of deaths does not indicate very effective warfare on the part of the invaders. The French governor was glad to get to Niagara and devote himself there to the building of the fort, and in the next year disasters rushed so thick and fast that he was compelled to abandon that stronghold.

Denonville's expedition became the text of communications with the governor of New York, and of appeals to King Louis for more soldiers for Canada and for strengthening the forts on the border. The Canadian rulers strongly urged the acquisition of New York, which " would render His Majesty master of all North America." The device of a treaty of neutrality had failed to preserve peace on the borders, and both parties were charged, and truly too, with gross acts of violation. The question of jurisdiction over the Iroquois was sharply contested between James and Louis in the old countries, as well as between the governors of New York and Canada.

The Iroquois, meanwhile, asserted their independence of both powers, and six hundred warriors, headed by Grand Guele, marched against Montreal. The chief warned Onontio of his danger, and told him that he could escape by accepting peace on the terms proposed by Corlaer. The French governor bowed to the necessity and a truce was agreed upon, and the chiefs sent to France as captives were returned. Before Denonville gave up the government he saw another war-party ravaging Canada almost to Montreal, and bewailed the capture of Fort Frontenac by the Iroquois.

The Stuarts had been driven from the English throne, and the accession of William broke the close connections which had existed with France. Count Frontenac was sent back as governor of Canada with instructions to arrange for a simultaneous attack on the English colonies at Hudson's Bay and in New York. He was welcomed as "the Redeemer of Canada," which was surely in need of help. His efforts were directed to restoring his old relations of friendship with the red men. The authorities of New York strove to check his plans. Eighty Iroquois sachems met at Onondaga in council to consider the rival propositions. Millet, a French priest naturalized among the Oneidas, held that tribe and the Cayugas from the alliance with New York in which the Mohawks, the Onondagas, and the Senecas joined. Frontenac was equal to the emergency. He threw three expeditions against the English colonies: one by way of Three Rivers against the settlements between Albany and Boston, a second from Quebec against Maine, while the third advanced from Montreal against New York. This third column included eighty of the praying Indians from Caughnawaga, under the Mohawk chief Kryn, with other red men, and a body of Canadian bush-rangers. They marched in February, 1690, and directed their assault against Schenectady. The town was without watch or preparation, although it was surrounded by a palisade and had a small fort. The inhabitants were asleep when the invaders fell upon them. Fire and slaughter met with little resistance, for the bravest were so surprised as to fight at disadvantage. Sixty persons were killed, and twenty-seven old men, women and children were taken prisoners. Thirty Iroquois were spared, to show that the English and not the red men were the enemies aimed at, and immunity was shown to neighboring settlers who had previously befriended French prisoners. Twenty-five whites sought safety by escaping through the severities of winter to Albany, and all froze limbs on their flight. The invaders made haste to retreat with their prisoners and spoils to Canada, and suffered from cold and hunger on the way.

Peter Schuyler, mayor of Albany, with two other leading men, in the emergency wrote a strong appeal for help from the authorities of Massachusetts. He spoke of the affair at Schenectady as a "dreadful massacre and murther," the like of which had " never been committed in these parts of America," and said: "the cruelties committed no pen nor tongue can express; the women big with child ripped up, and the children alive thrown into the flames, and their heads dashed in pieces against the doors and windows." The weather was so severe that "it was as if the heavens had combined for the destruction of that poor village." The French plan was to seek immediate alliance with the Mohawks, and presents were brought to purchase amity. The effect was, on the contrary, to arouse the tribe to renewed activity, and the alarm at Albany led to movements to ward off the attack which it was feared might be directed against that town.

The Mohawks, who had been assigned the duty of scouts, were blamed for carelessness in not detecting the approach of the expedition, and now they advised the invasion of Canada. At Albany, an appeal was issued to all the colonies for a united movement against Quebec in the spring. In May, French agents were seized among the Onondagas, and two were handed over to the red men, who burned them to death. In the same month, another invading party, coming by way of Lake Champlain, captured several Iroquois and several English women, but was attacked by mistake by Indians in the French service. Here was killed Kryn, the Mohawk chief, a devoted champion of France, constantly striving to form an alliance between the Iroquois and the governors of Canada.

The conflict had already changed its character from a simple attempt of the French rulers to control the Iroquois by diplomacy and force. It had become a war between the colonies separated by the St. Lawrence. Massachusetts had made a demonstration by water under Governor Phips against Quebec, while a land movement from Albany was conducted by Connecticut and New York. The result was hardly less than disgraceful in both the land and naval operations. The New York colonists arranged to take their full part in the attack. Captain John Schuyler, the youngest brother of the mayor of Albany, added to the laurels of his brother by leading a gallant assault, with forty whites and one hundred Mohawks, to a fort at La Prairie, opposite Montreal. After driving the garrison with great loss from the fort, he retired, destroying crops and holding his command in good order. The next year, in 1691, Peter Schuyler led a force of Iroquois and settlers northward from Albany, to test the designs of Frontenac, and to defend the frontier. His force consisted of 266 men — 120 whites, 80 Mohawks, and 66 River Indians. The rendezvous was for July 17, and the advance was not challenged until within ten miles of Fort Chambly. Plans were formed for a hasty march to La Prairie, but a party of French and Indians, which Schuyler places at 420, appeared at the fort, and a sharp fight compelled them to retire within their defenses. Schuyler destroyed crops, and a second contest occurred later the same day. Frontenac pronounces the fight at this point the " most hot and stubborn " ever fought in Canada. Schuyler says : " We broke through the middle of their body until we got into their rear, trampling on their dead, then faced upon them, and fought them until we made them give way ; then drove them by strength of arm four hundred paces before us." His little army opened the path homeward, and won a real victory. Losses on both sides were

exaggerated in various letters. Schuyler reports his killed at " 21 Christians, 16 Mohawks,
and 6 River Indians, and the wounded in all
25 ; " while, he says, "it was thought by all
that his expedition killed about 200 French
and Indians." The effect in Canada was an
offset to the alarm in New York from the burning of Schenectady. John Nelson, an Englishman, at the time a prisoner in Quebec, writes
that Schuyler's action was there accounted
"one of the most vigorous and glorious attempts that hath been known in these parts,
with great slaughter on the enemy's part, and
loss on his own, in which if he had not been
discovered by an accident, it is very probable
he had become master of Montreal." That
was beyond his design, for the time, but was
the incitement to all his plans.

Captive Iroquois were in 1692 taken to Montreal, and, on two occasions at least, by order of
Frontenac, some of them were tortured and
burned at the request of his Indian allies. The
purpose was to strike terror along the Mohawk
and on Onondaga Lake. Any such effect must
have been temporary, for the Iroquois were
soon again north of the St. Lawrence and
threatening Montreal. Frontenac organized
another winter expedition, with his Indian allies as its centre, supported by a hundred sol-

diers and a band of Canadians. The force numbered six hundred, and marched from Chambly
in January, 1693. Sixteen days were spent in
reaching the lower Mohawk castles, which were
easily taken, for the warriors were absent. The
third castle was surprised, the cabins burned
and prisoners taken. The French then found
it necessary to retreat, and at the end of two
days' march they put up defensive works.
There Major Peter Schuyler, at the head of
five or six hundred men, including a party of
Oneidas, came up with the invaders. He, too,
prepared defenses, and upon them repeated assaults were in vain made by the French. In
the night the latter withdrew in a driving
snow-storm. Schuyler's force was on the point
of starvation, and was not able to make successful pursuit. The invaders, after many trials and losses, straggled home. Yet Frontenac
pronounced the expedition a glorious success.

From this time for three years comparative
quiet was maintained between the rulers on the
St. Lawrence and the red men on the Mohawk.
Frontenac received deputations who proposed
peace, but he wanted it on his own terms.
The authorities in New York tried to keep the
Iroquois in hostility to the French. They were
in large measure successful. The governor of
Canada determined upon a formidable assertion

of French power. He had restored Fort Frontenac, and there gathered his forces in July,
1696. They numbered two thousand two hundred men, regulars, Canadians, and Indians, and
were well supplied with cannon. Frontenac
was himself in chief command ; Callières, who
was to be his successor as governor of Canada,
and De Vaudreuil, already noted in Indian warfare, also to become governor and the father of
a governor, were his main lieutenants. They
advanced by the Oswego River, and August 1st
reached Onondaga Lake. The Onondagas retired before the invaders. Among the stragglers
was a warrior of eighty years, who was burned
at the stake, taunting his captors as dogs, and
dogs of dogs. The castle of the Oneidas was
also destroyed, and some hostages seized, while
Frontenac gave as the conditions of peace that
the whole tribe should emigrate to Canada.
French valor exhausted itself on the growing
crops, for no foe could be discovered. These
were the results of this ostentatious invasion.
The Onondagas and the Oneidas sacrificed their
castles, which they were powerless to defend,
and in the winter depended for food largely
upon the authorities of New York. Frontenac
boasted in his despatches to the French king
that no force withstood him in ambuscade or in

the passes of the hills. The Iroquois strategy
was more cunning and effective. The French
force was compelled to retire without a fight,
and the Indian warriors nestled unharmed in
the wilderness.

The peace of Ryswick in 1697, between
France and England, ended hostilities with the
Iroquois on the soil of New York, for the time.
Controversy arose over the prisoners captured,
and the recognition of the dependence of the
Iroquois upon the British government. But the
chapter of Frontenac's exploits was closed.
New York had escaped from its most threatening danger of subjection to the French, and its
red men retained their wide domain. Frontenac died November 22, 1698, and his name is
indelibly marked in the annals of New York as
well as of Canada. Distinguished as a soldier,
far-seeing as a statesman, no other governor of
Canada approached him in skill in dealing with
the Indians or in power over them. He could
adopt their habits, and in a war council he led
the war-dance and whooped like a savage. He
was seventy-six years old at the time of his invasion of the Onondaga country, and on the advance was carried in a litter. He learned the
reverses of fortune, and his vast schemes for
the subjection of the Iroquois proved empty

visions. The fault cannot be attributed to him. The event was due to the courage and persistence and loyalty of the Five Nations and to the advantages which they enjoyed in their imperial domain.

II. A BRITISH COLONY.

CHAPTER XII.

BEGINNINGS OF ENGLISH RULE.

1674–1688.

THE representative of the British government to receive the province now finally to be known as New York, was Major Edmund Andros, a member of the royal household, distinguished in the wars in Holland, a major in Prince Rupert's dragoons, and already the commander of the king's forces in Barbadoes. To him a commission was given as lieutenant and governor of the territories of the Duke of York in America, and these James took pains to assure to himself by a new patent from the king. Elaborate instructions required Governor Andros to encourage settlement and foster trade, and imposed a tariff of two per cent. on all goods imported from England or its possessions, and ten per cent. if from any foreign country, with higher charges upon wines and liquors. Merchandise carried up the Hudson, except farmers' tools, was to pay three per cent. In addition, the excise and internal taxes imposed by Nicolls and Lovelace were to be continued. Courts were to be maintained in the king's name. A council of ten was to be appointed by the governor; " all persons of what religion soever " were to be treated alike, if they did not molest others. Anthony Brockholls, a Roman Catholic, was designated as lieutenant-governor, while Andros was a moderate Episcopalian. The Duke of York sent over a company of a hundred infantry to serve in the province.

When the vessels bearing the new governor and his staff, accompanied by a number of colonists, arrived in New York, Governor Colve and the burgomasters asked for guarantees to the Dutch inhabitants. These were accorded. November 9, 1674, Governor Colve made his formal farewell, and the next day the ceremonies of the transfer were consummated. Nine days later British officers were installed at Albany. Meetings on the eastern part of Long Island pronounced that their people owed allegiance to Connecticut, but Andros soon asserted the authority of New York over them. Matthias Nicolls was designated as secretary of the province and mayor of New York, and a council and board of aldermen were appointed.

Manning, who had surrendered the province to the Dutch fleet, was put on trial for neglect of duty, cowardice and treachery. He pleaded guilty to the first charge and appealed for mercy. His sword was broken over his head in front of the city hall, and he was pronounced incapable of filling any office of trust.

Governor Andros soon showed the temper of his administration. John Burroughs, town clerk of Newtown, was forced to stand an hour on the whipping-post in front of the city hall, for stating by direction of his fellow-townsmen the grievances under which they suffered. Many prominent burghers of New York objected to an oath of allegiance required of them, and eight asked to take a modified form or to be permitted to remove from the colony. The governor refused assent, and the signers of the petition, Steenwyck, Van Brugh, De Peyster, Bayard, Luyck, Beekman, Kip, and De Milt, were imprisoned for endeavoring to incite a rebellion, and were released only on giving bonds. They sent a memorial of their case to the States General. Trial was ordered before the court of assizes, and seven were convicted, but finally all yielded and took the oath, whereupon the penalties were remitted. Arrests for sedition were not a rarity. In 1678 Jacob Milborne was arrested as "a mutinous person,"

and going to London after his discharge, three
years later, recovered a verdict of £45 against
Governor Andros. His subsequent career may
indicate that the epithet was well applied.

The transfer of the colony, however, caused
less friction than might have been expected,
and moderation prevailed as a rule on the part
of the government, as well as of the settlers.
Governor Andros was busy in other ways in
confirming his powers. He landed in Saybrook
with a force to proclaim his title over Connecticut; he sent soldiers to Martha's Vineyard and
Nantucket; and he visited the red men at the
sources of the Mohawk, penetrating "nearly a
hundred miles beyond Schenectady." The Iroquois held a conference with him at Albany,
where they gave assurances of good will. Recognizing the importance of friendly relations
with them, he organized a board of commissioners for Indian affairs, and designated as
secretary Robert Livingston, a Scotchman now
twenty-one years old, who had come hither
from Rotterdam, and had already become town
clerk of Albany. While New England was engaged in the war with its Indians, resulting in
the death of King Philip, charges were made
that arms and ammunition were furnished to
the Indians from Albany. Andros indignantly
denied the slander, and sent six barrels of pow-

der and other supplies to Rhode Island, while
that colony fostered very cordial relations with
New York. In the crisis of the conflict, the
Mohawks struck severe blows against the eastern Indians. Edward Randolph, an agent from
England, investigated the charges that Albany had assisted the enemy in the war, and
pronounced them " without any just cause or
ground, but rather a report raised out of malice and envy," and King Charles confirmed this
judgment. But the relations between New
York on the one hand, and Connecticut and
Massachusetts on the other, continued to be
strained. With New Jersey also Andros had
trouble, and he refused to allow a port to be
opened in its territory. He was instructed by
the Duke of York to maintain the northern
bounds of New York " as far as the Lake or the
River of Canada." This claim brought on controversy with the French at Montreal, and with
King Louis, relative to jurisdiction over the
Iroquois. The Duke of York also asserted
rights in Maine, and as the red men there were
working harm, Governor Andros sent an expedition to Pemaquid, where Fort Charles was
built, and arrangements were made for a government dependent on New York.

The Iroquois were already and long continued
a source of very great anxiety and responsibility

to the province. In 1677, Massachusetts and Connecticut asked and were permitted to hold conference with them in Albany, and formed a treaty of friendship. Maryland and Virginia, in the same year, sent an agent, who agreed upon satisfactory relations with the confederacy.

Governor Andros went to England in 1678, perhaps notified that he was there to be knighted for his services, and left his lieutenant, Brockholls, in control of the province. The governor made a statement of its affairs when he reached London. The value of all the estates was about £150,000. A merchant having £500 or £1,000 was accounted substantial, and a planter " rich " with half that capital. There were " very few slaves," each worth £30 to £35. The exports were mainly provisions, furs, tar, and lumber, and the imports £50,000 a year in British manufactures. In all the province were about twenty churches, including Presbyterians and Independents, Quakers, Anabaptists, Lutherans, Reformed, and Jews, and all supported by "free gifts." The Duke maintained an Episcopal chaplain. Nicolaus van Rensselaer, ordained in both the Reformed and Episcopal churches in the old countries, had been recommended by James, and was made a colleague of Domine Schaats in the Reformed church in Albany. Charges were brought against him by

Jacob Leisler and Jacob Milborne for heresy, and he was tried in New York, on appeal, by the mayor and aldermen and the ministers of the city. The Albany authorities managed to adjust the differences, and the prosecutors were compelled to pay all costs. It was a fitting ending to one of our earliest religious controversies.

In 1679 a classis of the Reformed Church of Holland was organized to ordain·Petrus Tesschenmaker, a graduate of the university of Utrecht, who wished to serve as a clergyman on the Delaware. It is a curious incident that Governor Andros, an Episcopalian, gave an official order for the examination of the candidate, and that the ordination was approved by the authorities of the church in Amsterdam. Governor Andros also took the initiative for building a new edifice for the Reformed Church in New York, and contributed to the free gifts for the purpose; while Rev. Charles Wolley, an Episcopalian, who had come out as chaplain of the forces in the province, attended the meeting, with its pastor, Domine Van Nieuwenhuysen. Chaplain Wolley in 1701 published a " Journal of Two Years in New York," in which he praised the air and pronounced the " inhabitants, both Dutch and English, very civil and courteous," to whose " tables he was frequently

invited, and always concluded with a generous
bottle of Madeira."

New Jersey was a continual thorn in the
flesh of the New York authorities. Conflicting
claims led Governor Andros to send soldiers to
Elizabethtown, where Carteret, who held a
patent from the Duke of York, resided, and in
the dead of night he was taken a prisoner to
New York on the charge of assuming illegal
jurisdiction. Andros sat as judge, while Carteret showed his commission as governor of
New Jersey. The jury, against Sir Edmund's
efforts, recorded a verdict of not guilty, and
Carteret was conducted home with great pomp.
The authority of Governor Andros was, however, so far recognized that civil and military
officers commissioned by him were inducted
into office without question. In 1680 justices
from New Jersey, Nantucket, and Pemaquid
attended the court of assizes in New York.
Quakers had come into West Jersey, and
sought to set up a separate government. William Penn was among those who in London argued their case before the Duke's commission.
The matter was referred to Sir William Jones,
who found in favor of the Quakers, and the
Duke of York granted a deed to their leaders.
In 1680, the controversy over East Jersey was
settled by a similar instrument.

That controversy led to the recall of Sir Edmund Andros. Lady Carteret complained to the Duke of the arrest of her son, and the Duke disowned all responsibility. Farmers of the revenue were in favor in that age, and an offer was made to James to pay him large returns for the receipts of New York. Complaints were urged of the governor's action concerning trade, and his accounts were alleged not to agree with the actual revenue. The Duke sent out John Lewin to inquire into all the affairs of the administration. He prosecuted his investigations with sleuth-hound zeal, and the authorities of New York complained of his violation of personal rights. When his report was submitted to the Duke's attorney and solicitor, they found that the governor had not " misbehaved himself," nor " in any way defrauded or mismanaged the revenue." Andros received a substantial token of vindication in an order to serve as a gentleman of the king's privy chamber, and so was kept in London until he was sent out as governor general of all the northern colonies.

The administration in the absence of the governor was committed to Anthony Brockholls as commander-in-chief. Trouble befell him at once, because the customs duties had expired by limitation and had not been renewed. The merchants on this ground refused to pay any

duties on imports. The council advised Brockholls that he had no authority to collect them
without orders from the Duke. Dyer, collector
of the port, was arrested, and charged with trai-
torously exercising " regal power and authority," because he tried to hold goods to enforce
payment. He appealed to the courts at home,
but without trial finally received practical approval of his course by appointment as surveyor
general of customs in America. The jury, on
the other hand, declared to the court of assizes
that a provincial assembly was needed. Sheriff
John Younge, of Long Island, was designated to
draft a petition to the Duke of York for " an
assembly to be duly elected by the freeholders,
as is usual within the realm of England and
other of his majesty's plantations." The demand was urgent, because the inhabitants " were
groaning under inexpressible burdens of an arbitrary and absolute power," by which " revenue
had been exacted, their trade crippled, and
their liberties enthralled." Disaffection was
open and pronounced, especially on Long Island. Lieutenant-Governor Brockholls laid the
case before the Duke, and was censured for not
promptly renewing the order for the duties and
enforcing their collection.

The pressure for money led the Duke to intimate that he " would condescend to the desires

of the colony in granting them equal privileges
in choosing an assembly and so forth, as the
other English plantations in America have;"
but this was "on the supposition that the inhabitants will agree to raise money to discharge
the public debts, and to settle such a fund for
the future as may be sufficient for the maintenance of the garrison and government." James
had previously disapproved of any movement
for an assembly as fraught with "dangerous
consequences," while he pointed to the court of
assizes as adequate to hear and remedy any
grievances. Now he declared, March 28, 1682,
that he "sought the common good and protection of the colony and the increase of its
trade " before any advantages to himself, and
he promised that whatever revenues the people
would provide should be applied to the public
uses suggested.

The summons for an assembly was, however, left for a new governor to issue. Thomas
Dongan, who was permitted to inaugurate his
administration with this gracious act, arrived in
New York August 28, 1683, and on the next
day the city authorities welcomed him by "a
large and plentiful entertainment." He was
born in 1634, the youngest son of an Irish bar-
onet, was a colonel in the Royal Army, had
seen service in France, and been lieutenant-

governor of Tangiers. He was a Roman Catholic, and was to prove himself a man of prudence, of loyalty to the colony, and for that period a statesman of foresight as well as of ability.

His commission covered the land to the west side of the Connecticut River, with Pemaquid, Martha's Vineyard, and Nantucket. His instructions were to call Frederick Phillipse and Stephen van Cortlandt and other "most eminent inhabitants" as councilors, not exceeding ten in number, and to summon a general assembly, to consist of not more than eighteen persons, to be chosen by all the freeholders. This assembly was to "have free liberty to consult and debate for all laws," and its statutes were to be valid unless disapproved by the Duke. The governor was clothed with authority to establish courts similar to those in England, but the Duke's command was a condition for waging war, and revenue could be collected only under act of the assembly. The formal summons for this assembly bears date September 13, 1683, and was addressed to the freeholders of Pemaquid and Martha's Vineyard as well as of New York, Long Island, Esopus, and Albany.

The assembly met in Fort James, October 17, with Matthias Nicolls as speaker, and a letter from the Duke of York was read. In a session of three weeks fourteen acts were passed.

By far the most important was " the Charter of
Liberties," in which declaration was made that
under the king and lord proprietor " the supreme legislative authority shall forever be and
reside in a governor, council, and the people
met in a general assembly." It was the first
time " the people " were recognized " in any
constitution in America," as James when he
became king took occasion promptly to point
out. The whole document was in the same
free spirit. It provided in elections for liberty
of choice for all freeholders, and for entire freedom in religion. It embodied in plain words
the principle that " no aid, tax, custom, loan,
benevolence or imposition whatsoever shall be
levied within this province upon any pretense,
but by the consent of the governor, council and
representatives of the people in general assembly." An accompanying act granted certain
duties on imports to the Duke and his heirs.
In no other colony in America had the principle of representation of the people as a condition of taxation been so clearly asserted by statute at that day. Twelve counties were erected
— New York, Westchester, Ulster, Dutchess,
Orange, Albany, Richmond, Kings, Queens, Suffolk — within the present State, while Dukes
County included Nantucket and Martha's Vineyard and dependencies, and Cornwall covered

Pemaquid and adjacent territory. Courts were established and naturalization provided for. This assembly did its work well and promptly, and set a good example to its successors.

The boundaries of the colony gave Governor Dongan no little trouble. Its relations with Canada and the Iroquois presented the most serious difficulty. He met the controversy with courage and foresight, and bore himself well in complex and trying negotiations. The claim of New York to jurisdiction to Lake Ontario and the St. Lawrence he maintained with persistency, and the purpose to protect and control the red men in this territory was asserted in many forms. The raids of the Iroquois to the south brought Francis, Lord Howard of Effingham, to confer with the governor of New York, and together they met the chiefs of the Mohawks, Oneidas, Onondagas, and Cayugas in Albany, July 30, 1684. Stephen van Cortlandt represented Massachusetts in the consultation, which lasted for several days. The occasion was important, the speeches as they have been preserved were notable and eloquent, and the whole transaction was peculiar and picturesque. The results were far-reaching and impressive. The Four Nations represented submitted to King Charles, with the formality of signatures and seals, and the record was made on parchment, to be sent to England. Tomahawks were buried in behalf of the contracting parties, and "the Indians threw dirt upon them" in sign of enduring peace, and they "sang the Peace Song," and rejoiced over the treaty. The arms of the Duke of York were put upon the castles of the Four Nations. As the negotiations were closing, the Senecas appeared and were included in the adjustment.

Governor La Barre, on the part of Canada, refused to recognize the "pretensions" to the soil or its red inhabitants, and the case was reported to the governments of France and Britain. The governor of Canada did not deem it necessary to change his policy before he received orders from his home government to do so, and he kept up his hostile movements against the Iroquois, and complained that help was given them from Albany.

The accession of James II. to the throne boded no good to New York, or to popular rights in any of the colonies. He continued in the main the policy towards Canada and the Iroquois which had been inaugurated. He repudiated the charter of liberties, ostensibly in part because it recognized a "lord proprietor" who was now king, but also because it tended to abridge the king's power and traced authority to "the people met in general assembly," and he ordered " the government of New York to be assimilated to that of New England," where no assembly was authorized. He held on, however, to the revenue which had been voted as a consideration for the charter he now repudiated. Yet the colonists felt a sort of personal interest in the king whose ducal title was borne by their domain, and they gave cordial expression to their loyalty.

His reward to them, as to all the provinces, was to enforce the royal authority, without respect to petition or protests. For one thing he deserves credit. While previously in every form, even in the charter of liberties, liberty of conscience was confined to those " professing faith in God by Jesus Christ," now King James, in instructions to Governor Dongan, extended such liberty to " all persons, of what religion soever." He extended the ecclesiastical jurisdiction of the Archbishop of Canterbury over the colony, and schoolmasters were required to get licenses from him. At the same time, printing without leave of the governor was expressly prohibited. The provincial assembly, first prorogued for six months, was by proclamation of January 20, 1687, formally dissolved, and Governor Dongan and his council assumed power to impose taxes and frame statutes. But the right of represen-

tation was so vital and fruitful in the breasts
of the colonists, that the denial of it caused a
stir and ferment which soon compelled its restoration.

All the while the Iroquois kept busy the
wits and the resources of the governors of
New York and Canada, and compelled them to
make frequent resort to the home authorities.
Governor Dongan gave passes for trade and
hunting to young men to penetrate to the
western tribes, and this competition invited
protests from the French.   The French governors kept up their raids at intervals into the
Iroquois country.   The influence of French
missionaries prompted Dongan to seek for
English Jesuits to counteract it.   He held frequent conferences with the red men, and, by
moral means and occasionally by arms and aid,
strengthened them against the French.   His
plans were far-reaching.   He recommended the
erection of forts at Ticonderoga, Oswego, and
Niagara to serve as a cordon about the red men,
whom he recognized as the " bulwark " of the
colony against French assault.

Governor Dongan thriftily turned many a
penny from the change which had taken place
in the occupancy of the British throne.   He
required the several towns to take out new
patents, and collected fees on them.   New

York and Albany in 1686 each paid him £300 for their revised charters, besides fees to subordinates, and Rensselaerwyck paid £200. The charges created no scandals, and were accounted the proper perquisites of the office. Nor was Dongan a venal man. He pledged his personal credit and mortgaged his farm to raise money in aid of the expedition against Canada which brought so little of glory.

His official career was closed by the policy adopted by King James of consolidating the colonies north of Pennsylvania under a single head. He proved himself here a competent governor, faithful, of broad views and vigorous in action; his report continues to be a model of clearness and accuracy concerning the affairs of the colony. The principal towns were at this time New York, Albany, and Kingston, and the first two were maintained wholly by trade with the Indians, with England, and with the West Indies. England took beaver and other peltry, oil and tobacco, while to the West Indies flour, bread, peas, pork, and sometimes horses were exported. New York was far from an English or even a British settlement. Governor Dongan testifies that in seven years after his coming, not over twenty families arrived of English, Scotch, or Irish people, while of French families several had come, and several Dutch

families had been added to the population.
On such facts he based an argument for the
union of the Jerseys and Connecticut with New
York, "so that a more equal balance may be
kept between his Majesty's natural born subjects and foreigners, which latter," he adds,
"are the most prevailing part of this government." He states the case moderately.

German and French Protestants found welcome in New York, and after the repeal of the
Edict of Nantes the latter came in considerable
numbers, so that the Huguenots attained at
once to recognized influence both by reason of
their numbers, and the ability, worth, and thrift
of their leaders. The current of migration
from Canada was at times so strong as to lead
to appeals from Montreal for aid from Albany
to check it. The Quakers were those who fared
worst under the administration of Governor
Dongan. Their creed did not permit them to
take up arms for the colony in its needs, and
they were fined for refusal. For kindred reasons the privilege of voting was denied to them.
Their grievances now begun were long the subject of discussion.

After he gave up his position, Governor
Dongan retired to his farm at Hempstead.
When the anti-Catholic fever raged he was
brought under suspicion. Because he con-

structed a brigantine for a visit to England, he was charged with getting up a force to maintain the authority of James against William and Mary, and in Leisler's time a warrant was issued for his arrest. He withdrew across the border until the craze passed away. In his administration he was tolerant of all creeds, not only because his instructions so enjoined, but because his own spirit was generous and liberal. Those were evil times which chose such a man for a victim, and heaped false charges upon him, and drove him, even temporarily, from the rural home where he was illustrating the modest virtues of a private person.

CHAPTER XIII.

A REBELLION AND AN EXECUTION.

1688–1691.

THE colony was now to enter upon stirring experiences. James II. had ordered the consolidation of the northern colonies under the title of the Dominion of New England, and had designated Sir Edmund Andros, at the time governor in Boston, as Governor-in-Chief and Captain-General. He was to have a council of forty-two members, selected from the various provinces. No seat of government was designated, and Governor Andros exercised his power wherever he happened to be, whether in Boston, New York, or far-off Pemaquid. The majority of the population was east of the Hudson, and a close union of the colonies was for many purposes desirable. But New York did not take kindly to the apparent advantages which its eastern neighbors were likely to gain by the new policy. Its governor and the merchants at the seaport wanted Connecticut and the Jerseys brought under its jurisdiction. One of the first results of the royal plan was to carry Connecticut into the arms of Boston. It was inevitable also that the eastern towns of Long Island, largely settled from New England, should go east to trade more than the merchants of New York approved. New England was Puritan in creed, and its clergy directed its policy. New York was liberal, already cosmopolitan, and gave no special preference to priest or preacher of any creed.

Governor Andros had in this first council Anthony Brockholls, Frederick Phillipse, Jarvis Baxter, Stephen van Cortlandt, John Spragg, John Younge, Nicholas Bayard, and John Palmer, of New York. They took part in legislation and administration for all the northern colonies, while New York was equally subject to the joint authority of the councilors resident elsewhere. Andros came to New York August 11, 1688, to receive the transfer of power from Dongan, and was received with pomp, and kindly remembrance of his previous services. He visited Albany for a conference with the Iroquois, at the time when Denonville was threatening to subdue them. But the governor general soon found that the eastern colonies needed his care, and kept him in Boston, while Francis Nicholson, captain of a company of soldiers sent from England, represented, as lieutenant governor of the Dominion, the royal authority in New York.

When James Stuart, by his bigotry and arbitrary measures, threw away the crown of Britain, the American colonies were cast into a ferment of excitement. They had been warned to guard against invasion by foreign force. They were prompt to respond to the first summons to proclaim the new sovereigns. New England rejoiced because they were Protestants ; New York beheld in William a Dutchman, its former friend, and therefore the harbinger of a restoration of its local government. But the accession of William and Mary, as it was the immediate source of revolt in Massachusetts, led in New York to rebellion, open, armed, and for a while completely successful.

The colonies, the British law-officers held, passed from one sovereign to another by the same act which brought in William and Mary. They confirmed in the colonies the commissions of all persons "being Protestants." When Nicholson in New York learned by a shipmaster from Virginia of the change of government in England, he scouted at the "invasion," and forbade promulgation of the news. When Andros, who was in Maine, was informed of the revolution, he awaited official notification. This, it

was charged, was delayed by the intrigues of
Increase Mather, who was in London. By a
popular movement Governor Andros, on returning to Boston, was placed under arrest, and a
committee of safety for Massachusetts was
created. So the Dominion of New England
went to pieces, and New York was left to administer its own affairs. Andros had definitely
cut off Pemaquid, Martha's Vineyard, and their
dependencies from its jurisdiction, and confirmed
Connecticut in its separation.

Nicholson, the lieutenant governor at New
York, had no nerve to breast a storm. His title
to act at all was questioned. With his chief
under arrest, could he claim original authority?
The three councilors then in New York were
Phillipse, Van Cortlandt, and Bayard. They
summoned the aldermen and council of the city
to advise in the emergency, the justices and
military officers accessible were invited, and an
appeal was issued to royal councilors to assist
with their wisdom. Not one of the latter appeared, nor did the rural counties respond when
asked to appoint delegates for conference.
Nicholson sent a messenger to England with a
report of the situation and a request for instructions, and in the mean time he concluded
that it was " most safe to forbear acting in the
premises till the minds of the people become

better satisfied and quieted." Andros had no
suggestions for his lieutenant further than to
ask him to send commissioners to Boston to ask
for the governor's release from imprisonment.

But New York took no interest in petitions
to the committee of safety in Boston, and was
not disposed to "forbear acting." On the contrary, the rule of James II. had introduced into
the colony a dread of Catholic aggression. Dongan was a Catholic, and personally observed the
forms of his church, while he was tolerant to
every faith. Nicholson was nominally an Episcopalian, but he had in the camp of King James
reverently kneeled at the celebration of the
mass, and by a stretch of intolerance was denounced as a "papist." His three councilors
belonged to the Dutch church. The religious
fears and prejudices which had precipitated the
revolution in Britain were grotesquely para-
phrased in New York. "With his sword
William became King of England;" with his
sword Jacob Leisler became Dictator of New
York.

The story is for the greater part a comedy
rather than a tragedy; for the rebellion was
achieved without bloodshed, and only at its close
were lives sacrificed. At last the chief paid for
his brief exercise of power with his life. One
of the first needs of the government, when the

arrest of Andros occurred, was for funds, especially for the defense of the port. Nicholson
ordered the revenue from the customs to be applied to this purpose. Jacob Leisler, a captain
of militia, refused to pay duties on a cargo of
wine, on the pretext that the collector was a
" papist." The militia was called to keep guard
at Fort James, in apprehension of French invasion. Lieutenant Henry Cuyler ordered a
man to stand sentinel, and Nicholson called him
to account for exceeding his authority, and in
wild rage exclaimed: " I would rather see the
town on fire than commanded by you!" His
words were reported as a threat to burn the
town, and they started the flame of revolution.
The succeeding Sunday it came to be alleged
he was to order another massacre of St. Bar-
tholomew.

A conference was held May 31, 1689, when
Nicholson sought to explain his position. He
lost his temper, took Cuyler's commission away,
and afforded the occasion for open revolt. The
militia captains who were present ordered the
drums beat. The companies were soon under
arms, and on their demand Nicholson gave up
to them the keys of the fort. A declaration
was drafted by Leisler, signed by several, and
circulated in manuscript, repeating the grievances and dangers felt and apprehended, and

promising to hold the fort " in behalf of the
power that now governeth in England, and to
surrender to the person of the Protestant religion" sent to receive it. The charges grew by
repetition. By accident a sloop arrived from
the Barbadoes, off Coney Island, and it was represented to be the advance of a French fleet
with a Catholic army. The militia was gathered into the fort, and Leisler issued a proclamation, signed also by five other captains and
four hundred men, renewing the pledge to hold
the fort, with the specification that they awaited
" orders from His Royal Highness the Prince of
Orange." Official letters addressed to Nicholson and his councilors Leisler seized and read.
He and four other captains joined in an address
to William and Mary, reciting the events in
which they were actors, and giving assurance
of prompt submission to their pleasure. While
Leisler was acting with so much vigor, Nicholson went off to England, June 6, 1689, carrying
letters from clergymen and his councilors, and
abandoning the field.

Now, if not before, Leisler might claim the
right to act. He summoned first a committee
of safety, and then a popular convention. Delegates were chosen by a light vote from most of
the towns, excepting those in Queens, Suffolk,
Ulster, and Albany counties, and they assembled

in the fort in New York, June 26, 1689. Two
withdrew when the purpose became apparent;
but ten members constituted themselves into
a committee of safety, and designated Jacob
Leisler as captain of the fort, " till orders shall
come from their Majesties." He set to work,
built a battery, and organized a company of
soldiers. He sent out Sergeant Joost Stoll, a
"dram-seller," to "disarm the papists," and
several persons were arrested. No magistrate
could be found to administer the oath of allegiance to the existing power, and so the committee of safety designated Leisler as commander-
in-chief with full discretion. Report of these
transactions was carried to London by Stoll
and Matthew Clarkson, the latter of whom returned as secretary of the province. Orders
were issued for elections in the several counties,
which were only in part recognized. Albany
under the guidance of its mayor, Peter Schuyler, and the leading inhabitants, refused to
recognize the commander-in-chief, or to be
"subordinate to the city of New York." When
alarm arose from the operations of Denonville,
Albany sent an express to Leisler for help, and
in turn he declined to coöperate in the defense
of the northern borders. Nor was he content
with this refusal. He sent a force with three
sloops under his son-in-law, Jacob Milborne, up

the Hudson to bring the recusant town into subjection. Milborne did not fail for lack of speech or strategy. His arguments were set aside, and Mayor Peter Schuyler, in command of the fort, thrust him out, and, ordering the garrison to load its guns, he "read a paper." He had also at hand a body of Mohawks ready to help the Albany garrison against the New York assailants. Milborne was compelled to withdraw as he came, except as he had organized a faction among the young men with Joachim Staats as leader.

In New York Leisler's power was growing. The charges of "popish plots," and of hostile schemes on the part of Nicholson and his allies, were diligently exaggerated, and the usual devices of arbitrary power of searches and annoyances were employed, so that not a few persons of prominence fled from the colony. When special letters addressed to Nicholson arrived, or to "such as may bear rule for the time being," Leisler appropriated them, and acted on the orders they contained. He seized a messenger bearing other orders from England. Thereupon he claimed authority as lieutenant governor under the king's commission, and he tried to continue the government in the former grooves. By the seizure of private letters he claimed that he had "detected a hellish conspiracy" against

the king's government and New York, and on
this pretext he arrested the councilor Bayard,
who was carried in chains about the fort, and
William Nicolls, who had also aroused his hate.
They were kept in close confinement for thirteen
months. When Schenectady was burned, the
popular alarm prompted him to order many
other arrests.

The dread of the vigorous movements of
Frontenac for the moment brought recognition
of the sole government existing on the lower
Hudson. On the advice of Connecticut, the
Albany authorities accepted Leisler as governor, although the ink was yet fresh on their
protest that he was a "restless and ambitious
spirit," "acting without the least show of authority." To a summons to elect delegates to
an assembly, all the counties except Suffolk and
Queens responded, and it was held April 24,
1690, and provided for a revenue; but on receiving petitions for the release of political
prisoners it was prorogued until September,
when it met again to clothe Leisler with almost
absolute control of person and property in the
colony.

One of the anomalies of history is that the
call for the first Colonial Congress in America
proceeded from this governor, whose title was
won by his sword and his audacity, was always

in dispute, and was finally cancelled on the
gallows. The immediate suggestion was presented by the convention held in Albany in
February, 1690, and was inspired by the Five
Nations as the teaching of their experience.
The Colonial Congress met in New York, May
1, 1690, and Jacob Leisler and Peter de la
Noy were the members for that colony. Its
business was to organize joint expeditions
against Canada. The coöperation was far
from complete, and the movement became a
failure, to serve for a prophecy of a future
achievement, when union should be learned
and practiced.

William and Mary refused to listen to the
agents of Leisler, and appointed Colonel Henry
Sloughter to be governor of New York. But
the incumbent held his position firmly, though
once assaulted in the street. He grew more
arbitrary in his conduct, and delay in the arrival of the newly appointed executive produced serious complications. Sloughter's commission bore date September 2, 1689, but by
delay in England and mishaps to his vessel at
Bermuda, he did not reach New York until
March 19, 1691. In the mean time a vessel had
arrived which sailed when he did, and bore
Major Richard Ingoldsby, with two companies
of soldiers. These landed September 10, 1690.

Major Ingoldsby had no authority to act as
commander in the absence of his chief. Leisler professed himself as ready to welcome
Governor Sloughter, and offered quarters to
Ingoldsby and his soldiers in the town, but insisted on holding the fort until the governor
should arrive. Collision arose upon this
ground. Leisler collected the militia to sustain
him. Ingoldsby, on the urgency of persons
named of the new governor's council, prepared
for seizing the fort. Armed men were arrayed
against each other. Proclamations, addresses,
letters, were thick as rooks. March 17, Leisler
with his own hands fired a gun from the fort
at the British troops on parade, and volleys
of musketry followed. The force of Ingoldsby
returned the fire. Of the latter two were
killed, and several wounded. On Leisler's side
six were killed.

The bloodshed would have been prevented if
patience had held out two days longer, for when
the hostile forces were waiting to renew the
conflict, Governor Sloughter arrived, hastened
to land, and organized his government. Leisler
first asked for sight of the royal commission,
and sought to make terms, but he soon surrendered the fort, and was imprisoned with his
chief supporters. The next month they were
put on trial, charged with treason and murder,

for holding the fort after the arrival of Ingoldsby, and for the resistance offered to him.
A court was specially commissioned to conduct
the trial; all of its members were English or
Scotch, and nearly all with titles as officers.
Major Ingoldsby was one of the judges named,
and William Pinhorne, another of them, was
also designated on a committee, with Bayard
and Van Cortlandt, to prepare evidence for the
prosecution. The jury was all drawn from New
York, while the other counties were not represented at all. Then and afterwards it was alleged that the governor and council put only
the enemies of Leisler on the bench; and this is
substantially true. Leisler and his son-in-law
and main support, Milborne, denied the jurisdiction of the court, but they were found guilty as
mutes. Besides them were convicted Abraham
Gouverneur, Gerardus Beekman, Johannes Ver-
milye, Thomas Williams, Myndert Coerten, and
Abraham Brasher. Two others indicted were
acquitted. Most of these prisoners were after
a time discharged, but passion raged bitter and
violent against Leisler and Milborne. The
Dutch clergymen, who had felt the rebel's
power, led the demand for the enforcement of
the law, and the wealthier people, especially the
women, joined in the clamor. Petitions were
presented for pardon or mitigation of sentence,
but to no avail.

Leisler and Milborne were hanged, and their heads separated from their bodies, May 16, 1691, near old Tammany Hall, in New York. It was a cruel, unnecessary exercise of legal authority. When Sloughter arrived, the foundation and superstructure of Leisler's power were annihilated.

He was a rebel, it is true, but he had not used his usurped power corruptly or basely. Even his enemies rested their entire indictment against him on his conduct subsequent to the landing of Ingoldsby. If his authority before that time was not controverted in court, he can well be pardoned for insisting on some real title on the part of those who summoned him to surrender. The evidence is absolute that he had the support of a large and growing majority of the people. Of the three resident councilors whom Nicholson left, Phillipse early joined Leisler, and Bayard later recognized him. The Albany convention yielded after a while, and the other colonies all followed Connecticut in treating him as the governor of New York.

He was born in Frankfort on the Main, and came to New York as a soldier in the pay of the West India Company. He engaged in trade and took sea ventures, on one of which in 1678 he was captured by the Turks, and compelled to secure his freedom by a large ransom. His education was limited, but he became connected by marriage with both Bayard and Van Cortlandt. He caught the wild fever of the times against the Catholics, and like other zealots denounced as " papists " all who crossed his path. The divisions which he caused weakened the colony in its contests with the French in Canada; but he put forth wise and broad efforts to correct that evil, and to organize the forces of New York, and to make it a centre of a union of all the colonies.

His faults were those of all usurpers. He was arbitrary and violent, and pursued his personal enemies with public enginery. Yet until that unfortunate last day before the arrival of Sloughter, he shed no drop of blood to get or to hold his place. He appealed to popular forms for carrying on his administration, and expressed himself at all times as ready to hand it over to any duly accredited representative of the British crown. His logic was natural that King William could not deem him guilty for maintaining the Protestant faith in New York by the same instrument that asserted it in England. But the Protestant faith was in no danger in New York. The Catholics were few in number, had never been aggressive, and could have exercised no control if they had tried to do so. But Dongan had several Catholics in prominent places, and he was charged with putting a Jesuit over the Latin school. Those who saw in Canada and in France the incarnation of the papal power were easily alarmed, although New York was far less bigoted than other countries. Race controversies facilitated the schemes of Leisler. The English rule was not yet so firmly established but that those of other blood and other birth found occasion for complaint. They had probably their fair share in the colonial council and local offices, but the difference was a convenient pretext for a rallying cry.

Leisler was overthrown by no popular uprising. He felt strong enough to hold the fort against two companies of British regulars. He succumbed to the royal seal, but not to actual force. His dying speech was that of a sincere man, not without a touch of heroism, and with a deep desire for the welfare of the colony. It puts his religious character in a favorable light. Milborne was less resigned to the gallows, and had less of the stuff of leader or martyr. The British parliament passed in 1695 an act reversing the attainder of Leisler and his associates, and annulling all the convictions. The act not only recognized Leisler's appointment by the assembly, but treats it as confirmed by the royal letters addressed to "such as bear rule," and expressly declares that Ingoldsby's demand for possession of the fort was "without legal authority," while the transfer to Sloughter was gracious and in due time. If the severity of the court and of the governor, council and assembly had been mitigated by the generosity which at that late day parliament exhibited, the record of New York might have been spared the stain of cruelty and of the sacrifice from political malice of two brave and active lives.

CHAPTER XIV.

A REACTION IN ADMINISTRATION.

1691–1708.

COLONEL SLOUGHTER had a council appointed for him at Whitehall, made up of the pronounced opponents of Leisler, or, as the phrase was, of members of the "party of aristocrats;" for already wealth was a claim to distinction, and certain families began to assume eminence and influence. He was authorized to summon a general assembly, abolished by James II. When that body assembled, it appealed to the king to give back Connecticut and the original Jerseys, including Pennsylvania, to this colony, and it re-enacted substantially the old charter of liberties, with the exclusion, however, of the right to worship according to the "Romish religion."

So the government of the province was put again on a regular track. Relations with its neighbors were growing more close in various ways. The questions which were arising were not unlike those which the settlers elsewhere had to deal with. The conditions were not identical; for the inhabitants were in large part different in origin, in training, and in many elements of character, and their views of British authority were not the same. By geographical position, now that the colonists recognized a common sovereign, New York became a link between those to the east and those to the south, and the activity and importance of the Iroquois, and the continual conflicts with Canada, made it a centre of colonial conference and operations.

History often turns on the character and conduct of the rulers. At this period New York affords no wide field of that sort. Its governors moved over the stage almost as rapidly and with little more substance than the Scottish kings appeared to Macbeth. Their terms were more brief than those in other colonies. While Virginia had twenty governors in the century before the Revolution, Massachusetts twenty-one, and Pennsylvania twenty-five, the executive authority in New York underwent thirty-three changes, counting the lieutenant governors serving temporarily as heads of the government. Governor Sloughter died suddenly July 23, 1691, whereupon Major Ingoldsby conducted the administration until Colonel Benjamin Fletcher came out as governor, August 29, 1692. Richard, Earl of Bellamont, appointed in 1695, did not arrive until April 2, 1698, and died

March 5, 1701. John Nanfan, lieutenant governor, acted as chief executive from May 19 of that year until Lord Cornbury entered upon the government in 1702. He gave place, December 18, 1708, to John, Lord Lovelace, who died very soon after his arrival. Then Major Ingoldsby acted again until April 10, 1710, when Gerardus Beekman, who had been indicted with Leisler, was chosen by the council to await the arrival of General Robert Hunter, who was transferred from Virginia, June 14, 1710.

The governors were graciously treated by the people and the assembly. When Fletcher arrived in New York, he was welcomed with a " treat costing £20," and on return from a tour no farther than the Jerseys, public entertainment was extended to the head of the government. The salary paid to Governor Fletcher was £780, while at the same time (1692) Chief Justice William Smith received but £130. The state and parade of some of the titled occupants of the executive chair, notably of Lord Cornbury, were imposing and extravagant.

In so young a colony, with all its struggles, and with inhabitants with fortunes to make, much civility and social outlay would hardly be looked for. To Captain John Miller, who was for nearly three years chaplain to his Majesty's forces in the province, it presented in 1695 an

aspect sufficiently rude. Besides the Episcopal
church in the fort, there was also a Reformed
Dutch church, and in the city of New York were
a large French Protestant congregation, one of
Dutch Lutherans, and a Jewish synagogue,
while English dissenters, although somewhat
numerous, had no meeting-house. Long Island
had meeting-houses in almost every town, but
the ministers were Presbyterians or Independent, or without orders at all. At Albany and
Kingston were Reformed Dutch churches. To
the grief of Captain Miller, voluntary contributions were the only source of support for religion, and the ministers " did more harm in
distracting and dividing the people than good
in amending their lives and conversations."
The chaplain pronounced the people little con-
cerned about religion, inclined, " so soon as the
bounty of God has furnished them with a plentiful crop, to turn the money into drink," and to
" ride ten or twenty miles " for " sottish engage-
ments." Like habits prevailed in New York
city, where " ruin and destruction of many
merchants " followed from frequenting taverns.
The marriage relation was not always respected,
separation was easy, and chastity was sometimes
disregarded. The absence of ministers of his
own church, Chaplain Miller deemed the cause
of these evils, and perhaps gave depth of color

to his statement; for his conclusion is that "the great, most proper and effectual remedy" was to "send over a bishop to the province of New York," to be appointed by the governor on a salary of £1,500, with the king's farm as an Episcopal seat. He should have also five or six sober young ministers, with Bibles and prayer-books. But the chaplain was not appointed bishop, as perhaps would have been every way proper.

Religious activity there was, however, although of the dissenting sort in such large measure, and not without the practices incident to adventure and new settlements. The movement so vigorously pressed in these years, for missions among the Iroquois, must have been inspired in no small degree by religious zeal. Political motives there were, for the "praying Indians," who had migrated across the St. Lawrence, gave as a reason for removal to French jurisdiction the desire for religious instruction; and they promised in 1698 to return to their castles, if good teachers should be furnished to them there. Rev. Godfrey Dellius, the Dutch minister at Albany, had visited the Mohawks occasionally for several years, on religious missions. Rev. Bernard Freeman, also a minister of the Dutch church, in 1700 began his work in Schenectady, under the auspices of Governor Bellamont, with chief regard to instruction of the Mohawks. During the five years of his residence he learned their language, and translated into it the liturgy and parts of the Old and New Testaments. He testified that thirty-six of the Mohawks had embraced the Christian faith. Rev. Mr. Lydius, the pastor at Albany, labored zealously among the Indian tribes. The first missionary of the Church of England sent to them was Thorougood Moor, who came in 1704, but he met with discouragements, and after beholding the promised land from Albany withdrew the next year. The authorities of the colony, it must be confessed, were more steady and urgent for mission work among the Iroquois than the clergymen and churches proved to be.

The question of revenue was the first for each governor in turn to meet, and it gave rise to constant collisions with the assembly, both concerning the power and mode of raising it and the control of its expenditure. The amount raised at this period, for a population of twenty thousand, scattered from New York to Schenectady, was less than some of the minor cities of the State now devote to their fire departments, and less than one fourth what they expend for lighting streets. In 1692, the total revenue was £3,202 17s., derived from customs, excise, quit-rents, weigh-house, and fines, and for several years the average was about the same, except as special appropriations were made for military purposes. In 1700, the total revenue and from like sources was £5,400, and did not vary greatly for several subsequent years.

The assembly, when Sloughter first summoned it, voted the revenue for a period of two years; under Fletcher the period was extended to five years, under Bellamont to six years, and under Cornbury to seven years. This last administration was well calculated to show the mischiefs of such long grants. In 1711 and afterwards, the assembly voted only annual appropriations for four successive years. The assembly in 1709, and again in 1711, voted, in order to provide for an expedition against Canada, to issue £10,000 in bills of credit, and they passed into circulation as money.

Domestic matters well deserved attention, and they were growing to a magnitude which, if royal governors were to be sent out, was quite adequate to engross all their energies. Yet Fletcher's jurisdiction extended over Pennsylvania and Delaware, and he had the titular command of the militia of the Jerseys and Connecticut. The Earl of Bellamont was governor also of Massachusetts and New Hampshire. Fletcher's title to remembrance lies in his zeal and

activity as a soldier, which was recognized by
the assembly by placing at his disposal £6,000
for the defense of the frontier, and by the Indians by the title of " the Great Swift Arrow."
The assembly had less regard for his wishes
when he sought to secure provision for an established ministry, a revenue for the king during
life, and repairs for the fort in New York, and
the erection of a chapel. A quarrel arose over
the governor's demand for authority to " approve and collate," and of course to reject ministers, and he vigorously scolded the legislators
convened before him, and then dissolved the
body. The act as passed applied to four counties, and contest at once arose over its construction, which was not settled, by a formal resolution of the assembly, " that the vestrymen and
church-wardens have power to call a dissenting
Protestant minister, and that he is to be maintained as the act directs." The claim was
long urged that only clergymen of the Episcopal
church were entitled to the public maintenance,
and in fact the endowed churches generally became attached to that denomination. Governor
Fletcher, although such a champion of the church
under State care, was sent to England under
arrest on charges of malfeasance, from which he
was never relieved, and on allegations that he
was a partner with pirates on the coast, which
were never verified.

The Earl of Bellamont was of a far nobler type. His opening speech to the assembly gave assurance of reform, where he found " a divided people, an empty purse, a few miserable, naked, half-starved soldiers, not half the number the king allowed pay for ; the fortifications and even the governor's house very much out of repair, and in a word the whole government out of frame." For himself, he declared : "I will take care there shall be no misapplication of the public money; I will pocket none of it myself, nor shall there be embezzlement by others." One point of significance about the attitude of Bellamont is, that he at once dismissed the chief councilors, and brought grave charges against some of them, while he called the friends of Leisler about him. As he had been a member of the committee in parliament which favored the reversal of the act of attainder on Governor Leisler, his choice of supporters from that side must be accepted as the result of investigation and deliberation. Councilor Nicoll was put under bonds, charged with collecting money for protecting pirates. Councilor Bayard was suspended for cause : for conniving at commissions to pirates, for advising "Fletcher's frequent embezzlements of the king's revenue," for taking to himself a grant of land belonging to the Mohawks as large as one of the middle

counties of England, without a reasonable quit-
rent, and for raising scandalous reports against
the new governor. Bayard responded with an
elaborate defense, denying several of the charges
and justifying the acceptance of the land patent.

His case was only one of many. Land began
to promise large returns, and speculation reached
out for vast tracts. Robert Livingston, who
had begun his career in Albany, on a visit to
England secured grants for many thousand
acres on the Hudson, which became known as
Livingston's Manor. Transactions with the red
men led more and more to purchases of land,
or acquisitions less regular. Clergymen were
members of combinations such as would now
be known as "Indian rings and land rings."
Domine Godfrey Dellius, the Dutch pastor at
Albany, was a zealous politician, bitter in his
hostility to Leisler, and yet appointed by Leisler a commissioner of Indian affairs. He was
charged with fraudulently securing deeds from
the red men for vast tracts. Pinhorne, a member of the council, with associates, obtained
patents for the Mohawk Valley, two miles on
each side of the river, for fifty miles along its
banks. Peter Schuyler was one of several who,
at first interested in buying these lands, had
withdrawn from the transactions on account of
the frauds practiced. The courts vacated the

patents, Dellius was suspended from the ministry, and a temporary check was given to the
greed of the land jobbers. But the vast domain
of the Iroquois continued to offer temptations,
and governors and officials of various grades,
and capitalists, small and large, grasped for a
share of it, until only scanty reservations remained to the original owners.

Party spirit suffered the prosecution against
the land operators to lack nothing of activity
and thoroughness. They had been leading
opponents to Leisler, while a reaction in his
favor set in when Bellamont came. Leisler's
remains and those of Milborne were disinterred
in 1699, were exhibited in state, and were re-
buried in the Dutch church. Acts of indemnity
were passed for such of this party as had not
been pardoned, and popular favor ran strongly
in favor of what was styled the " popular cause."

This was made especially manifest in 1702
by the arrest and trial for treason of Nicholas
Bayard, chief in influence under recent governors. He was arraigned under a statute enacted by his procurement in 1691, aimed against
Leisler, pronouncing all persons " rebels and
traitors " who should by arms or otherwise " disturb the peace, good and quiet " of the colony.
The specification was that in an address, with
warm protestations in honor of Lord Cornbury,

already appointed governor, but not arrived,
he had joined imputations upon Bellamont
and accused Nanfan of bribing the assembly.
With him was brought to trial, for circulating
the address, a tavern-keeper named Hutchins.
Chief Justice Atwood and two associates of the
supreme court, designated to preside at the trial,
were avowedly hostile, as was the prosecuting
attorney; and of the jurors it was alleged, one
had declared that, " if Bayard's neck were gold,
he should be hanged." An indictment was
found, but Bayard's son objected that a sufficient number of the jurors did not agree to it ;
that those who did were Dutch, and several could
" neither read nor write nor understand the
English language." He objected, too, that most
of the petit jury, all Dutch, were " handicraft
and laboring men." The trial, however, proceeded. Weaver, the solicitor, appealed to the
race prejudice of the jurors by accusing Bayard
and his English associates of seeking to introduce popery, and as a nest of pirates, and directly alleged that they had offered Bellamont
£10,000 " to connive at their piracies, and £100
to himself to solicit it." Both prisoners were
convicted under the indictment, and they were
sentenced to be punished for high treason.
Hutchins was released on bail, but Bayard was
kept in prison until Lord Cornbury arrived.

Then the chief justice and solicitor, in fear of their lives, fled to England, although they had been appointed members of Lord Cornbury's council. All the proceedings against the prisoners were nullified, and the statute under which they were conducted was repealed, by order of Queen Anne.

Connivance at piracy was a charge not infrequent against prominent persons in the colonies at this time. Privateering was encouraged by the government, and reputable persons became partners in vessels sent out under daring sailors to seize prizes. The sailors did not always observe nice distinctions when rich captures were possible, and privateering not infrequently fell more and more into audacious piracy. This was the case with William Kidd, whom the ballad represents as confessing, " most wickedly I did," and whose career is closely connected with New York. He was a navigator who won confidence and fame. In 1691 he was employed by the council, and the assembly on its restoration voted him £150 " for many good services done to the province." During the war with Spain, a vessel was provided for him for privateering, and King William, the Earl of Bellamont, Robert Livingston, and others in England and New York, were shareholders. He swept the seas with little regard to laws of

property, and his achievements became the
theme of story and invention. He captured
considerable treasure, which he turned to his
own use, and some of it he buried on Gardiner's Island. " Kidd's treasures " have tempted
speculators to dive and dig at various points,
from the exaggerations which have found ready
currency. He cannot have deemed himself a
criminal in any great degree, if at all; for after
selling his ship he appeared openly in Boston,
where the Earl of Bellamont recognized him
and put him under arrest. He was sent to
England, and put on trial for murder and piracy
under a law specially enacted to supply a deficiency in the statutes which did not cover such
transactions as he had been engaged in. The
Earl of Bellamont was accused of partnership
with Kidd, as he was in fact with the king and
others in privateering, but not in piracy. An
investigation in parliament gave signs that New
York merchants pressed the charge against
Bellamont, because as governor he had shown
vigor in enforcing the acts of trade.

Lord Cornbury, who became Earl of Clarendon, held a higher rank at home than the Irish
peer Bellamont. But he was impoverished by
his vices, intent on gain without regard to
methods, and possessed little capacity for administration. He threw himself into the arms

of the aristocratic party, and was at once conspicuous for his zeal for the Episcopal church.
He insisted that no preachers or teachers should
practice their vocation without a license from
the bishop of London. In Jamaica, a contest
arose between the original Dutch settlers and
the Episcopalians of the town for the possession
of a church edifice, and resulted in violence.
The governor sustained the Episcopalians, and
having borrowed the parsonage house of the
Presbyterian minister for his own use, deceit-
fully handed it over to the sheriff and the Episcopalians, who held it for their denomination.

The temper of administration and people is
well illustrated by the trial of Francis McKemie,
a dissenting minister, for unlawfully preaching
without a license, and for using other ceremonies
than those prescribed by the Book of Common
Prayer. The claim was urged by the prosecution that the governor's directions had the force
of law, and that the statutes of uniformity applied to the province. For the defense this was
denied, and it was insisted that preaching was
no crime by the common law. McKemie closed
the argument for himself with such effect that
he was acquitted, and yet by some legal device
he was not discharged until he paid the fees
for his prosecution. The doctrine of religious
liberty was asserted with a force and clearness

worthy of any tribunal in any age. And yet
an act passed in 1700 was on the statute books,
providing for the hanging of every "popish
priest" who came voluntarily into the province.

The province had grievous occasion to learn
that Lord Cornbury was a spendthrift even
more than a zealot. As soon as the assembly
was organized, as it was by the party to which
he allied himself, it granted him £1,800 for the
defense of the frontiers, and made a personal
gift of £2,000 for the expenses of his voyage.
Although a like gift of £1,500 had been made
to Bellamont and £500 to his lieutenant, this
liberality was so scandalous that Queen Anne
forbade any more such donations. But Cornbury was not content even with this lavishness.
He diverted to his own use £1,000 of the ap-
propriation for the frontiers, and £1,500 raised
for batteries at the Narrows. His waste and
greed brought him into collision with the assembly. He sought to prolong his power by a
claim of the right of the council to amend money
bills, which was promptly rejected, and the assembly passed a series of resolutions denouncing
as a "great grievance for any officer to extort
any money whatsoever not positively established," as also was it to "compel any man upon
trial to pay any fees" beyond his own counsel.
It was pronounced a "great discouragement to

trade, to screw excessive sums from masters of vessels," and to send to vessels " supernumerary officers taking extraordinary fees." The principle was plainly declared further, " that the imposing and levying of any moneys upon her Majesty's subjects of this colony under any pretense or color whatsoever, without consent in general assembly, is a grievance and a violation of the people's property." This resolution was elaborated in an address previously presented to the governor, in which these eloquent words were used: " Whatsoever else may admit of controversy, the people of this colony think they have an undoubted, true, and entire property in their goods and estates, of which they ought not to be divested but by their free consent, in such manner, to such ends and purposes, as they shall think fit, and not otherwise." Possibly such misconduct as that of Cornbury was required to call forth such enduring expression of popular rights. New Jersey, also under the same governor, appealed for his removal. Queen Anne listened to the cry, although Cornbury was her cousin. His creditors thrust him into prison, but his earldom of Clarendon now fell to him, and by its privileges he was released to go home, carrying with him the contempt of the colonists.

CHAPTER XV.

A DECADE OF DEVELOPMENT.

1708–1720.

THE province was slowly growing in population in the years following Leisler's rebellion. Governor Hunter in 1716 "cannot say that the inhabitants increase as in the neighboring provinces, where the purchase of land is easier." He adds that "great numbers of the younger sort leave Long Island yearly to plant in the Jerseys and Pennsylvania." From the interior of New York settlers were practically excluded by the hostility of the Canadians. Yet the militia, which Colonel Fletcher reported at 2,923 in 1693, Governor Hunter officially stated to be 6,000 in 1720, owing probably in part to closer enlistments. The population in 1720 was reported to the Lords of Trade at 27,000 whites and 4,000 blacks. The total population for all the colonies was 434,600.

Negroes were systematically imported into New York by private traders. In 1701, 1,014 were brought in from the West Indies and 626 from Africa; but this was an exceptional year, for from that time to 1726 the importation was 1,573 from the West Indies and 828 from Africa. They became the cause of alarm and cruelty. They were aliens, not closely identified with the families whom they served, and were the object of the race hatred, then much more intense than now. In 1712 New York was stirred with rumors of organized insurrection, and suspicion welcomed and exaggerated every charge. One house was burned, and several whites were killed. The vengeance was prompt and sweeping. Many negroes were arrested, and nineteen were tried and executed. The assembly passed an act for preventing, suppressing, and punishing the conspiracy and insurrection of negroes, and thus illustrated the dread which prevailed and the severity on which dependence was placed.

Trade was extending in various directions, especially with the Indians. From 1717 to 1720, the total imports averaged £21,254 a year, against exports of £52,239, including furs valued at £8,443. The British merchants did not receive the benefits which they desired from the trade of the colony. The device which was suggested to help them, in addition to the rigid enforcement of the navigation laws, was the restriction of all forms of manufactures in this as in the other colonies, and the fostering of the production of naval stores. Caleb Heathcote, a member of the council, wrote in 1708 to the Lords of Trade in London, referring to former urgent correspondence: " My proposal was to divert the Americans from going on with their linen and woolen manufactories, and to turn their thoughts on such things as might be beneficial to Great Britain. They are already so far advanced in their manufactories that three-fourths of the linen and woolen, especially of the coarser sort they use, is made amongst them." He feared " they would carry it on a great deal further," although he was exerting " all his interest and skill to prevent the making of fine stuffs." His apprehension led him into some exaggeration, for Governor Hunter in 1715 declared that very few in New York or Albany wore American fabrics; and of the colony at large he said: " Few that are able to go to the expense of English manufacture wear homespun, and a law to oblige such as are not able to go to that expense to do it under penalties, would be equivalent to a law to compel them to go naked." He agreed with Heathcote in advocating a policy for producing naval stores, " because these provinces raise much more than serves for their own consumption

and that of the West Indies," and except in
naval stores he saw "no solid way to prevent
the decay of trade."

Zeal to develop the production of naval stores,
with a thrifty eye to profits, prompted Governor
Hunter in 1711 to enter upon a large scheme
for introducing laborers into the province. He
found them in the German districts known as
the Palatinate, where the French had ravaged
the country and impoverished the people. He
secured from the British government a grant
of £10,000 for the project, and entered into a
contract to transport the immigrants, and to
maintain them for a while, in return for their
labor. The number is commonly stated at
3,000 persons, but authorities differ on the
subject. At a hearing in London, in 1720, a
committee of the Palatines, as they were called,
placed the original migration at between 3,000
and 4,000, and Governor Nicholson placed it at
3,200. Statistics show that 2,227 went upon
the lands provided upon the banks of the Hudson, while 357 remained in New York. These
came in two shipments about the same time,
while a third immigration occurred in 1722.
Their coming was a marked event, for it added
nearly ten per cent. to the total population.
The first Palatines, except such as remained in
New York, located on both sides of the Hudson,

" about a hundred miles up," as Governor Hunter says, in five villages, three on the east side of the river, on lands belonging to Robert Livingston, and two on royal lands on the west side.   They were to produce tar and turpentine. Governor Hunter contracted with Livingston to furnish bread and beer to them, and trusted to local overseers.   Trouble soon began.   It was alleged that money promised was not paid to the immigrants, that the land was barren, and that enough food was not provided.   Certain it is that complaints were loud and long, and the Palatines within the year refused to do the work required of them, and wished to move to other lands.   They organized a strike, and Governor Hunter went among them with troops to subdue them and enforce his contracts.   He found that his receipts were far from meeting his outlays.   In July, 1712, he cut off the supply of beer from all except men actually engaged in work, and the following September he notified them that " everyone must shift for himself, but not outside of the province."   He declared that his money and credit were gone, and later investigations prove that the enterprise involved a loss of £20,000. His accounts and conduct were long in controversy.   In England the Palatines did not command the sympathy which their appeals sought

to arouse, because it was urged that in a new
country a livelihood was easily gained. Lord
Clarendon said "that every person who will
work, man or woman, above fifteen years of age,
may earn 2s. 3d. a day in New York money,
that is 18d. sterling; while handicraftsmen,
joiners, masons, blacksmiths, and the like, may
earn 5s. a day." The fallacy was that these
people had mortgaged their wages, and were
crippled by their contracts.

The red men offered the Palatines land in
Schoharie on easy terms, and thither many of
them soon removed and created a settlement.
Some at different periods, and a hundred families in 1722, with additions from the third
migration, found homes in the Mohawk Valley,
where Palatine Bridge and the town of German
Flats and their original patent of Stone Arabia
preserve their memory. The contract system,
and not the character of the Palatines, was the
cause of the failure of Governor Hunter's
migration scheme. As independent laborers
the immigrants proved themselves industrious,
thrifty, and prosperous, and they became useful
and in many cases eminent members of the
community, and their numerous descendants
perpetuate their virtues.

Settlement was advancing up the Mohawk
Valley with slow but sure steps. Tradition

locates Hendrick Frey, a native of Zurich, Switzerland, west of Palatine Bridge before 1700. In 1712 Fort Hunter was built at the mouth of Schoharie Creek, and in the succeeding year a like centre for trade and defense was constructed at Onondaga. These forts were one hundred and fifty feet square, with breckhouses, and served for small garrisons, while they became the resort of traders and the nucleus of a few daring pioneers. The Dutch current spent its main force not far from Fort Plain, where the Palatines established their lines, and opened and held the route by the Mohawk for adventure and traffic.

The movements against Canada from the advent of Frontenac lost the character of operations by New York alone. Virginia found its interests in the west threatened by French aggression, and New England actually suffered from invasion. Yet New York was by its position most frequently assailed, and by reason of its intimate relations with the Iroquois was the chief reliance for any campaign, whether of assault or defense. Since it had to bear the brunt of the conflicts, it asked the other colonies for contributions to a common fund. The request was obviously equitable. It was not always met with generosity, although with some quibbling and delay response was made, frequently with a condition that the command of expeditions should be yielded. The concession was costly, as the event proved. Possibly failure in such expeditions was inevitable, but in New York it was attributed to the leadership of men not familiar with the kind of warfare needed, as when in 1693 Phips, of Massachusetts, over the fleet, and General Winthrop over the land forces, met with disaster; and even greater shame was incurred in 1710, when an expedition for which New York had made preparations was abandoned, and in 1711, when a movement met with an utter failure. Then Governor Nicholson, of Virginia, led an army of 4,000 men, coöperating with a British fleet under Walker, which was wrecked on the St. Lawrence. Great Britain rendered New York a greater service by the Treaty of Utrecht than it did by military or naval resources; for peace, even though transient, was of priceless value.

The preparations for the campaign of 1711 afford a glimpse of the markets and prices of the period. Commissioners were appointed to purchase provisions, and they were allowed to pay not exceeding £3 "for each barrel of good, firm pork well saved, 31½ gallons;" 5s. per bushel for peas; 8d. per pound for bacon; 7d. for buttock of beef, smoked; 6d. for cheese;

2*s*. 6*d*. per bushel for Indian corn ; 17*s*. 6*d*. per hundred for " well-baked biscuit, made of meal, as comes from the mill, with all the flour, only the bran taken out, without mixture of cornell ; " and 3*s*. 6*d*. per gallon for rum. The articles bought for the soldiers, and their cost, let light into the larders and upon the tables of many of the colonists.

The burdens which the expeditions against Canada had cast upon New York were very heavy. It was to meet them that it first issued paper money. In 1714, to pay debts incurred chiefly in these expeditions, a new issue of bills of credit was authorized to the amount of £28,000. In 1717 another issue of £48,000 was ordered, on like pretexts, and for claims for services running back thirty years which had only lately been discovered. The ugly áspect is that nearly all of the claims allowed were in the name of partisans of Governor Hunter. With such methods it is not strange that the general assembly voted the revenue for five years, breaking down the precedent of annual appropriations. In our own days the scheme of the sweeping allowance of resurrected claims would be denounced as a corrupt job. The grand jury then remonstrated, as well it might, against the issue of the paper money, for the bills were current at the rate of three for one in coin ; its members were reprimanded for their pains. The home government forbade the issue of any further paper money except for current expenses of the colony.

Robert Hunter is one of the most marked figures on the list of royal governors of New York, and, except George Clinton, his administration covers the longest period, extending over nine years. He was by birth Scotch, by training a soldier, by taste and habit devoted to literature and literary men, and known as a friend of Addison and Swift. By his career under King William and Marlborough, he had won the rank of major-general, and by marriage with a peeress he had established connections which gave him political promotion. In 1707 he had been appointed governor of Virginia, but was captured by the French and taken back to Europe. When in 1710 he came to New York, he reported that it had "the finest air to live upon, but not for me ; for according to the customs of the country, the sachems are the poorest of the people," and he pathetically exclaims, " Sancho Panza was a type of me." His administration was in many respects successful, and he has not been charged with enriching himself, although the assembly in which his friends were dominant passed extravagant, wasteful, and corrupt measures, to which he gave his approval.

He was himself a communicant in the Episcopal Church, but he did not satisfy its clergy in enforcing the law for the maintenance of ministers, and in Jamaica he was charged with favoring the dissenters. His fault was that he tried to be tolerant and even-handed, and reasonable members of his own church sustained him. Lewis Morris, with a vision worthy of a statesman, pointed out that in Pennsylvania the Episcopal Church was, without legislative support, much stronger than in New York, and argued that here " she would be in much better condition if there were no law in her favor," and he showed that the statute was open to a construction recognizing all denominations for maintenance. He dwelt cynically on the extent of dissent here, for " as in New England the greatest part of the people, except a few families, was the scum of the old, so in this province the greatest part of the English is the scum of the new." The evidence he cited was their tendency to other religious faith and practice than his own.

In the main, Governor Hunter managed to get on in his position with comparative quiet and harmony. Yet it was not without understanding the temper and drift of the people. As early as 1711 he wrote to St. John, afterwards Lord Bolingbroke : " The colonies are

infants at their mother's breasts, but such as
will wean themselves when they become of
age." In that year the assembly denied the
authority of parliament to tax the colony, and
of the council to amend money bills, while it
asserted its own "inherent right to act not
from grant of the crown, but from the free
choice of the people, who ought not, nor justly
can be divested of their property without their
consent." The Lords of Trade declared that the
claim " tended to independency of the crown."
The logic was inevitable, as events were moving on to prove.

Governor Hunter himself opened a new channel for such events, by establishing a court of
chancery in 1712, and thus began the education
of the province in a jurisprudence which has
been one of its marked features. The courts
of the justices of the peace, of sessions, of common pleas, and the supreme court did not
wholly meet the views of the governor. By
advice of the council, without consulting the
assembly, he set up all the machinery of a
court of chancery, of which he was chancellor, and appointed masters, an examiner, a
register and clerks. The scheme promised considerable returns in fees, while it added largely
to the power of the governor, and to the same
degree diminished the authority of the assem-

bly. The Lords of Trade sustained the claim that the power to establish courts belonged to the crown. The assembly asserted its own rights in behalf of the people, and the independence of the courts from executive control became one of the principles for which the province struggled, and to which various incidents gave especial prominence. Such a principle was, in addition to power over the revenue, one of the branches of the doctrine of self-government which New York was working out so thoroughly.

When Governor Hunter, June 24, 1719, announced his purpose to take a leave of absence, his address to the assembly was very cordial. " The very name of party or faction seems to be forgotten," he said, and he expressed a wish coupled with praise: " May no strife ever happen among you, but that laudable emulation who shall approve himself the most zealous servant and most dutiful subject of the best of princes, and most useful member of a well-established and flourishing community of which you have given a happy example." The answer was even more glowing in compliment to the " just, mild and tender administration " which was closing, and assured General Hunter, " You have governed well and wisely, like a prudent magistrate, like an affectionate

parent," and a shower of good wishes followed
for "our countryman." He returned to Eng-.
land, and received the appointment which he
desired, on account of a climate better fitted
for his failing health, of Governor of Jamaica,
where he died in 1734. His success in New
York was in no slight degree owing to his intimacy with the strong men who were developed as the real leaders. He won the confidence of most of them, and he had the tact
which court favorites did not possess, of enlisting their talents for the province, and of securing their coöperation with himself personally.

In the generation divided by the beginning
of the eighteenth century, Peter Schuyler
stands forth as the most prominent New
Yorker. He was designated under the charter
granted by Governor Dongan as mayor of Albany, and he served in that capacity for more
than eight years. He led the movement against
Leisler at that point, and was commander of
the fort, but was nevertheless retained as mayor
on the recognition of that governor's authority.
He was called into the provincial council in
1692 under Governor Fletcher, and long served
in that body. He was lieutenant of a troop of
horse as early as 1684, and was colonel of the
Albany county militia in 1700. He was urged
for commander of the movement against Canada

in 1693, and was admitted to be the foremost
soldier of the province. His exploits during
the campaigns of Frontenac, when he was the
chief in command of the colonists, endeared
him to red men and whites. As a commissioner of Indian affairs he was of the utmost
service. He welcomed the red men to his home
and table, and won and held their confidence, so
that his presence was for a generation essential
to a successful conference with the Iroquois.
They knew him as Brother Quider, and he had
trust in them and friendship for them. His
views were broad and sagacious. His conviction that dangers were threatened from Canada
was prompted by intelligence secured from the
red men, and his counsel was zealous and persistent to guard against such dangers by carrying the assault across the St. Lawrence. To
enlist the British government in this policy,
and to counteract the discouragement consequent on the abandonment of the proposed expedition, he went to England in 1710 at his
own expense, and took with him five Iroquois
chiefs, whose visit created general and lasting
interest among the English people. Upon his
departure for his voyage, the general assembly
passed unanimously a resolution accrediting
him to the queen, as "a person who not only in
the last war, when he commanded the forces of

this colony in chief in Canada, but also in the present, has performed faithful services to this and neighboring colonies, and behaved himself in the offices with which he has been intrusted with good reputation, and the general satisfaction of the people in these parts." The British court gave heed to Schuyler's argument; but the expedition ordered for the ensuing year, by sea and land, added another to the series of failures, and charges are on record that the British ministry was responsible by neglect or jobbery. Schuyler's policy was postponed by the peace between Britain and France, but no British minister and no colonial authority gave it up until it was finally carried out to a triumphant result. In New York Schuyler retained and extended his influence, and when Governor Hunter retired, he became, as president of the council, acting governor of the province. As such he was called to meet the renewed activity of the French and the Iroquois. Chevalier Joncaire, a skillful and dangerous emissary, had been adopted by the Onondagas, and was never idle in stirring up the tribes in the interest of France. Schuyler urged the Iroquois to exclude him from among them. He could not secure this point, but a new treaty with the red men marked his brief occupancy of the executive office. Schuyler

was born in Albany, the son of another Peter
Schuyler, an immigrant from Holland, whose
descendants were many, and their services to
the province and to the Union precious and
.enduring.   Peter's nephew, Philip Schuyler,
soon to come upon the stage, adorns our annals as commanding general, and a senator of
the United States.   Peter Schuyler's second
wife was a daughter of Petrus van Rensselaer.
The several branches of the Schuyler family
intermarried with the Hamiltons, Livingstons,
the Van Cortlandts, and other influential persons, and continued very strong in social and
political position for a long period.

Associated with Schuyler for many years,
and allied to him by marriage, was Robert
Livingston, son of a Scotch preacher, who, for
conscience' sake, had fled to Rotterdam.   Town
clerk of Albany, and commissioner of Indian
affairs, he took part in the Albany movement
against Leisler, was arrested and outlawed by
him, and in turn favored his execution, and
was denounced by name by Milborne from the
gallows.   In London, however, he advised the
reversal of the act of attainder, and advocated
at home indemnity to the associate rebels.
George I. in 1715 confirmed to him a grant
of land which he had received under Governor
Dongan, included in Dutchess and Columbia

counties as they now are, and established the manor and lordship of Livingston. While he supported Bellamont and was his close friend, Livingston joined with Schuyler in seeking to make William Smith, senior councilor, acting governor to the exclusion of Nanfan. To punish him for this course, a partisan prosecution was waged for his removal from his office of commissioner of Indian affairs, and for an alleged deficiency of £28,000. But he triumphed over his enemies, and became mayor of Albany, a provincial councilor, often a member of the general assembly, and a representative to other colonies. His descendants and those of his brothers kept the name on the rolls of New York and the Union for a long period, by ability and worth and patriotism, by remarkable gifts in legislation and administration, and generous devotion to the public welfare.

In the administration of Governor Hunter, a third personage of eminence was Lewis Morris, born in Morrisania, of Welsh descent. He possessed large estates in New Jersey as well as in New York, and devoted himself in large degree to public affairs in both provinces. He was a scholar, a lawyer, and a natural leader. He was especially influential in the general assembly, became chief justice, and exerted a lasting influence. He was one of the closest supporters of Governor Hunter, who owed not a little of the success of his administration to him. By his efforts a separate administration was accorded to New Jersey, and he became its governor in 1738. His descendants furnished many notable names to the roll of New York and the Union.

These, and such as these, gave promise of further development, already so auspiciously begun.

CHAPTER XVI.

1720–1736.

WILLIAM BURNET, son of the distinguished bishop, exchanged with General Hunter the office of comptroller of customs in London for the position of Governor of New York, and began his career in the latter capacity September 17, 1720. He was a civilian of considerable culture, an astronomer, and an author. He was one of the multitude who had lost money in the South Sea Bubble. He sought the governorship to retrieve his fortunes, but no base or corrupt devices are attributed to him. He sought to continue the policy of his predecessor, and the council was not radically changed. He accepted the friends of Governor Hunter, and identified himself with the province by wedding a daughter of Abraham van Horne, a prosperous Dutch merchant, and a member of the council. He met with no difficulty in securing a grant of revenue for five years, which was extended for three years.

He had the zealous support of the colony in the chief measure of his administration, which was the prohibition of the trade in Indian goods between Albany and Canada. The French traders found profit in buying their supplies in Albany for their trading excursions among the red men. They fostered intimacy with the tribes, and sought to alienate them from New York. The design of the new statute was not merely to secure the profits of trade for Albany, but to hold the red men by every tie to the authority of this province. The London merchants complained on the ground that their exports would be reduced, and Canada would get supplies elsewhere. The colonists responded in an elaborate report, urging that the effect was to increase the volume of British trade in America. Already forty young men had engaged in traffic with the red men. Indians from Mackinaw and a branch of the Mississippi had come direct to Albany for merchandise. The assurance was given that more beaver would be exported than ever before, and more goods would be imported into New York for the Indians. The province through Albany felt quite adequate to meet all demands of the Indian trade, and to increase it. In pursuance of this policy, a trading post was established at Oswego in 1722, and a fort built there

in 1727. The French saw the meaning of such
acts, and in 1726 launched two large vessels on
Lake Ontario and rebuilt the fort at Niagara,
where Joncaire and the historian Charlevoix
represented their interests.

These projects disturbed the Iroquois. When
Governor Burnet called upon them to explain
if they encouraged the French at Niagara, their
representatives declared at Albany : " We speak
now in the name of the Six Nations, and we
come to you howling because the governor of
Canada encroaches on our land." They were
not content to permit New York to build at
Oswego, but finally they renewed an old grant
of the land, ceded a strip sixty miles wide from
Oswego to Cleveland, on Lake Erie, " to be protected " by the British government. Governor
Burnet was so zealous for his plans, that he
paid from his private funds for building the fort
at Oswego, where trade became at once active.
The British authorities at home repealed, December 11, 1729, the prohibition on the trade
in Indian goods between Albany and Canada,
and traffic with the red men fell back in some
measure into French hands. The British merchants were finding the colonies, and not least
New York, a good market, for from 1720 to
1730 England sent to this province £657,998
worth of merchandise, and to all the colonies

£4,712,992. The sanguine trader might already discern the signs of the growing commerce of New York.

A congress of governors and commissioners from the various provinces met in Albany in 1722 to consider relations with the red men. A recommendation was made for a line of trading posts on the northern and western frontier. It was not acted upon, perhaps because the poverty of the colonies was more keenly felt than the need of a defensive policy, which would have saved them in the future much blood and treasure. The alliance with the Iroquois was confirmed, and they threatened to wage war against the Eastern Indians if the latter kept up their raids on the New England settlers. The habit of conference and united action between the colonies was of more significance than any specific results. The leadership of New York in the movement was due in this case to the importance of the Iroquois, in view of the increasing activity of the French from Canada among the Western tribes, as well as on the borders of this province.

Popular discussion doubtless existed in the province, for it goes forward wherever men have minds and tongues, and the taverns of Dutch days and public resorts of various kinds of later years afforded a sort of forum. In

1693 the council, feeling the need of preserving and multiplying copies of official papers within the province, passed a resolution inviting a printer to establish himself here, and offering "£40 a year and half the benefit of his printing besides what served the public." William Bradford, who had already the distinction of the earliest printer in Philadelphia, accepted the invitation to come to New York, and was retained as official printer for fifty years. His first work was to fill orders for broadsides, pamphlets, and proclamations. The prohibition against printing without a license forbade the establishment of any newspaper. In 1696, Governor Fletcher ordered the reprinting of a number of the London "Gazette," with news of a battle with the French. Among productions of Bradford's press preserved are the trial of Nicholas Bayard, under date of 1702, and the Laws of the Colony, 1710. The latter was probably the first bound book printed in New York. About 1723, Benjamin Franklin called on Bradford, looking for work, but the business did not justify the employment of additional help. So the young printer was referred with kind words to Bradford's son in Philadelphia, and New York lost the man who was to call lightning from its home, and to stand before Europe as the representative American.

In 1725 Governor Burnet felt the need of communicating with the people in a semi-official channel, and the New York " Gazette " was started by Bradford to serve as an organ of the administration. It was a weekly sheet, printed on foolscap paper, from the type known as English in size. As has so often happened since, one partisan organ called forth a rival. The New York " Weekly Journal " was started November 5, 1733, by John Peter Zenger, for checking the influence of Governor Cosby. It was, like the " Gazette," of foolscap size, but was printed in pica type, and so contained more matter. Its publisher, when a boy, came over in the Palatine migration, and was an apprentice to Bradford in Philadelphia. He had scholarly attainments and approved courage and ability as an editor.

The two newspapers at once engaged in conflict. The " Journal " criticised Governor Cosby with severity, and reveled in innuendoes concerning the character and acts of rulers. Before that paper was a year old, the governor decorated Zenger by a proclamation for publishing " divers scandalous, virulent, false and seditious reflections, not only upon the whole legislature in general and upon the most considerable persons in the most distinguished stations in the province, but also upon his Majesty's lawful and rightful government," and £20 reward was offered for the discovery of the author of two ballads, "highly defaming the administration of his Majesty's government in this province." Zenger was arrested and imprisoned. He continued to edit the "Journal" while a prisoner, and the popular sympathy was strongly aroused in his favor. The "Journals" containing the alleged libels and the sheets of the offensive ballads were ordered to be burned by the hangman. The mayor and council refused to attend the burning, as required. The assembly stood aloof, while the court of sessions forbade the hangman to obey the order, and a negro slave belonging to the sheriff burned the offensive matter. Governor Cosby appealed to the courts to punish the audacious editor and to put down his newspaper. The controversy constitutes one of the most notable chapters in the struggles for liberty in America.

The court of chancery was the delight of Governor Burnet, and it was the source of his chief troubles. He exercised the powers of chancellor with a flippant vivacity, and with the habits of a layman, for he was not a lawyer. One of his decrees affected the estate of Phillipse, the speaker of the assembly, who had been a devoted supporter, but was now dismissed from the council. The assembly seized the occasion to express "the general cry of his Majesty's subjects inhabiting this colony," that this court's "violent measures" had ruined some persons and driven others from the colony, and that "its extraordinary proceedings and the exorbitant fees countenanced to be exacted by the officers thereof are the greatest grievance and oppression this colony hath ever felt." Resolutions were passed, November 25, 1727, denouncing "the erecting and exercising" of such a court, as a manifest oppression and grievance to the subjects, and of a pernicious consequence to their liberties and properties. The assembly also announced the purpose to declare all the orders and proceedings of the court to be null and void. The only action taken at the next session was, however, to correct certain abuses in practice, and greatly to reduce the fees of the court. Governor Burnet had striven to secure fixed salaries, by permanent appropriations, for all the officers of the province, so that they might feel free from the influence of the assembly. In increased measure the representatives held firmly to the purse-strings, and abolished the crown. office of auditor-general.

This controversy over the court of chancery with other incidents alienated the governor's previous supporters. He dismissed Peter Schuyler from the council, and even DeLancey went over to the opposition on account of a quarrel in the rich French church in New York. In a trial of this case, two lawyers appeared who were to become eminent. For the minister who held the pulpit James Alexander was counsel, for the elders William Smith. The former was of Scotch descent, the latter of English birth and blood, and both came over in the same ship. Smith challenged the jurisdiction of the court, on the ground that the matter was ecclesiastical, while Alexander sustained the court, and the governor took the same side. In the new divisions, Alexander, already a member of the council, became one of the leading champions of the executive authority. Smith arrayed himself with the advocates of popular liberty, and was for years prominent at the bar and in public affairs. A son and grandson bearing the same name, wrote a History of New York, but chose British protection and official favor in Canada, when the colonies asserted their independence. It was he who in 1734 delivered an elaborate argument before the assembly, that the assembly, and not the crown or its representatives, should establish courts and determine their jurisdiction, and judges should serve during good behavior, and not at the pleasure of the governor.

Prompted probably by the bitterness arising from the church quarrel, Governor Burnet lifted Stephen DeLancey to the position of a martyr. The latter was a Huguenot refugee from Caen in Normandy, and had amassed wealth as a merchant in New York. He was chosen in 1725 to fill a vacancy in the assembly, when the governor refused to administer the oath to him, on the pretext that he was an unnaturalized alien. DeLancey was able to prove that he was a British subject, and the assembly challenged the governor's action as an infringement of its privileges. That body always afterwards asserted and maintained the exclusive right to determine the qualifications of its own members.

The denunciations of the court of chancery so offended Governor Burnet that he dissolved the assembly, which had existed for eleven years. The new members are stated to have been " all ill affected to him." They were opposed to his broad claims of executive power, and he had his full share of personal antagonisms. He was glad to be transferred to the governorship of Massachusetts, and to surrender the chair of New York and New Jersey to John Montgomerie, April 15, 1728. The new governor was a Scotch soldier, who had served in parliament and as groom of the bedchamber to King George I. His career in the province

was uneventful and brief, for he died July 1,
1731, and was succeeded by Rip van Dam, who
was the senior member of the council. He occupied the executive chair for thirteen months,
awaiting the arrival of Governor Cosby, who
came as Governor of New York and New Jersey,
August 1, 1732.

Over the trifling matter of the adjustment of
fees between these two officers arose a controversy which affected the whole current of events.
Governor Cosby brought an order from the
king for an equal partition between his immediate predecessor and himself of the salary,
emoluments, and perquisites of the office for the
period of Van Dam's incumbency. The Dutch
merchant bowed before the royal order, but
asked its literal execution. He had received
the salary, but Cosby had received the fees.
His receipts had been £1,975 7s. 10d., which
he was willing to share with Cosby, but the
latter in turn must divide his receipts, alleged
to be £6,407 18s. 10d. The royal governor
applied the order of partition to Van Dam, and
not to himself. Both sides appealed to the
courts to enforce their construction. Van Dam
sought to proceed under the common law.
Cosby asked the supreme court to proceed according to the rules of the English courts in exchequer, and he designated the judges " barons

of the exchequer." Smith and Alexander were
the counsel for Van Dam, and excepted to the
jurisdiction of the supreme court in equity.
Chief Justice Morris sustained their claim, while
DeLancey and Phillipse overruled them. Governor Cosby, in order to carry his case, as he
succeeded in doing, removed the chief justice,
and appointed in his stead James DeLancey, a
native of Albany, but a graduate of the University of Cambridge, England, son of that
DeLancey over whose seat the rights of the
assembly had been asserted.

While the Dutch settlers had made provision
for education, their English successors had been
occupied with other things. Schools there
were, but so poorly supported, that our historian
Smith testifies, that after he was born, " such
was the negligence of the day, that an instructor
could not find bread from the voluntary contributions of the inhabitants." It was high time
to care for the youth of the province, for its
population had become, in 1731, 50,289. Yet an
act passed in 1732 to " encourage a public school
in the city of New York," went no further. It
was the beginning of our broad system of public
schools, and provided especially for teaching
" Latin, Greek, and mathematics." The school
was free to all pupils.

Advance in religious liberty was made in the

struggles of these times. In 1734, the assembly
granted to the Quakers the privilege of making affirmation, instead of taking the usual oath.
It was a great step forward. Quaker members
from Queens county were excluded from the
assembly of 1691 for refusing the oath, and
the exclusion continued in effect for this whole
period. The contests between the governor and
his opponents served to teach the assembly the
need of recognizing the rights of the individual
conscience.

The assembly of 1734 was called to meet other
demands for consideration for the rights of the
people. In 1728 a declaration was formally
passed that " for any act, matter, or thing done in
general assembly, the members thereof are ac-
countable and answerable to the House only, and
to no other persons whatsoever." The notice
was directed to governor and council, but logically it crossed the sea and echoed in Whitehall and in the ears of King George. The
salaries of all the officers of the province were,
by act of 1729, determined by the assembly.
The treasurer who paid the money appropriated
was appointed by the governor ; but already ap-
pointments were made, as Lewis Morris charged
when Philip van Cortlandt was named, of persons " inclinable to give up the rights of the
crown." This control of salaries carried other

powers with it, for Attorney-General Bradley charged that the assembly attached to every vote for money "some bill injurious to his Majesty's prerogative and interest, which must be complied with or no money can be had for the necessary support of the government." He told the Lords of Trade, November 22, 1729, " Most of the previous and open steps which a dependent province can take to render themselves independent at their pleasure, are taken by the assembly of New York." His words are a testimonial of fidelity and patriotism such as it was not his purpose to perpetuate.

In 1734, a further demand was made. At that time representatives once elected served, in fact, at the pleasure of the governor. Until he was pleased to dissolve the assembly, no new election could take place. It was now proposed to provide for elections every three years. The measure was too radical to pass the governor and crown at once, but the proposal was a proof that the province was reaching out for all the substance of power.

The controversies, which had been confined to speech and letters and broadsides, found a larger audience when rival journals entered upon their discussion. Party spirit borrowed bitterness from personal quarrels. Governor Cosby was greedy, arrogant, and strong-headed. The council had a will of its own, denied his right to preside at its meetings, and commanded the popular favor. He dismissed such of its members as he pleased, and removed from the bench those who failed to carry out his schemes. He died March 10, 1736, and left an order not before promulgated suspending Rip van Dam, the senior member, from the council.

Governor Cosby had served in a like executive capacity in Minorca before he came to New York, but experience had not taught him wisdom as a ruler. He sought to derive all available profits out of the colony. The revenue was voted under his administration for six years, and he received a salary of £1,560, with payments of fees of £400, £150 for a trip to Albany, and £750 for services in London in opposing a bill inimical to the colony relative to trade in sugar.

In an address to the assembly, he admitted that discouragements were upon trade and the prosperity of the province. These his opponents charged to his misgovernment. He recommended as remedies, assistance to ship-building and a transfer of some of the taxes from trade to legal documents, while he condemned " too great importation of negroes and convicts." This address is in better spirit than his personal conduct. He destroyed deeds

which fell into his hands for land in Albany,
and he aimed to overthrow the old patents on
Long Island, in order that in the re-adjustment
he might get gain in fees, and perhaps also in
land. In like spirit, when the Mohawks submitted to him a deed by which they had conveyed a valuable part of their domain to be
held in trust for them, and objected to grants
to private persons in defiance of this trust, he
by deceit secured possession of the paper, and
threw it into the fire, where it was burned.
The name of " Cosby's manor," covering vast
tracts of land in the upper part of the Mohawk
Valley, and perpetuated in the title-deeds,
proves that his greed brought rich and ripe
fruit into his lap.

A strong effort for his removal was pressed
in London by Lewis Morris, who had gone
abroad with leave of the assembly, and therefore spoke to some extent in its name. But
the Lords of Trade reported that the reasons
urged did not call for action on their part. And
so Cosby ruled until death befell him. The
best that can be said of his character is that it
developed an opposition which established a
free press in the province, and lifted up the
courts into an independence which his successors could not destroy. His tyranny was so
gross, and his self-seeking so offensive, that he

served the province better than a more prudent governor could have done. The people learned to look out for their own rights, to assert their own convictions, to defend the integrity of the judiciary, and to regard their rulers not as representatives of a sacred majesty, but as simple instruments for carrying on the government. The teaching was rude, but the lesson was learned.

CHAPTER XVII.

THE PRESS MADE FREE.

1734–1735.

JOHN PETER ZENGER had no heroic aim when he printed political ballads, and admitted severe censure of Governor Cosby into the columns of the New York " Journal," and indulged in the criticisms which events and measures seemed to him to justify. The specific libel with which he was charged was an article in answer to the " Gazette," declaring that " the people of New York think, as matters now stand, that their liberties and properties are precarious, and that slavery is likely to be entailed on them and their posterity, if some past things be not amended." The " Journal " also reported a person moving from New York to Pennsylvania as saying : " We see men's deeds destroyed, judges arbitrarily displaced, new courts erected without consent of the legislature, by which it seems to me trials by juries are taken away, when a governor pleases ; men of known estates denied their votes, contrary to the received practice of the best expositor of any law. Who is there in that province that can call anything his own, or enjoy any liberty longer than those in the administration will condescend to let them do it? for which reason I left it, as I believe more will." This report of the criticism of an emigrant, and still more the words of the editor, were little more than a repetition of some of the phrases of the assembly denouncing the court of chancery, with a fresh application, and a verbal expansion. The language did not go beyond that often used in political discussion before and since, and it embodied none of the charges against the personal integrity of the governor which were current and have come down to posterity. It was, however, too bold and too comprehensive for the royal representative to endure.

When Zenger was arrested, November 17, 1734, he was at first denied even pen, ink and paper. A writ of *habeas corpus* was sued out for him, when he swore that " he was not worth £40 in the world," but bail was fixed at £800, which he did not raise ; but his liberty was enlarged, so that he was able to edit the " Journal " from his room in the city hall, then used as a jail. The grand jury refused to find a bill for libel, and proceedings were instituted by information, by the attorney-general, Richard Bradley.

At the April term of the supreme court, Alexander and Smith, his counsel, excepted to the commissions of Judges DeLancey and Phillipse. They were met by an order of the court excluding them from practice at the bar, and assigning John Chambers as counsel to Zenger, while a struck jury was summoned for the trial. The case aroused all the more attention from this action of the judges. It was everywhere discussed, and the friends of the prisoner took pains to excite sympathy. Three years later, when the disbarred attorneys were prosecuting suits for damages against the judges, they were restored to practice on abandoning all such claims. Thrust out of court, they enlisted all the more heartily in behalf of Zenger, or perhaps more truly against his assailants, and were the real advisers in legal proceedings, and quite as much in the popular movements which gave courage to the defendant and to his supporters.

Probably in connection with this case, certainly about this time, an organization was formed, destined to wield vital influence on the affairs not only of the province, but of the continent. To express and maintain opposition to arbitrary power, and at this time especially to the acts and policy of Governor Cosby, the " Sons of Liberty " were established. The leaders in the movement have left no memorial of their services. The records of the society at that time were secret, and it was felt rather than heard. At a later period it became the nucleus of deliberation, correspondence, and action.

When the case of Zenger was called the judges were surprised to see as leading counsel for Zenger, Andrew Hamilton, speaker of the assembly of Pennsylvania, a Quaker, venerable in years, and, as he soon proved, skilled in law, and master of a glowing and powerful eloquence. He admitted the publication charged, but denied that it was " scandalous or seditious." The attorney-general argued that the "jury must find a verdict for the king," whether " the libel was true or false." He pronounced it a very grave offense to revile those in authority, and declared that Zenger had offended in a most notorious and gross manner in scandalizing the king's immediate representative. Hamilton charged the attorney-general with going back to the odious Star Chamber for his precedents, and ridiculed the claim that the governor could arrogate the prerogative and exemptions of the sovereign. The information charged the publication to be false ; the defense did not ask proof to this effect, but offered to give testimony that it was true. The chief justice ruled that the defense could not be " permitted to

prove the facts in the papers." Hamilton cited
authorities in support of his position, and then
appealed to the jury as witnesses of the facts.

He went further. He charged thus: "The
practice of informations for libels," adopted by
the prosecution, "is a sword in the hands of a
wicked king and an arrant coward, to cut down
and destroy the innocent." He declared that
the representatives of a free people "are not
obliged by any law to support a governor who
goes about to destroy a province or its privileges which by his Majesty he was appointed
and by the law he is bound to protect and encourage." Referring to the right of protest he
asked, "Of what use is this mighty privilege if
every man that suffers must be silent, and if a
man must be taken up as a libeler for telling
his sufferings to his neighbor?" He dwelt on
the abuses of executive power in general, in
controlling legislatures and courts. He averred
that "prosecutions for libel have generally
been set on foot by the crown or its ministers;
and it is no small reproach to the law, that
these prosecutions were too often and too much
countenanced by the judges, who held their
places at pleasure, — a disagreeable tenure to
any officer, but a dangerous one in the case of
a judge." He insisted that the jury should consider the truth of the publication.

In conclusion he asserted the principle un-
derlying the case: " It is not the cause of a
poor printer, nor of New York alone, which the
jury is now trying. No! It may in its consequences affect every freeman that lives under
a British government on the main of America.
It is the best cause, it is the cause of liberty;
and I make no doubt but your upright conduct
this day will not only entitle you to the love
and esteem of your fellow-citizens, but every
man who prefers freedom to slavery will bless
and honor you as men who have baffled the
attempt of tyranny, and by the impartial and
uncorrupt verdict, have laid a noble foundation
for securing to ourselves, our posterity, and our
neighbors, that to which nature and the laws
of our country have given us a right, — the
liberty both of exposing and opposing arbitrary
power, in these parts of the world at least, by
speaking and writing truth."

After such an appeal the argument of Attorney-General Bradley fell like idle words on the
ears of the jury; and the charge of Chief Justice DeLancey, that the court and not the jurors
must decide whether the words were libelous,
had no effect. The jury promptly rendered a
verdict of not guilty.

The significance of the result was perceived
at once, and the report of the jury was greeted

with deafening shouts. Chief Justice DeLancey rebuked the crowd, and threatened to imprison the offenders, whereupon a son of Admiral Norris called for more cheers, and they were given. The chief justice succumbed to the demonstration of popular enthusiasm, and ordered no arrests. The advocate Hamilton was the hero of the hour. A banquet was served and a salute was fired in his honor, and the common council voted to him the freedom of the city for "the remarkable service done by him to the city and colony by his learning and generous defense of the rights of mankind and the liberty of the press." The gold box containing the certificate bore the mottoes: "*Demersae leges, timefacta libertas, haec tandem emergunt;*" "*Non nummis, virtute paratur;*" and on its front: "*Ita cuique eveniat ut de republica meruit.*"

In advance of action in any other province, in a clearer, stronger tone than anywhere else in the world, the liberty to print the truth was thus asserted in New York. The occasion arose out of the struggle over the partition of executive emoluments. That incident led Governor Cosby to interfere with the independence of the bench. It put Van Dam forth as battling for the legal privileges of the citizen. The divisions in the council aggravated, while they were in part caused by, this controversy. The governor created a council to support all his acts. The suspended members and the assembly, arrayed first against his aggressions, inevitably used the language and became the champions of legislative and individual rights. The establishment of the " Journal " afforded a channel for their criticism, their satire, their arguments. The trial of Zenger was not the prosecution of an editor simply. It was the effort of arbitrary power to suppress free speech, to hold the courts in leash, to rule by royal prerogative and executive assertion.

The strength of the popular determination can be measured by its overwhelming triumph. The jury spurned the direction of the chief justice, and decided the case independently of his claim to apply the law. The court yielded without protest, and the audience turned the chamber into a scene of tumultuous rejoicing. Zenger was sustained in the right to criticise the administration. The jury went further, and proclaimed that his criticisms were true and just. The triumph, however, did not belong to him. Hamilton attained a success in his profession rare in any land. A stranger in the city, he had spoken the words, had given utterance to the purposes, had crystallized the convictions and aspirations of the people. They recognized in him the voice eloquent for the present emergency, and prophetic of that liberty which on province and continent was already beginning to dawn.

With the declarations of the charter of liberties, with the protests against interference with the power of the assembly over the revenue, with the recent denunciations against the establishment of the court of chancery, and against the designation of judges of the supreme court as barons of the exchequer, the people of New York were ready to accept the bold eloquence of Hamilton and his appeals for the rights of mankind, in their full scope and logic. Already the seed was sown which was germinating to become Declaration of Independence and National Constitution.

For the doctrine of this case went far beyond the decisions of the courts in England up to that time, and far in advance of any claim then asserted in other colonies. In Massachusetts the authorities were agreed in censuring James Franklin for articles in his "Courant," and had forbidden him to print it further, "except it be first supervised." This New York verdict cast to the winds all the tyranny of requiring license for printing, and maintained the liberty of the press up to the highest standard which even this century has proclaimed.

Viewed in the light of that day, before the
colonies had learned the use and power of newspapers, before John Wilkes had defied parliament and crown in behalf of the right to deal
in type with public questions, the case and its
results marked a complete change in theory
and practice. It was the development of a
new motor in affairs. It was the creation of
an implement for the people, which rulers and
courts must forever regard. The Christian era
doubtless would have come without John the
Baptist and his preaching. So American independence would have been wrought out, without this triumph for the liberty of printing the
truth. But as events have occurred, the trial
of Zenger and his acquittal stand forth as the
one incident which molded opinions, which
strengthened courage, which crystallized purpose on this continent in the grand movement
whose termination perhaps no man foresaw,
whose direction few suggested above a whisper,
and yet whose logic was as direct as the laws
of the universe.

Why should the press be wholly free, if this
continent was to bow before a king seated beyond the ocean, and to receive its statutes from
a parliament in which it could have no representatives? A generation was required for the
question to stir men's minds, and to bring them

face to face with the answer. If Zenger had been convicted, no estimate can determine the time which would have been demanded to strike the fetters from discussion, and therefore from deliberation and action for the rights of the people.

This verdict in New York was an achievement for the freedom of the press, and so for the liberty of man, of which the colonies soon began to reap the benefit, and for which the thought and speech of mankind all over the globe are braver and more affluent of noble life.

CHAPTER XVIII

RIP VAN DAM denied the efficiency of Governor Cosby's posthumous order for his removal, on the ground that it had not been confirmed by the crown. On that claim he was, as senior councilor, acting governor of the province. The next councilor in order was George Clarke, who also claimed the executive chair. They carried their contest to the eve of actual violence. An election for alderman in New York city showed a majority for Van Dam's friends. The grand jury was publicly urged to indict Clarke for high treason, and he in turn summoned the militia into the fort to maintain his title. The assembly responded to a proclamation issued by Clarke, but by repeated adjournment postponed decision on the controversy until orders should be received from the home government. Van Dam's magistrates in New York resolved to assert his authority by arms on October 12, 1736. But Leisler's tragic comedy was not to be reënacted; for just in the nick of time a vessel arrived with official despatches to Clarke, as president and commander-in-chief of the province, and soon afterwards he was appointed lieutenant governor. Arms were stayed; the contest was shifted to the field of discussion and politics.

Clarke was disposed to exercise his power shrewdly and with moderation. He refrained from sitting with the council when it met as an upper house of legislature, and thus set a precedent which his successors followed. His opening address to the assembly exhibited intelligent consideration for the welfare of the province. In view of settlements which had extended into the Mohawk country beyond Fort Hunter, he recommended that its garrison be removed to a fort to be built " on the carrying-place," where Rome now stands, both to encourage the " settling of the rest, which is most the greatest part of the Mohawk country," and " to fix an easier communication between all the frontier garrisons from Albany to Oswego."

The assembly did not comply with his recommendations, particularly to provide for a considerable debt of the province; and May 3, 1737, he dissolved the House, which had been

elected nine years before, and writs were issued
for an election in the succeeding June. His
trust in the new assembly is evidence of his
courage and confidence in his own influence.
He was recognized as the successor of Cosby
in tendencies as well as in place, while the
opponents of that governor, and especially the
friends of Van Dam, were active and numerous. Clarke proved himself able to conduct
affairs, not so as to satisfy either faction, but so
as to secure support for his measures, and to
prevent rival leaders from rising to power over
his failures.

The new assembly began well, by recording
for the first time the ayes and noes on the passage of bills. Its response to his address was
long, bold, and critical of past rulers, and threatening to the governor. It called for frequent
elections, a settling of the courts, and, while
recognizing the royal prerogatives, claimed the
right of the people to be " protected in the en-
joyment of our liberties and properties." The
debts of the province, the address alleged, existed, although the legislators " had been lavish
beyond their abilities ;" and they felt called upon
to say: " We therefore beg leave to be plain
with your honor, and hope you will not take it
amiss when we tell you, you are not to expect
that we either will raise sums unfit to be raised,

or put what we shall raise into the power of a
governor to misapply, if we can prevent it ; nor
shall we make up any other deficiencies than
what we conceive are fit and just to be paid, or
continue what support or revenue we shall raise
for any longer time than one year; nor do we
think it convenient to do even that until such
laws are passed as we conceive necessary for the
safety of the inhabitants of this colony, who
have reposed a trust in us for that only purpose,
and which we are sure you will think it reasonable we should act agreeable to, and by the
grace of God we will endeavor not to deceive
them." The sentence was sinuous, but the
meaning struck home like a winged arrow. It
was a declaration of independence which any
governor could understand. Clarke took it well
to heart.

The legislation of the assembly which was dissolved October 20, 1738, covered a large number
of bills. A law was passed ordering triennial
elections of assemblymen, but it was vetoed by
the authorities in England. New paper money
to the volume of £48,350 was created, of which,
to comply with the rule established, £8,350 was
appropriated to current uses, while £40,000 was
apportioned to the counties, to be loaned on
mortgage, in sums not less than £25 nor more
than £100, at interest of five per cent., which

was two per cent. below the legal rate. The interest was set aside to pay the sum of £8,350, and afterwards for current uses. Perhaps as a sop, the governor's salary was raised to £1,560, only to be reduced at the next session to £1,300. To a bill granting revenue for one year only, as was always thereafter the limit, was tacked a provision that the paper money of 1714 and 1717, and the excise for sinking fund, should be continued for some years. That was the measure which led to the dissolution.

This assembly, in the case of a contested election for a vacancy in the city of New York, set up two principles which have been since rejected. Adolph Phillipse had received the certificate, and protest was made in behalf of Cornelius Van Horne, on the ground that Jews and non-residents had been allowed to vote. The eloquence of William Smith for Van Horne, and Murray for Phillipse, has passed into a tradition. Smith succeeded in having the votes of Jews rejected; but the votes of non-resident freeholders were counted, and Phillipse was confirmed in his seat, and in the next assembly was chosen to be speaker. Less serious is an incident gravely recorded in the quaint type of the journal of the assembly for 1738, for the last day but one of the session. A formal preamble recites that, " whereas on the complaint of Colonel Chambers that one Samuel Bevier had calumniated him by saying that he was a rogue and liar, and likewise a fool and no fit person to be an assemblyman, and that he was always drunk, and that the other assemblymen could always make him do as they had a mind," and that Bevier could not be arrested before the dissolution; thereupon " the House unanimously certified that the said Colonel Chambers has duly attended the service of this House in a sober and discreet manner, and that he (as far as is known to the other members) always acted as a free representative for the public service of this colony." Colonel Chambers had been seated after a contest as the member for Ulster county, and his name appears as that of one taking his due share in the public business. His example has not served to establish a rule for certificates of character from fellow-members to legislators accused of bad conduct, nor is it the practice to-day to spread on the records charges that a member is a rogue, a fool, and unfit for his place.

Scandal arose over the immigration of a body of Scotch Highlanders under the leadership of Captain Laughlin Campbell. He sold his estate in Scotland, and brought over eighty-three families, including four hundred and twenty-three adults besides children, and his plan was to maintain a settlement to defend Lake George against French incursions. In his behalf it is alleged that he acted under a promise from Governor Clarke of a grant of 30,000 acres, and impoverished himself to carry out his scheme of immigration. On the other hand the statement is put forth that many of his company came at their own cost, and on landing claimed that they sought relief from the vassalage they were under to lords in Scotland, and would not become vassals to Campbell in America. Some were certainly bound to serve him for the expenses of their transportation. Governor Clarke, October 13, 1738, asked the assembly to provide for the support of such families who were " poor and unable to do without some assistance." A motion was offered by Mr. Livingston, who remembered the experience with the Palatines, to give £7 to each of seventy families, and the historian Smith avers this proposition was to offset the claims of the governor and his subordinates for extortionate fees and a share of the lands. The over-sanguine expectations of Campbell, and the pressure of the contract system, are enough to explain a large share of the complaints. The trials of a new country and the homesickness of immigrants may serve further in the same direction. Campbell was ruined by his speculation. Many

of the Highlanders enlisted in the war with
Spain, and were sent on the expedition to Car-
thagena.

By this immigration the province secured a
much-needed addition to its population, and
these Highlanders must have sent messages
home not altogether unfavorable; for they
proved the pioneers of a multitude whose coming in successive years was to add strength and
industry and thrift and intelligence beyond the
ratio of their numbers to the communities in
which they set up their homes.

Affairs with the Iroquois, Governor Clarke
was wise enough to foresee, required once more
the most serious attention. The French had
been permitted in 1731 to erect Fort Frederick at Crown Point, on Lake Champlain, and
the New York assembly had contented itself
with a declaration "that this encroachment, if
not prevented, would prove of a most pernicious
consequence to this and other colonies." But
at that time neither the home government nor
the province took any action to repel the invasion, except as new supplies of ammunition
and cannon were secured from England. Irondequoit, on Lake Ontario, was marked by the
French for another foothold, and Governor
Clarke tried to induce the Iroquois to keep
them out, and to permit a settlement there by

New York as an advance post of the garrison at Oswego. He could not secure the assent of the red men to his project, for they would permit settlement there by neither side. The assembly on its part refused to repair the chapel at the first Mohawk castle, or to advance money for strengthening any post on the frontiers, yielding reluctantly to a demand from the red men themselves for the repair of Fort Hunter.

Struggles over the revenue between governor and assembly are a constant feature in the chronicles of New York. The assembly of 1739 gained another step towards control by insisting upon making its appropriations in definite sums for specific purposes, and even for salaries for officials by name. This was a radical change from the grant of money in gross to be paid on the governor's warrant, according to previous custom. Discussion between the governor and the legislators at this period was sharp, radical, and prolonged. Governor Clarke gave warning that "a jealousy had for some years obtained in England as to this province that the plantations are not without thoughts of throwing off their dependence on the crown of England," but he "hoped and believed that no man in this province had any such intention." In its exhaustive address in reply, the assembly, insisting on popular rights, declared in words then construed as full of unreserved loyalty, that it "vouched that not a single person in the colony has any thoughts or desires" for separation from the crown; for "under what government," it was asked, "can we be better protected, or our liberties and properties so well secured?" The satire included in the question was not, perhaps, meant by the authors, as it was not discerned by the readers at the time. It is possible, in the light of subsequent events, to read beneath the words a doubt whether liberty was not reaching out for new forms and a better substance. So asseverations of loyalty become sometimes challenges and defiance. But the assembly of New York did not thus construe its own declarations.

While the colonists were exhibiting in so many ways so much of common sense, and even of profound sagacity, a tragedy occurred which proved that superstition and frenzy found among them, as among so many other intelligent communities, ready victims, whom panic could drive into cruelty and blood-thirstiness. March 18, 1741, a fire occurred in the chapel and barracks at Fort George, on the Battery, in New York. It was generally believed to be accidental, but charges were set afloat that it was set by negroes. Before April 6, eight other fires startled the entire community, and a negro was detected escaping from near the last flames. Belief in a plot by negroes for burning the town seized upon the population generally. Experience has shown that among the ignorant and excitable a series of accidental fires may start a passion for looking upon flames, and thus for kindling them. The proof of a conspiracy was the flimsiest; but popular suspicion and fear took the place of evidence. The entire case rested on the testimony of Mary Burton, a " bought servant " — that is, an immigrant bound for service for her transportation — to John Hughson, shoemaker, and keeper of a tavern frequented by sailors and negroes. Mary Burton was prompted and encouraged to add to a charge against a sailor, three negroes and a fellow-maidservant, Peggy Carey, of bringing and receiving stolen goods to the tavern, the pretext for the judicial madness which was to stain the records of the colony. She was inspired to testify that some slaves had met and formed a conspiracy for setting fire to the town. Peggy Carey, under threats and promises, poured forth numerous stories of plots, but afterwards contradicted all her testimony except such as related to thefts and corrupt living.

The common council met and offered freedom to every slave with £20 reward, and to every white £100, for the conviction of any incendiary. The grand jury was diligent in holding every person charged with petty crime as a possible conspirator. In a proclamation for a fast day, May 13, 1741, the governor joined to the war with Spain, and the cold of the preceding winter, as cause for prayer, the fact " that many houses and dwellings had been fired about our ears, without any discovery or occasion of them, which had put us into the utmost consternation." There could be no doubt about the consternation. All the blacks were put under surveillance, and thus every household which kept a slave had the terror at its own hearth. Every lawyer in the city was enlisted for the prosecution. The negroes were kept without any counsel. Informers were set at work to extort or to manufacture confessions from the prisoners. These were numerous enough. Twenty-one whites and over a hundred and sixty slaves were thrust into jail. The woman Burton was carried away by excitement, and finally inculpated persons of such character that danger from that direction checked the fury, and in time led to reaction. Religious fanaticism added to the violence and extent of the panic.

One of the accused was a zealous preacher named Ury, against whom was brought the indictment of "officiating as a popish priest," as well as of engaging in the conspiracy, and some of the negro slaves arrested were discovered to be Catholics, who had been captured as prizes from Spanish vessels. Governor Oglethorpe of Georgia wrote to Governor Clarke, giving "intelligence received of a villainous design of a very extraordinary nature." It was no less than that "the Spaniards had employed emissaries to burn all the magazines and considerable towns in English North America, to prevent the subsisting of the great expedition and fleet in the West Indies, and for this purpose many priests were employed, who pretended to be physicians, dancing-masters, and of such other occupations, and under that pretense to get admittance and confidence in families." This was regarded as confirmation, strong as holy writ, of a conspiracy, with dangerous leaders, who were trusted in every home, with support from a powerful government and an all-pervading church organization.

As Cotton Mather seriously narrates the proofs and repression of witchcraft in Massachusetts, so Daniel Horsmanden gathers the proceedings in detail to justify the prosecutions for this alleged conspiracy in New York. He was a recognized leader in the affairs of the colony, a member of the assembly, and active in shaping

legislation and public policy. At this time he
was recorder of New York, as well as third in
rank of the judges of the supreme court, and
later he rose to the position of chief justice. He
wrote, therefore, with an air of authority, and
his record is full and elaborate, as it is certainly
pervaded by strong convictions of the guilt of
the accused. While he sat during the trials as
third judge, James DeLancey was chief justice, and Frederick Phillipse was second judge.
Judge Horsmanden recites the examinations,
the confessions, the contradictions, the entire
processes, which, until the common frenzy was
exhausted, drove judges and jurors and legislators into unreasoning panic and cruel.injustice.
We are enabled to understand, but not to excuse,
the phenomena. Now, it is easy to perceive that
many of the confessions were mere ravings ex-
torted by fear or promises, and many others
fanciful exaggerations of loose talk or petty
criminality. Some of the testimony seems to
point to a sort of Voodooism, and other parts
would be comical but for the tragic consequences.

One remarkable feature is that the witnesses
tell each his peculiar story, as if each were vy-
ing with the other for sensation, and thus they
convey the impression that invention is the inspiration of the shocking details. An ignorant
fellow named Kane, who swore that Ury tempted

him to become a Roman Catholic, describes the
ceremony of swearing the negroes to the conspiracy. He avers: " There was a black ring
made on the floor, about a foot and a half in
diameter, and Hughson bid every one put off
their left shoe and put their toes within the
ring; and Mrs. Hughson held a bowl of punch
over their heads, as Hughson pronounced a fear-
ful oath, and every negro repeated its words,
and then Hughson's wife fed them with a
draught of the bowl." This was calculated to
disturb excitable natures, and to convince persons already certain that a conspiracy existed.
Unfortunately for the case, however, no other
witness knows anything about this ceremony,
and in not one of the other confessions is there
any sign of it. Common sense concludes that
the scene was due wholly to Kane's imagina-
tion or to the fumes of the liquors of the tavern. We have the advantage, which the court
and the jury had not, of viewing the testimony
as a whole. Thus its contradictions, the inherent impossibility among such creatures of a
conspiracy for wholesale incendiarism, and the
manifest manufacture of a case out of the shreds
of thieves' and carousers' gatherings, stand forth
against the conclusions of the tribunals. The
trials were a travesty of justice, and the community after a while became ashamed of them.

The book of Horsmanden is a defense on the part of the courts for their action, and he is so far impressed with the weakness of his case that he argues that the " history of popery " proves the probability of the alleged plot.

When reason fully returned, few pretended that any conspiracy existed for burning the town, while the proof seems conclusive that such fires as were not accidental were kindled to facilitate schemes for petty thefts and sometimes burglary. The Spaniards were in no wise connected with the matter, and it is needless to say that no priests were engaged in any incendiarism. Many innocent lives were sacrificed under the forms of law. The preacher Ury was hanged, protesting that he was free from guilt. The tavern-keeper Hughson and his wife and servant Peggy Carey may have deserved the gallows on general principles, for they were doubtless allies of thieves and burglars, and receivers of stolen property. No good reason exists for believing that of thirteen blacks burned at the stake, eighteen hanged and seventy transported, more than a few were engaged in sporadic incendiarism, while all were punished for a conspiracy which had no existence.

The tragedy of the alleged negro plot led to an increase in severity in the laws already vigorous and cruel towards the blacks. It also added to the hostility to slavery as an institution, and led to the substitution of free white labor for that of slaves in no small degree. The chronicles for this period are dark enough for New York. The courts of 1741 dealt with colored people with brutality not paralleled in that city, except by the mob during the draft riots of 1863.

After the extremely severe winter of 1741, and the terror over the alleged negro plot, followed a malignant epidemic fever in 1742, by which out of a population of less than 10,000, 217 persons died. The disease is described as resembling the yellow fever of our Southern States. The succession of afflictions was long remembered, and determines the color of the annals of the period. Even controversies between the governor and assembly gave way before such competition, and the condition of the colony and the estimate made of it by its own people and in the old country were affected by these incidents.

The administration of Governor Clarke terminated September 2, 1743, when he was superseded by Admiral George Clinton, who was to challenge the colonists to the fight for self-government, for which they were well prepared. With Clarke they had been engaged in discussion, and perhaps if he had remained he

might have been forced by the claims urged in
Britain to aggression equal to that of his successor. He had not, however, what Clinton
brought, the temper of a sailor, the assumption
of the son of an earl, the creed and purposes
of one bred and trained and living in the circle
of British nobility. So the era of Clarke was
rather one of preparation for the conflict. He
had much more capacity for affairs than Clinton,
and was assiduous and diligent and watchful,
which his successor was not. In habits, regard
for popularity, in disposition to mingle with
the citizens, the contrast was equally marked.
Clarke's personal qualities enabled him to put
off the struggle which was already threatening.
In one respect Clarke and Clinton were alike.
They both illustrate how without gross scandal
the executive office in the province could be
used by a thrifty person for personal profit.
Clarke came out as secretary of the province
under Cosby, whose favor he won by zeal and
devotion, and he became clerk of the council,
and then a member. When he reached the executive chair, he took every means to gather in
fees and to increase his fortune by operations
in lands. He had no broad education, and his
influence in England came chiefly from his wife,
who was a Hyde, and a distant connection of the
famous family of that name. He sent home so

poor a picture of the prospects of the colony, and especially of the emoluments of the governor, that candidates for the place were discouraged, and he managed to gather in his profits for seven prolific years. He returned to England with a fortune estimated at £100,000, chiefly gained in the province. The sum was immense for that period; but Clinton was to exhibit almost an equal measure of the possibilities of the executive office in New York, for the fortune he amassed was estimated at £80,000 at least.

CHAPTER XIX.

NEW YORK was under Governor Clinton in
many respects more completely an integral part
of the British Empire than it had ever been
before, while the centrifugal forces were active
which were to lead to independence. The
reason for this union with the government in
England is to be sought in the plans for extending French power westward, involving attempts to secure the active coöperation of the
Iroquois, and such a pressure along the northern and western waters of New York as taught
the keen-eyed colonists to allege that the effect
of success must be to "crowd them into the
sea." Britain was preparing for the war with
France, of which these French aggressions on
this continent were among the chief causes,
and the formal declaration in March, 1744, recognized hostilities which had been hardly concealed by either side. The British government
assented at last to the plan, so often urged by

the colonists, for the capture of Louisburg and the invasion of Canada, and promised to pay the chief part of the cost. It failed signally to fulfill that promise, and within three years New York contributed £70,000 to the war. Its northern borders bore the chief share of the French operations. Oswego was abandoned by the traders, and the settlers drew closer under the shelter of military power. Cannon and money were contributed to the expedition, which gave the colonists a decided victory over the French at Louisburg, June 17, 1745. The governor asked for close alliance with New England, and for defenses on land and water, beyond the disposition of the assembly to vote. It was a dangerous economy, as was proved by a raid by French and Indians from Crown Point upon Saratoga, November 16, 1745. The surprise was so complete that the settlement of twenty houses was for a time destroyed. Only one family escaped, twenty persons were scalped and killed, and a party including one of the Schuylers was led away into captivity. All the savagery of border warfare was exhibited in its bloody horror.

The assembly soon learned that prudence demanded liberal expenditures and a broad policy, while it was none the more ready to exalt executive authority, and to yield to dicta-

tion from England. Instances can be cited in
which jealousy of executive suggestion was carried so far as to interfere with the best interests
of the colony. The desire to check expenditures defeated some measures, but others were
obnoxious because they strengthened a power
which the legislators dreaded. Governor Clinton regarded New York chiefly as it could serve
British purposes and enrich himself; yet it must
be confessed that his plans for defense and for
keeping the Iroquois loyal deserved support, if
lives and property were to be protected, and the
rule of France was not to be welcomed. The
assembly was willing to defend the province,
even to help conquer Canada, but it wanted
at the same time to assert and maintain control over the finances and to hamper the royal
governor at every point. If the governor was
regarded as wasteful in his suggestions, if
legislators felt that in a war between Britain
and France the home treasury should meet the
whole outlay, if criticisms of executive action
were more liberal than gifts of means for defense and attack, there was much in the experience and situation of the province to justify
such views and feelings and criticisms. If incidental harm befell, this self-assertion of the
assembly and its constituents was with all its
mistakes the training, costly it may be, for in-

dependent existence. The assembly had gained something also by the act to which the English authorities gave reluctant assent, in 1744, requiring elections for members at least as often as seven years. This period was then, as it still remains, the limit of the existence of British parliaments, and New York could secure no more frequent elections for legislators.

Immediately after the raid upon Saratoga, the assembly declared that it would at all times concur in every reasonable measure not only for the defense of the province, but for the assistance of its neighbors, and " this was and ever had been the unanimous resolution of the House." It did provide for men and subsistence of a company of militia, and for a reward for scalps in retaliation " in case the enemy shall commence the cruel and inhuman practice of scalping," and a report was made for the impressment of slaves into the military service. Six block-houses were ordered to be built between Saratoga and Fort William, afterward Fort Stanwix, Mohawk country, and the defenses of New York harbor were strengthened. When the aggregate expenditures of these years are considered, no charge of parsimony can be maintained against New York. For the expedition against Louisburg the province had contributed £3,000, and Governor Clinton, who had asked for more, bought provisions by private subscription, and sent artillery from the royal magazines. In 1746 a bounty of £6 was voted to all men enlisted for the movement against Canada, and this was soon increased by "40*s.* and a blanket" to every recruit. For the same purpose the sum of £40,000 was appropriated, and the total was soon raised by separate bills to £70,000 for various military operations within three years, and to this sum £28,000 was soon added. With a population of only 61,586 the province kept 1,600 men in the field, and the impressment of mechanics for war purposes was authorized.

The preparations against Canada were the occasion of serious troubles. Against the protests of the Duke of Bedford, soon to be premier, who feared that the colonies might by so great an expedition of their own learn their own resources, the Duke of Newcastle pledged the home government to pay the troops that might be engaged, while a British fleet was ordered to coöperate. Parliament finally appropriated £184,000 to settle the accounts; but the money was not paid at the time it was needed, and Governor Clinton was in constant anxiety for current resources. He was charged with embezzling presents meant for the Iroquois and with diverting funds voted for a specified purpose to other objects, while the troops clamored for their pay, and their subsistence was seldom furnished promptly in proper quantity. As commander-in-chief of the expedition he had ordered the seizure by force of an unlimited supply of provisions, and his agents were charged with "high crimes and misdemeanors" in obeying his orders. Governor and assembly charged each other with the neglect which permitted the burning of Saratoga, and with fault in general policy.

The time had not arrived for the conquest of Canada, and the preparation added no particular credit to the colonies or to the home government. The French fleet, sailing in American waters, directed attention to defense of the coasts. The alarm was relieved by storms, which scattered the vessels. By the Treaty of Aix-la-Chapelle, October 8, 1748, even Louisburg was given back to the French, and the New York assembly was fully justified in its conviction that success could not come to the operations as they were conducted.

The preparations for the Canada expedition had already brought the Northern colonies into close relations, and these were continued and improved after that expedition had been abandoned. The Six Nations came also into renewed importance, and evidence was not lacking that

French emissaries were artfully at work among them. Governor Clinton was blamed for interfering with the influence of the commissioners of the province, and especially for sending his chief adviser, Cadwallader Colden, to negotiate with the tribes. They were restive, and questions affecting them arose frequently. In 1744, an important council was held in Albany to adjust matters of which Virginia complained. The greed of the land speculators was bearing its natural fruit. Hendrik, a Mohican chief adopted by the Mohawks, who was one of the " kings " whom Schuyler presented before Queen Anne, to appeals for his aid retorted: " You have taken the land of the Mohicans (in New England), and driven us away," and he predicted the same result with the Mohawks. When the French Indians ravaged Western Massachusetts, the appeals of New York to the Iroquois became more urgent, and the presents more liberal. In a council in 1746, the tribes were divided in sentiment; but the Mohawks, Onondagas, and Senecas favored alliance with the English, and the confederacy was arrayed on that side. In October, 1746, a skirmishing party crossed the St. Lawrence and returned with scalps, and nine warriors went to Montreal and so deceived the French officers as to be employed to bear to Crown Point despatches which they handed over to the authorities at Albany.

Governor Shirley of Massachusetts had proposed an expedition against Crown Point in the winter of 1747, and Governor Clinton approved the plan; but the council learned that it would be impossible to bring the Iroquois into the movement in season, and by general consent the project was abandoned. In a letter dated May 30, 1747, Colonel Johnson asked for means to pay for twenty-nine scalps and prisoners brought in by his skirmishers that spring. The defense for such a ghastly record was that the routes into the province were infested by hostile war parties, and in the interior the ways were dangerous for the conveyance of supplies. Murders were reported even as far inland as Herkimer, then known as Burnetsfield, and near Schenectady a trading party was surprised and many killed by enemies who escaped before their pursuers. On Lake Champlain and at Saratoga, signs were frequent that the French and their red allies were watching for opportunity for successful attack. As a part of the French activity south of the St. Lawrence, a mission was established in 1749, at the mouth of the Oswegatchie, and called La Presentation, and on its site Ogdensburg has grown. There and at Fort Levi, built ten years later on Chimney

Island, was a centre of French operations, and
there finally the last resistance was offered to
British arms in 1760.

The struggles relative to control over raising
and expending the revenue kept the treasury
at a low ebb, and as a consequence means were
lacking to feed and pay the troops on the frontier. Officers were resigning, and some of them
were sued for pay by their soldiers. The men
were barely restrained from open mutiny.

The Treaty of Aix-la-Chapelle came at the
right moment to enable the province to confront
serious internal controversies. Governor Clinton lacked tact to adjust them, even if they had
not been by their nature sure to culminate at
last in deadly conflict. He received from Whitehall instructions which he relied on such leaders of the colony as he for the time accepted
as advisers, to carry out. His confidant, when
he first entered on his administration, was Chief
Justice DeLancey, a man of ability and skill in
affairs, with a will of his own, and not content
to echo the behests of anybody, even of a royal
governor. The story is that he went into opposition on account of a personal quarrel with
Governor Clinton "over his cups." He was
able, in the controversies that followed, to show
other cause for support of the privileges of the
assembly and the people, and to render good

service to them. Before Clinton's retirement
DeLancey was found again in approaching accord with the governor, in order, as the gossip
of the times alleged, to make sure of the post of
lieutenant governor, for which a commission had
been issued for him and not delivered. Clinton
had the power to withhold the commission, and
thus make Cadwallader Colden, who was president of the council, acting executive.

Colden had in recent years proved himself
an adviser even more conversant with colonial
business than DeLancey, and not inferior in
talent and acquirements, diligent and aggressive
to the last degree. He had already been engaged in the affairs of New York for a generation. He was a scientist and author of no mean
qualities, and had studied the history of the
Iroquois and the resources of the province with
a scholar's thoroughness. His writings on these
themes are of enduring value. A Scotchman
by birth and a graduate in medicine of the University of Edinburgh, he illustrated the qualities
of his race and his education. He migrated to
Philadelphia in 1716, and Governor Hunter invited him to become surveyor-general in 1718.
He had since that time been intimate with every
administration. Introduced by Governor Burnet as a member of the council, he had often
acted as its chief in fact. He gave especial at-

tention to Indian matters, but he was at home in all branches of colonial administration. The addresses of Governor Clinton were attributed to him ; and no important executive act for a long time was, in the opinion of the assembly, taken without his suggestion and direction. In 1749, Colden gave way as practically premier to Alexander and Smith, whose rank as lawyers and influence as leaders of opinion previous events had developed.

On the popular side the pen was wielded for formal arguments and popular appeals by Judge Horsmanden, whose special pleading relative to the alleged negro conspiracy proves how intense were his zeal and devotion to the cause which he espoused. David Jones, speaker of the assembly, took a large share in the controversies of these times against executive dictation.

More busy, and prominent in more fields than any factional leader in these times, was Colonel William Johnson, who was appointed to the chief command of the New York levies, and was already accounted as exercising a wider and more direct control over the Iroquois than any other person. He was born in county Down, Ireland, in 1715, and in 1738 was brought over to take charge of an estate belonging to his uncle in the Mohawk Valley. This uncle was Sir Peter Warren, who commanded the British

fleet in American waters in the early years of
Clinton's administration; and, as he was a
brother-in-law of Chief Justice DeLancey, he
was able to push forward his energetic and
sturdy nephew. Johnson made his home in the
town which still bears his name, and lived with
the Mohawks as one of them, and was adopted
by them as a war-chief. He identified himself
with the cause of the governor, and through his
long career was intense in his loyalty to the executive of the province and to the British crown.
Governor Clinton soon introduced him to the
council, employed him in dealings with the Iroquois, and raised him in military affairs over
the heads of all other colonial officers. In 1746
he was appointed by Governor Clinton superin-
tendent of Indian affairs. While in command
of the troops and holding these relations to the
red men, he also prosecuted the incongruous
business of a contractor of supplies for both.

The controversies between the royal governor
and the assembly involved no new principles,
but became more grave by the persistence of
both sides. Clinton was blunt and defiant in
his language. He told the assembly that it
" had no authority to sit but by the king's commission and instructions " to him. " Every
branch of this legislature may be criminal in
the eye of the law; and there is a power able

to punish you, and that will punish you, if you provoke that power to do it by your misbehavior ; otherwise you must think yourselves independent of the crown of Great Britain." The assembly was no less bold, and passed a remonstrance which Clinton refused to receive, and forbade Parker, the public printer, to publish. The governor was plainly told that his order "was arbitrary and illegal, in open violation of the privileges of the House and the liberty of the press." The remonstrance was published, and aggravated hostility to the governor. The assembly held fast to its control of the revenue, and after several refusals Clinton was glad to accept the appropriations with the restrictions affixed.

From Whitehall, April 2, 1751, came a report asking for an act for a perpetual revenue "upon the plan of that which had been passed in Jamaica," and "all the claims of present factions" would be set at rest. Clinton appealed to the king to "make a good example for all America, by regulating the government of New York ;" for he was convinced that "the remedy must come from a more powerful authority than any in America." The assembly advanced a step when it refused to grant Indian appropriations unless it was allowed to nominate the commissioners, and it claimed that the " powers of the militia can only be put in execution by the authority of the assembly." Clinton grew weary of these "graspings after more power" by the legislature, and the home authorities attributed some of the friction to his hostile relations with that body.

The peace with France was proving itself unreal. Bands of French and Indians on the frontiers and lakes were causing frequent alarms. The Iroquois were growing restive under the pressure of the greed and fraud of the land speculators. The Mohawk Hendrik, with several other chiefs, in 1753 carried their reproaches to governor and assembly in New York, and receiving little satisfaction, declared: " By and by, you will expect to see the Five Nations, which you shall not see ; for as soon as we reach home, we will send a belt of wampum to our brethren to acquaint them the covenant chain is broken between you and us." Colonel William Johnson was appointed to visit the tribes and win them back, and he succeeded in preventing an open outbreak.

This was the condition of affairs when Governor Clinton was summoned to the honorable repose of governor of Greenwich Hospital, and Sir Danvers Osborne came out to succeed him, October 10, 1753. Disappointed in the colony, and despondent by reason of domestic grief, Osborne was barely inducted into office when he committed suicide. James DeLancey, whose commission as lieutenant governor had been delivered by Clinton just before his retirement, entered on the executive authority October 12, 1753.

The colony was showing signs of life outside its activity in politics and in the field. A bill was ordered, October 22, 1746, to raise £250 by lottery towards erecting a college, and from that humble start Columbia College, known at first as King's College, has grown. Trinity Church gave the college a part of its estate in 1752, and over an effort to place the control under Episcopal supervision a controversy arose which divided parties and arrayed partisans, so that in politics as well as in religion Presbyterian and Episcopalian served as distinctive titles. At this time the assembly contained no college graduate except DeLancey, and in public life only another person, William Smith, held a collegiate diploma. Thirteen young men who were to impress themselves on affairs, and who are named in Smith's History, had secured a liberal education.

Among the devoted missionaries who came to labor among the Iroquois as teachers of the arts as well as of the Gospel, college graduates were conspicuous. This work, after the brief visit of

Rev. Mr. Moor, lapsed for eight years, and was taken up again among the Mohawks in 1712, by Rev. Mr. Andrews, who was assisted by Rev. Thomas Barclay, the English minister at Albany. Of the services to the red men of Rev. Peter van Driersen, minister of the Dutch church at Albany, the record is brief. Rev. Henry Barclay, a graduate of Yale College, an Episcopalian clergyman, labored efficiently among the Mohawks from 1736 to 1746, and at his departure a congregation of five hundred Indians, including eighty communicants, assembled to bid him farewell. Two years later, from the schools at Stockbridge, Mass., under the direction of the noted Jonathan Edwards, and at Lebanon, Conn., under Dr. Wheelock, began that stream of educated missionaries who adorn the annals of the province. In 1752, Rev. Gideon Hawley made his first visit to the Iroquois, and has left interesting journals of his services as evangelist among them for many years. Other zealous men engaged for brief periods in the difficult work, until in 1764 Samuel Kirkland went forth to preach to the Senecas, and became identified especially with the Oneidas, leaving his name in the churches, affecting the current of events, and commemorated by Hamilton College, which has risen on the foundation of an academy established by him for Indians and their instructors. The last of the missionaries to the Mohawks was Rev. John Stuart, who served among them from 1770 to 1775 with fidelity and usefulness.

The contrast between the broad plans and steady persistency of the French fathers and the fitful zeal of the Protestant missionaries is not flattering to the churches and the political authorities who claimed to sustain the latter. If the decision had been left to the religious elements opposed to each other, the Iroquois and through them New York would have been won to France and to Catholicism.

CHAPTER XX

BY the accession of James DeLancey to executive control, the affairs of the province were put on a new footing, and it was able to make preparations for the imminent struggle which involved the fate of the continent. The acrimonious charges by the assembly against Clinton were continued after his departure, and the royal instructions did not lose anything in their imperative tone. DeLancey possessed the arts of conciliation, and avoided conflict where that was possible. He advised the Lords of Trade that the assembly would not vote support for more than one year at a time, while he urged the legislators to place the money at the discretion of the governor and council. His relations with both parties enabled him to dull the edge of controversy, while they subjected him to criticisms for duplicity hardly deserved. Comparative peace in the province was compelled, and the significance of local quarrels was diminished, by the difficulties which arose with France and culminated in a great war. The English were charged with aggressions in Nova Scotia, while complaints were urged that the French were crowding viciously on the frontiers, and especially along the Ohio. The comprehensive strategy of the far-sighted French governors and their home authorities had placed a series of fortresses from Crown Point around by Fort Presentation (now Ogdensburg) to Forts Frontenac and Niagara and to Fort Du Quesne, which surrounded New York, and threatened it, in case of conflict, with invasion from all sides except the southeast, where a naval attack was conceivable, and even the Indians looked for it.

The attitude of the Iroquois was the first factor in preparations for defense. It was primarily to secure their alliance, and with that to bring all the colonies to united efforts, that a congress of deputies was summoned by Lord Holderness, the British secretary of state, to meet in Albany, June 14, 1754. Lieutenant Governor DeLancey presided, and with Joseph Murray, Colonel William Johnson, John Chambers, and William Smith, represented New York. The New England colonies, Pennsylvania and Maryland, with New York, sent delegates, and chiefs of the Iroquois came for negotiations. The extent of the domain of these tribes was admitted by Pennsylvania by the payment of £400 for lands within its boundaries, and their title was recognized beyond the Ohio, and their claims extended to the peninsula of Michigan. Chief Hendrik rebuked the English for their weakness and neglect, and bade them, " Look at the French : they are men ; they are fortifying everywhere ; but you are all like women, bare and open, without any fortifications." By July 11, the Indians were dismissed with presents after promises of co-operation against the French. On July 4 — a day to become historic by a deed of which this was a prophecy — a plan of union of all the colonies was agreed upon. It was proposed by Benjamin Franklin, and resembled a project suggested by William Penn as early as 1697. The draft was reported by a committee of one from each colony, on which William Smith represented New York, but the form and substance were the work of Franklin. DeLancey and Murray of the New York deputies opposed the plan. Beyond adoption by this congress, this plan of union received no further approval. The authorities at Whitehall were alarmed by it ; not a single colony favored putting it into operation. It served a valuable purpose in pointing out the possibilities of the future.

Events were already forcing a union closer than written forms could establish. Although war with France was not yet declared, hostilities were in progress, and New York had voted to obey the injunction from Whitehall to repel force by force in case of invasion. To encourage Pennsylvania and Virginia to check encroachments on their western borders, the assembly of New York appropriated £5,000 in August, 1754. George Washington was already engaged in operations against Fort Du Quesne, which the French were able to retain. The French were active also on the Kennebec in Maine. Hoosick in Massachusetts was burned. War parties advanced south of Crown Point. French vessels bearing troops were assailed by a British fleet, and two were captured. General Braddock, whose defeat and death were to follow speedily, was upon the sea with a military force from England, landing in February, 1755; and Baron Dieskau with 4,000 men arrived in May of the same year, to hold for France the route by Lake Champlain and Crown Point. In April, a conference of governors, called by General Braddock in Alexandria, Virginia, at which Governor DeLancey was present, agreed on four expeditions : one to reduce Nova Scotia; one under Braddock to recover the valley of the Ohio ; a third, to be commanded by Governor

Shirley of Massachusetts, was to drive the
French from Fort Niagara; and a fourth, under
William Johnson, now major-general, was to
strive to capture Crown Point.

This conference also recognized the difficulty
of raising money by vote of the colonial assemblies, and expressed the unanimous opinion that
"it should be proposed to her Majesty's ministers to find out some method of compelling them
to do it, and of assessing the several governments in proportion to their several abilities."
DeLancey at home rather favored duties on
imports, and the suggestion of stamps was recommended by Colden. Since expenses were
growing, and heavy charges were falling upon
the home government, the question of revenue
was attaining larger and more threatening proportions, and, as would appear, especially in
New York.

By the original plan, New York was to be the
centre of the military movements of 1755; and
the failure of Braddock's expedition, which occurred July 9, cast the burdens of the conflict
still more on this province. Invasion swept over
its borders and into the interior to the head
of the Mohawk, and so as to cast its shadow
even to Albany. The lines of assault from the
side of the colonies extended to Niagara on the
west, across the St. Lawrence to Fort Fron-

tenac, and to the defenses of Lake Champlain at Crown Point and Fort Ticonderoga. New York had thus to bear much of the brunt of the war.

The assembly began in 1755 by voting £45,-000 in paper money, and authorizing a levy of eight hundred men, and soon added £8,000 for enlisting men in Connecticut for the armies under Shirley and Johnson. Another vote of £40,000, and raising the force to seventeen hundred men, exhibited the zeal and energy of the assembly. In 1759, the quota was further raised to two thousand six hundred and eighty; a bounty of £15 was offered, with twenty shillings to the recruiting officer, and an emission of £100,000 in paper money was ordered, to be cancelled in nine annual installments. These provisions do not measure the impositions on the people. When Acadia was conquered and its inhabitants scattered, companies of them were brought to New York, to be fed and supported; and the practice of billeting troops on the citizens aggravated the cost and miseries of the war.

The campaign of 1755, in which the defeat of Braddock was the chief tragedy, was disastrous in New York at every point save one. Shirley, who paraded as commander-in-chief, had showed zeal and energy in urging this movement and

in making preparations for it, but he marched
no further than Oswego for the conquest of
Niagara. Colonel Philip Schuyler led the first
regiment of the expedition. Boats were built
at Oswego to convey six hundred men by lake.
Shirley followed by way of the Mohawk, and
reached Oswego August 21. He was delayed
from various causes, and in October a council of
war decided that the attack on Niagara should
be postponed for a year. Shirley was to have
met Braddock in victory at Niagara. Both
branches of the plan had been shattered. The
great western scheme sank to a mere strengthening of the defenses of Oswego. Colonel Mercer was left in command of a garrison of seven
hundred men, with instructions to build two
new forts, and General Shirley took the re-
mainder of his force back to Albany. The piti-
ful failure led to criminations relative to the
causes of the fatal delays.

In the summer of 1755, for the movement to
the northward from Albany, a fort was erected
on the east bank of the Hudson River, on the
carrying-place on the way to Lake Sacrament,
and it became known as Fort Edward. General Johnson was to have started on his expedition at this time; but trouble with General
Shirley at Albany, over leadership of the Iroquois, and a lack of boats, added to the shock

caused by Braddock's defeat, for weeks paralyzed the movement. August 8, General Johnson was able to set out with stores and artillery,
and with him were fifty Mohawks with chief
"King Hendrik," and Joseph Brant, then a
lad of thirteen years. At Fort Edward were
gathered New England troops under General
Lyman and Colonel Williams, with two hundred
and fifty red men. August 26, Johnson marched
with three thousand four hundred men to the
lake, which he now styled Lake George, as an
assertion of the title of the British king. To
this point General Lyman followed with his
entire force, leaving two hundred and fifty New
England troops and five New York companies
at Fort Edward.

The French governor, De Vaudreuil, had
taken his precautions early. He sent Baron
Dieskau with a force of three thousand men, of
whom eight hundred were French grenadiers,
to Crown Point to hold the route by Lake
Champlain. From Crown Point Dieskau led
two hundred French regulars, seven hundred
Canadians, and six hundred Indians, to the head
of the lake with the purpose to capture Fort
Edward, and thus to cut off Johnson's retreat,
and even destroy his army. The French commander, as is alleged, through the treachery of
Iroquois guides, failed to surprise the fort; and

his Indian allies refused to make an assault against cannon, but were willing to march against the encampment on the lake.

September 8, Johnson, under the advice of a council of war, sent out one thousand men in three parties for the relief of Fort Edward, with Colonel Ephraim Williams and Chief Hendrik in command. The advance at a distance of two miles from camp fell into an ambuscade in a defile, and both Williams and Hendrik were killed, with many others. The retreat was immediate, and was covered by a relief sent out from camp. There Johnson had his cannon in position, and had formed a rude breastwork. The French regulars began the attack, and tried centre, left, and right, but were met by men who, Dieskau said, "fought like devils." The whole French force was brought into the battle, but it could gain no foothold. The colonists seeing the enemy waver, leaped over their defenses, and by their bold onset drove before them the French, who fled to the woods with broken ranks. Dieskau fought close to the breastwork, and received four bullets in his legs, and was again shot in the moment of personal surrender. He was taken prisoner, and died in England of his wounds. Johnson was badly wounded early in the action, and the command fell upon General Lyman. The battle raged from half past ten in the morning until four in the afternoon. Later in the day Captain Maginnis, with two hundred New Hampshire troops, on their way from Fort Edward, came upon the remnants of the demoralized French army, and completed the rout. The designs of De Vaudreuil and Dieskau were utterly thwarted. The French loss was four hundred, in killed and wounded; and among the killed was St. Pierre, the victor on the Monongahela. Of the army of the colonists, two hundred and sixteen were killed and ninety-six wounded, and forty of the Iroquois. The Indians insisted on returning home. The French army retired at its leisure to Crown Point, and was not molested.

General Johnson has been criticised for not yielding to General Lyman's appeal to pursue Dieskau's routed army, and for failing to move promptly against Crown Point. Such censure is easy after the event. The colonial troops were new, and their commanders were learning how to fight battles. The enemy included veterans of France, and artillery and defenses were strong at Crown Point. The battle of Lake George was a decided victory, won by a superior force, it is true, but not pressed to the conceivable advantages. It was the one gleam of triumph within the colonies in the campaign of

1755, and checked the demoralization which
the disaster to Braddock was threatening. The
home government rewarded Johnson with a
baronetcy, although he closed the campaign with
this battle, and set about building Fort William
Henry, on the site of the battle, while the
French erected works at Ticonderoga.

In December, Shirley, who had become commander-in-chief of the British forces in America, summoned the governors to a conference in
New York, and proposed a winter campaign
against Ticonderoga, but the attempt was not
made. Shirley was, on the contrary, held cen-
surable for the lack of success in the Niagara
expedition, and was removed from command.

Sir Charles Hardy came out as governor of
New York, September 3, 1755, but DeLancey continued as lieutenant governor, dividing
emoluments with his chief ; and the interruption of his executive power was only nominal,
until June 3, 1757, when, as Rear Admiral, Sir
Charles took command of the expedition against
Louisburg, and did not return to the province.

Parliament decided to maintain a permanent
army in America, and the commander-in-chief,
the Earl of Loudon, arrived in New York July
23, 1756. War between France and England
had been declared. General Abercrombie and
General Webb were already in the province,

and the British regulars under them numbered three thousand. These troops were quartered on the inhabitants, and their officers gave more attention to quarters than to military service. Lord Loudon had over ten thousand men subject to his orders, and there was need for prompt movement. Savages were ravaging the counties of Ulster and Orange; the French were showing dangerous activity ; and soon a new commander, the Marquis de Montcalm, assumed the aggressive. They held their position on Lake Champlain. They were threatening the supplies which were conveyed by way of the Mohawk, Oneida Lake, and the Onondaga River to Oswego. March 27, 1756, a party of four hundred French and Indians under De Levi penetrated to Fort Bull, where Rome now stands. Three small works had been built at this point. Lieutenant Bull destroyed two to prevent their falling into the hands of the enemy. The third De Levi captured and razed to the ground, and bore the garrison of thirty prisoners to Montreal, where he reported with the loss of three men. In May, De Villiers with eight hundred followers, from a thicket near the mouth of Sandy Creek, struck out at the parties bearing supplies to Oswego. Colonel Bradstreet, a New York officer, repulsed one of such attacks made July 12. He kept in motion between Albany and

Oswego on the line of the Mohawk and Oneida
Lake, forty companies of boatmen of fifty men
each. He succeeded in throwing into Oswego
abundant provisions and ammunition. He foresaw the coming invasion, and gave early warning
at Albany of the gathering of an army of thirteen
hundred French regulars, seventeen hundred
Canadians, and many Indians, on the upper St.
Lawrence. General Webb was ordered to lead
his regiment for the relief of Oswego, but he
dawdled on the way, and advanced no further
than the head-waters of the Mohawk. He was
afraid of attack even there, and felled trees for
defense. He received at this point word of the
disaster he was sent to prevent, and fled in haste
to German Flats, where he was met by Sir William Johnson, who started from Albany, August
20, with two battalions of militia and three hundred red men, to aid in relieving Oswego; but
news of its fall prevented his further advance.

Montcalm acted differently from the English
generals. August 5, he reviewed his army at
Fort Frontenac, and the same evening trans- ·
ported it to Sackets Harbor. August 13, he
captured Fort Ontario, an outpost at Oswego,
and turned its guns on the main fortifications,
in which Mercer, the commander, was soon
killed, and a breach made in the walls. The
next day, the entire force of sixteen hundred

men, including Colonel Peter Schuyler, surrendered, with one hundred and twenty cannon,
six war vessels, three hundred boats, stores,
ammunition, and three chests of money. The
prisoners were protected by Montcalm from
butchery by the savages, and were taken to Montreal. In order to appease the Iroquois the conquerors destroyed all the works at Oswego, and
abandoned the site. The consequences of the
French victory were grave, and put the colonial
alliance with the Six Nations in peril. The Earl
of Loudon began and ended his active career in
New York with this disastrous campaign.

In 1757 he started on an expedition against
Louisburg, and abandoned it, returning to New
York to bluster and lie idle. New York and
the neighboring colonies were anxious to furnish
militia to act with the regulars. But the royal
commanders were shamefully incompetent, and
would not let the provincial leaders take the
necessary measures. Disaster and even disgrace
were invited on Lake George and the Mohawk,
to such an extent that the enemy seemed to
operate at pleasure. July 23, Lieutenant Marin,
a Canadian, with two hundred men, bore away
thirty-two scalps and a prisoner from under the
guns of Fort Edward. Four days later Lieutenant Corbiere, another Canadian, with a small
party destroyed twenty boats on Lake George,

and showed one hundred and sixty scalps as trophies. Montcalm was the inspiration to such achievements. At the close of July he was drawing his lines about Fort William Henry, and with him were eight thousand French and Canadians and two thousand Indians. He cut off communication with Fort Edward by a detachment of Canadians and Indians. He directed his main army against Fort William Henry, and a fortified camp, where afterwards stood Fort George. In the former, Lieutenant-Colonel Monro had four hundred and forty-nine men, and in the latter were seventeen hundred. Montcalm used artillery with effect, and Monro replied as he could by day, and repaired breaches by night. General Webb lay at Fort Edward with four thousand men, but repeated the neglect of which he had been guilty in the preceding campaign. General Johnson brought up a considerable force, and was advancing beyond Fort Edward, when Webb ordered him back and sent a letter to Monro advising him to surrender. Montcalm intercepted the communication, and forwarded it to the victim whom he was sure now he had within his toils. But Monro fought on for two days, when with cannon burst and ammunition nearly exhausted, August 9, he yielded to necessity, after a siege of eight days. Fair terms were made, but after the surrender drunken Indians assailed fear-stricken prisoners, and thirty were killed before Montcalm could check the barbarism, while in the siege his own army had lost only fifty-three in killed and wounded. Fort William Henry was destroyed. This disaster was the result of criminal stupidity; for within a week, Webb and Lord Howe, who had just arrived on the scene, dismissed to their homes many of the militia, and others in disgust abandoned their camps. They had been ready, and they ought to have checked the operations of Montcalm.

He was left to strike where he chose. The autumn added to the disasters of the summer. November 12, a party of three hundred French and Indians, under Belletre, penetrated as far into the interior as Palatine Village, and at three o'clock in the morning fell upon the sleeping inhabitants. Forty were killed and one hundred and fifty taken into captivity. Three thousand cattle and as many sheep, with grain and the autumn store of provisions, were carried away. The village had received warning from the Indians, and General Johnson had appealed to General Abercrombie, now in chief command, to keep a force of rangers in the field. Both counsels were unheeded, and the Mohawk Valley was left open to such devastation and to the consequent panic.

Pitt, the British prime minister, perceived
the situation in America, and said, " Every
door is open to France." New York was surely
naked on every side, and was suffering from the
presence of British troops, who did not shield
her from repeated and almost fatal blows. Pitt
rose to the occasion, and resolved to pay the
price of the defense of the colonies, and the conquest of Canada. He accorded American officers, up to the rank of colonel, equal command
with those sent from Britain. He asked New
England, New York, and New Jersey to furnish
twenty thousand men to march against Montreal and Quebec. The year 1758 opened with
the capture of Louisburg by Amherst and Wolfe.
The largest army yet seen in America was
assembled on Lake George, and began to move
July 5. Seven thousand British regulars were
supported by more than ten thousand provincials. General Abercrombie was in command,
Oliver DeLancey was colonel-in-chief of the
New York forces, and Lord Howe was the idol
of the army. Lake George has witnessed no
more splendid spectacle, and no waters have
been the scene of a more tragic result. The
troops landed in good order to storm Ticonderoga. They became confused in the woods.
Lord Howe was killed in a skirmish. Abercrombie hesitated for the night. In the morn-

ing of July 8 he ordered an attack by bayonet on the enemy's works. Montcalm had three thousand six hundred and fifty men, whom he sheltered with breastworks of trees, with branches outward. The British could not get through these branches, and in their confusion were shot down in multitudes. The attack was brave and persistent, for it cost nineteen hundred and sixty-seven in killed and wounded. It was not renewed. Abercrombie retreated and his army followed him. Colonel Bradstreet alone preserved a semblance of order among the demoralized troops. The panic swept through the province and into all the colonies.

Courage was restored by another service rendered by Colonel Bradstreet. He had in the early spring asked permission to lead a swift attack against Fort Frontenac ; but Abercrombie did not see the advantage of diverting the attention of the French from Lake George. After the disaster there the commanding general yielded his consent, and Bradstreet hurried forward. August 10, he was in consultation with General Stanwix, who was building the fort which was to perpetuate the latter's name. For the projected movement eleven hundred and twelve New Yorkers, under Lieutenant-Colonel Charles Clinton of Ulster, and Lieutenant-Colonel Isaac Corse of Queens, with nineteen hundred and twenty-three other colonists, and forty-two Indians under the chief Red Head, hastened to Oswego, and thence in open boats crossed Lake Ontario. Bradstreet succeeded in landing without opposition within a mile of Fort Frontenac, August 25. The next day he turned his cannon on the works, and its artillery responded. During the ensuing night entrenchments were carried within two hundred yards of the fort, in spite of the activity of its guns. August 27, the French garrison capitulated. One hundred and fifty prisoners with abundant stores, several cannon, and all the armed vessels on the lake, were the spoils, which cost not a single life on the provincial side, and only two or three slightly wounded. The French loss of life was also small. The exploit was won by the sudden demonstration of a force large enough to be sure of success. Fort Frontenac was destroyed, and the strategic line which connected Fort Du Quesne with Montreal was broken. The achievement shattered the plans of Montcalm, and went far to remedy the blunders and defeat of Abercrombie. The victory at Pittsburg followed in November, and redeemed the fame and the fortunes of the colonies.

The French from Canada had, with inferior numbers, and resources crippled by dearth and the death of domestic animals, almost snatched victory by the audacity of genius and the splendor of courage. In the campaign of 1759 Sir Jeffrey Amherst was commander-in-chief of the British forces. The plans included the occupation of posts at the west from Pittsburg to Lake Erie by General Stanwix; the capture of Fort Niagara by General Prideaux, and the concentration of a large army under Amherst, to advance into Canada by way of Lake Champlain, while a fleet was to coöperate, sailing up the St. Lawrence. The expedition for Niagara gathered at Oswego, and included two British regiments and a detachment of royal artillery. It numbered twenty-two hundred regulars and provincials, and seven hundred Iroquois. Colonel Haldimand was left with a New York battalion to hold Oswego. Prideaux sailed July 1 for the west. July 5, an army of fifteen hundred French, Canadians, and Indians attacked the garrison at Oswego, but was repulsed and retired the next day. At Niagara, General Prideaux was killed by the bursting of a cohorn, July 15, and Sir William Johnson succeeded to the command. He prosecuted the siege, and three days later a breach was made in the fort by the artillery fire. General D'Aubry attempted to raise the siege by marching from the western garrisons with twelve hundred men and hosts of Indian auxiliaries. Johnson met them, and in the

battle the French lost one hundred and fifty
killed and one hundred and thirteen prisoners,
including General D'Aubry. Fort Niagara was
surrendered to Johnson, with its garrison of six
hundred and eighteen, July 25. Its fall severed
the connection of the French authorities at
Montreal with the Ohio Valley and Lake Erie.

General Johnson left a garrison at Niagara,
and returned to Oswego, with a view of attack-
ing the French posts at La Galette and Oswegatchie; but General Gage, who was now in
command on the northern frontier, forbade the
movement.

On the eastern border, General Amherst began operations July 22, with an army of eleven
thousand. He invested Ticonderoga, and after
four days the French blew up their works and
fell back to Crown Point, whence they again retreated as Amherst advanced. He was delayed,
rebuilt forts, and failed to carry out the plans
of moving forward by this line against Montreal,
in coöperation with General Wolfe's expedition
up the St. Lawrence. A raid was made, September 13, by Major Rogers with one hundred
and forty-two men, on the Indian village of St.
Francis between Montreal and Quebec, which
was annihilated with all the barbarity of savage
warfare.

The great tragedy of the Plains of Abraham

was enacted, Wolfe and Montcalm were killed, and Quebec fell September 17, closing the campaign of 1759. June, 1760, three columns moved forward to capture Montreal, one up the St. Lawrence under General Murray, a second under Colonel Haviland down Lake Champlain, and the main army from Oswego under General Amherst. July 16, Oswegatchie was occupied by the forces of the last named, and La Galette was surrendered to him, July 25. The Indian tribes on the St. Lawrence were won over, and August 30 the three columns met before Montreal. September 8, the French governor, De Vaudreuil, gave up all of Canada and its dependencies to Great Britain. The policy of Peter (Quider) Schuyler was consummated by the iron will and brilliant energy of William Pitt.

The strain of this conflict on the province of New York cannot well be exaggerated. The victories of the French arms encouraged the Iroquois to neutrality and some of them to hostility. They always had grievances over the seizure of their lands by speculators and the breach of treaties, and all the arts and influence of Sir William Johnson were needed to manage them, and especially to get them to aid the province when invaded. Armies moving across the whole extent of country from New York to Lake Champlain and from Albany to Niagara, left their traces everywhere. The arbitrary system of quartering troops on citizens was ruinous as well as oppressive, especially to the two chief cities. Settlements were driven back by the ravages of the French and Indians. Manufactures were interrupted, agriculture was checked, commerce was paralyzed. Here and there blockhouses and small forts were built, which became the nucleus of hamlets and then of towns. Thus Fort Schuyler, erected in 1759, at a ford on the Mohawk, well known to boatmen and to engineers of the army, was chosen after a while as a point of departure for the north and southwest, as it was naturally for the west, and about it gradually gathered, beginning in 1785, a hamlet which has spread out into the city of Utica.

Other topics seemed petty in the presence of the great war between the two foremost nations of the world, in which New York was in so large a measure the field of battle. When the French power fell in Canada, the importance of the Six Nations as allies was greatly diminished, the apprehension of invasion was removed, and New York especially, and the other colonies in less degree, were relieved of external pressure, and the path was open for the freedom and independence which were to insure prosperity and greatness.

CHAPTER XXI.

PREPARATION — FIRST STEP TOWARDS UNION.

1760–1765.

THE fall of Montreal closed the immediate interest of New York in the war against France, although the Treaty of Paris, surrendering to Britain the French possessions in America, was not signed until February 10, 1763. It was high time for the province to devote itself to the tasks of peace. Its white population was in 1756 only 83,233, with 13,542 blacks, and yet it had kept in the field a force of 2,680 men, and when the war debt was summed up in 1762, it was found to exceed £300,000 and a tax of £40,000 a year was assessed to meet it. Under great exhaustion and stress the people showed commendable vitality and spirit. An election for members of assembly in 1759 developed a division which long affected the affairs of the province. To the Episcopalians, it was alleged, too much favor had been shown by the governor in organizing King's (Columbia) College, and members were

chosen to the new assembly to check such tendencies. This opposition expressed the popular
feelings, and was called the Presbyterian party,
or, from its chief leaders, the Livingston party,
while the supporters of the administration were
styled by the name of Governor DeLancey, or
the Episcopal party, or the aristocrats. The
lines were already drawn which deepened and
broadened into the great struggle for independence, and were continued after a state constitution was adopted. The home government
was moving rapidly in the course which drove
the colonies into revolt, and in New York and
elsewhere men were rising to leadership to resist the stamp tax and to organize a union.

The popular party had more than an ordinary
title to a personal designation. In the assembly
of 1759, consisting of twenty-seven members,
no less than four Livingstons sat: Philip for
New York, William for the manor, and Robert
R. and Henry for Dutchess. By alliance by
marriage with the Schuylers and the Jays and
by its wealth the Livingston family held a pre-
eminence rarely equaled in this country. In
the aristocratic party Lieutenant-Governor De-
Lancey was supported by his brother Oliver, by
his cousins Philip Verplanck of Cortland manor,
and John Baptist van Rensselaer of Rensselaerwyck, and other relatives and personal friends.

This family element was shattered by the sudden death of Governor DeLancey, August 2, 1760, when Cadwallader Colden, then seventy-three years of age, emerged from his plantation in Ulster County, to assume the executive power as president of the council. He sought to win friends by courtesy and concessions, when the death of George II. created the occasion for a new election, in 1761, by which the popular party gained additional strength.

New York had more than once insisted on the independence of the courts against the executive power. This question now took on a new form, and led to serious consequences. The assembly sought to compel the appointment of judges of the supreme court with terms running during good behavior; but Colden vetoed the measure, and insisted that their commissions should be at the pleasure of the appointing power. The difference was radical: should the judges be removable only upon impeachment or be the mere creatures of the royal authority? The Lords of Trade declared that the former policy tended "to lessen the just dependence which the colonies ought to have upon the mother country." Except for temporary purposes, jurists could not be found in New York to accept places on the bench at the executive pleasure. To fill the vacancy

caused by the death of DeLancey, a chief justice was imported from Boston in the person
of Benjamin Pratt, who arrived in October,
1761, with a commission "during his Majesty's
pleasure."

The assembly refused to pay salaries to judges
serving under such commissions, and would provide from year to year if the terms were during
good behavior. The quit-rents were set aside
for the payment of Pratt, while the other places
were left vacant. In this contest William Livingston, John Morin Scott, and William Smith,
"educated in Connecticut," as Colden says, at
Yale College, were leaders, and "maintained
the doctrine that all authority is derived from
the people."

The quit-rents from which Chief Justice
Pratt was to be paid were the receipts of the
king from the vast tracts of uncultivated lands
which had been granted before 1708. In the
assembly of 1761, by the efforts of Sir William
Johnson, an act was passed for accurate survey
of these grants and for the collection of these
rents. Contests had arisen with the Indians
over the excessive claims of the holders of
patents, and scandals were numerous over the
manner in which patents were secured by the
early governors and their favorites. The claimants held their lands for speculation, and so

checked the incoming of settlers of small means, who relied upon their earnings for support. The evils were brought within bounds by the official surveys which were at this time inaugurated and enforced.

Major General Monckton was designated captain general and general-in-chief of the province, in 1761, but he preferred military service, and took command of the expedition against Martinico ; Gates, Montgomery, and Lyman went with him, and among his force of 12,000 men, 1,787 were enlisted in New York. The emoluments of the executive office were divided between Monckton and Colden, while the latter exercised the authority. Monckton returned in June, 1762, and remained until June 28, 1763, but left no impress on affairs. The victories over Spain in the West Indies enabled Great Britain to extort a treaty of peace from France, November 3, 1762, and it removed from the British ministry all restraint in dealing with the colonies.

Peace was gaining some triumphs amid the din of war. New York city was the chief town, but the county of that name was in 1756 the fourth in population. The chief counties were in their order by this test : Albany with 14,805 whites and 2,619 blacks, total 17,424 ; Dutchess with 13,289 whites and 859 blacks, total 14,148 ;

Westchester, 11,919 whites and 1,338 blacks, total 13,257; New York with 10,768 whites and 2,272 blacks, total 13,040. By the census of 1771 New York stood at 21,863 and Westchester at 21,745, with Albany at 42,706, and Dutchess at 22,404. In 1756 the whites in the whole colony numbered 83,223, and the blacks 13,542; total, 96,765. In 1771 Ulster had a population of 13,950; Suffolk of 13,128; Queens, 10,980; Orange, 10,092; Kings, 3,623; Richmond, 2,847; Cumberland and Gloucester, afterwards set off for Vermont, had 4,659. The total of the colony in that year was 148,124 whites and 19,883 blacks, making 168,007 in all. Albany at this time, it will be understood, included all north and west of the present capital to the St. Lawrence and Niagara.

The slow growth of New York, as compared with the other colonies, indicates the check given to commerce by the navigation laws, the imposition of duties, the stamp act, and the consequent controversies. Yet New York continued to be the chief centre of imports, while it lost in exports. In 1770, of the total exports of all the colonies, amounting to £1,014,725, New York sent out only £69,882, while of total imports of £1,925,570 New York received £475,991. The shipping of the colony increased from 1762 to 1772 by 232 vessels, reaching 709 in the latter year, and by 9,618 tons, mounting up to 29,132 tons ; but the men engaged in seafaring fell from 3,552 to 3,374 during the decade.

New York city was in politics, in culture, in social display, the capital. The governor resided there, and the general assembly met there unless driven out by sickness or some other cause, as it was once or twice to Greenwich or Jamaica. The British commander-in-chief and the only garrison in the colonies for some years after the close of the French war, added the peculiar influences which gather about military quarters. Newspapers had risen and fallen in the city, where at this time three — the "Post Boy," the "Mercury," and the "Journal"— were printed, while the colony had no others until the "Gazette" was established in Albany, in 1771. King's College fostered a literary atmosphere, as it taught loyalty to the throne. A company of English actors visited the town in 1753, and in 1769 a company with headquarters there set up its stage for a while in Albany, where twelve years before army officials had given theatrical performances in a barn, to the scandal of many of the inhabitants. A plan was proposed in 1767 for an academy to promote architecture, sculpture and painting, and the useful arts, and in the next year it gave Philip Schuyler a medal for erecting a flax-mill in Saratoga. Benjamin West came from Philadelphia to practice painting in New York, and doubtless from associations here obtained inspiration for one of his best known works, " The Death of Wolfe," painted in 1771. The bar of the colony was always strong, and furnished several of the leaders in the struggle for colonial rights. It gathered in the capital and on the lower Hudson in chief part; but licenses to practice were easily obtained, so that pettifoggers also abounded. The bench was subject to political influences, and was therefore not always maintained at the highest standard, although brilliant names adorned it, even at this period and in larger measure afterwards.

In 1760 rigid provisions were enacted for licensing physicians, and in 1767 a medical school was established in connection with King's college ; but the doctors took part in the work of settlement, and if some were rough and uncultured it would not be strange. Smith's and Colden's histories and the political papers of the day prove that the colony was not destitute of writers of a high order. The pulpit from the earliest days had included men of broad education and marked ability, and the controversy between the Episcopalians and other denominations tended to render ministers prominent and influential.

While New York was the seaport and centre
of commerce, Albany was the seat of the fur
trade and of traffic with the Indians, and from
Schenectady boats started on their slow way
up the Mohawk. Attempts were made to work
iron in the spurs of the Adirondacks along
Lake Champlain, and at points in the High-
lands of the Hudson, and some pig and bar iron
was exported. In 1773 the colony built £30,-
000 worth of ships for English buyers, while
ventures were made in other manufactures, to
which British repression proved fatal. The fur
trade prospered, and agriculture was gradually
improved.

The vast estates which fell to the patroons
and were continued in their families, and in
those of the Schuylers and Cuylers, and the
manors established by the Van Rensselaers and
Livingstons and Phillipses and Johnsons and
Cortlandts constituted a peculiar feature in this
colony. They were the centre of almost feudal
power. They interfered with the settlement
of small farmers, while they introduced better
cattle, horses, seeds, and modes of culture than
could otherwise be used. The manor-houses
were the seat of courtly hospitality in summer,
and the landlords commonly spent their winters
in New York, where they contributed to give
that city the reputation of gayety and display,
and devotion to recent London fashions.

Sir William Johnson was a landlord who lived with his tenants and the Indians. He had before 1762 gathered a hundred families about him, in the neighborhood now known as Johnstown, and had built a villa and a lodge becoming his wealth. He introduced sheep and blood-horses into the valley of the Mohawk, and developed intelligent agriculture. He gave land to Lutherans and Calvinists whereon to build churches, and exerted himself to promote the education of the Six Nations, assisting in the labors of Rev. Dr. Eleazer Wheelock, of the Indian school at Lebanon, Conn., and of Samuel Kirkland, whose influence for good became so wide and enduring.

Although communication depended on the natural waterways, for the roughly worked roads permitted the passage only of saddle-horses or stout two-wheeled vehicles, the settlements had been considerably extended. They reached the head of the Mohawk Valley, where Bradstreet had established considerable works at Rome, and they were scattered along the waterways to Oswego. They even had beginnings westward toward Niagara. In the Seneca country and in the Susquehanna Valley a few whites found homes. In the valley of the St. Lawrence, about Oswegatchie, and along Lake Champlain and the upper Hudson, hardy im-

migrants had followed the armies, and had remained after their withdrawal. Fort Presentation was the centre of considerable trade with
the Indians.

Sir William Johnson, by reason of his personal standing and official relations, found no
little occupation in adjusting differences between the whites and the red men. Controversies over the claims to lands threatened more
than once to lead to appeals to arms on the part
of the original owners, and apprehension of
outbreaks was constant. At Fort Schuyler a
drunken Indian alarmed a household, and the
members in a panic fled, with the cry that the
savages were loose for slaughter, and the settlers
were not restored to calm until a strong force of
militia marched to the scene. When Pontiac
stirred up war in the northwest, and the Dela-
wares ravaged the frontiers, the Six Nations
were at first believed ready to join in the assault
on the whites, but Sir William Johnson maintained armed watch from Crown Point to Oswego, and fortunately the tide of conflict was
turned away from New York, although the
Senecas espoused the cause of the great western
chief. A conference at Niagara, and the march
of troops under General Bradstreet into the
Seneca country, with the personal influence of
Johnson, brought treaties and quiet for a time.

The British ministers were busy with their schemes for getting revenue out of the colonies, and New York held no secondary position in their estimates. New York city was engaged in a commerce, not allowed by law but known to the Lords of Trade, with the French and Spanish possessions, and it was looked upon as a proper source of revenue. This province had felt more keenly than any other the burden of providing quarters for British troops, and was most alarmed at plans for a standing army in the colonies, while the mixed population never cherished special affection for the crown of Britain. The strife over the tenure and pay of the chief justices led New York to take the first step of formal opposition. December 11, 1762, the general assembly adopted a memorial to the king for the " independency of so important a tribunal," which otherwise would be " an object beheld with terror," and asking for a royal hearing on the subject. This document was one of a series adopted by the New York legislature in this and the succeeding year, bearing on the relations of the province to the kingdom. It was reported and doubtless prepared by Frederick Phillipse of Westchester, and Robert R. Livingston of Dutchess, chosen justice of the supreme court this year, and father of the famous chancellor of the same name.

The memorial received no attention from the ministry; for the plan had been adopted to use the judges as a part of the machinery for British control in the colonies. But New York had found its voice, and kept on with its appeals to the authorities in Great Britain. Alderman Philip Livingston, in behalf of the merchants of the chief city, in the preceding April had prepared a strong argument against the sugar act; and the assembly unanimously approved its summary of the hardships under which the trade of the colony was suffering, as well as its appeal for relief. The plea was urged in behalf of every interest of the colony, and was full of statistics, and exhaustive in its treatment of the subject. The same able writer and far-seeing statesman, September 11, reported an address to Lieutenant Governor Colden, protesting, with many expressions of loyalty, against the acts of the British parliament, which "threatened to reduce the province to the deplorable state of that people who can call nothing their own," and calling on the executive in these strong words, "We hope your Honor will join in an endeavor to secure that great badge of English liberty of being taxed only with our own consent," a privilege which the sugar act invaded. The address was designed for the authorities in Whitehall, but they were not wise enough to heed it.

New York, like the importunate widow, kept on with its petitions. October 18, Philip Livingston reported another " representation to the king's most excellent majesty," which the assembly adopted. On the same day also addresses reported by William Bayard were adopted, to the lords temporal and spiritual, and to the house of commons. These papers were not excelled in clearness and vigor of thought or force of language by any utterances in the colonies at that time. James Otis, it is true, had raised his voice against writs of assistance ; but Samuel Adams' draft of instructions by Boston to its representatives in the general court followed in the month after Livingston's arraignment of the sugar act; and Virginia was to wait until 1765 for Patrick Henry's resolution and stirring warning to the king.

The New York assembly was systematic and vigorous in its discussion of the relations of the colony to parliament, and its petitions embody a complete and effective statement of the convictions and purposes which actuated the patriot leaders. Far less than justice has been done to their authors, and to the assembly of New York, for their courage and fidelity, for their eloquence, for their worthy championship of a great cause. While Massachusetts and Virginia have coined for current use the speeches of their writers and orators, it is still necessary to dig out of the official records the text of these documents, in which New York advocated high principles in a grand way. The petition to the king, after reciting the services of the province in the late war, proceeds : " For besides that involuntary taxes and impositions are absolutely and necessarily excluded from a state of liberty ; that it would be the basest vassalage to be taxed at the pleasure of a fellow subject; that all real property is lost whensoever it becomes subordinate to laws in the making of which the proprietor does not participate, and that thus to treat us would be to sink us into a subjugation infinitely below the ignominious rank of the most tributary states ; besides all this, we have the welfare of the nation, that most powerful advocate with a wise king, to plead our cause before your Majesty." The damaging effects of the policy of taxation then pursued were strongly shown in relation to immigration, industry, and trade. Then turning to the courts, the address proceeds : " Though we could, with the most becoming alacrity, submit our lives and property, and that we hold dearer than both, that inestimable liberty with which our ancestors have set us free, to your Majesty's royal clemency and princely direction, yet the unavoidable delegations of that royal authority which necessarily expose us to .the rapacious designs of wicked men, leave us neither rest nor security, while a custom-house officer may wantonly seize what a judge of your Majesty's court of vice-admiralty may condemn in his discretion," and " we tender our humble petition to the throne, that this great, this growing, this mighty evil may be removed from among us."

To parliament arguments and appeals no less clear and forcible were directed. " We have enjoyed," declared to the lords these evangelists of liberty, " the uninterrupted privilege of being taxed only with our consent, given by our representatives in general assembly. This we have ever considered as the inextinguishable right of British subjects, because it is the natural right of mankind, and so inseparable from the very idea of property as not to be divested even by conquest itself, without totally despoiling the vanquished and reducing them to a state of absolute vassalage." To the commons the case is stated fully and at length. The colony had since 1683, through its representatives chosen by the people, " enjoyed the right of taxing the subject for the support of the government." The design to induce the parliament of Great Britain " to impose taxes upon the subjects here by laws to be passed there," was an "innovation," of which the assembly sought to state its "foresight of the tragical consequences to the crown, the mother country, the colony, and to posterity."

With sturdy self-confidence, the authors of the address proceed : " Had the freedom from all taxes not granted by ourselves been enjoyed as a privilege, we are confident the wisdom and justice of the British parliament would rather establish than destroy it, unless by our abuse of it, the forfeiture was justly incurred; but his Majesty's colony of New York can not only defy the whole world to impeach their fidelity, but appeal to all the record of their past transactions, as well for the fullest proof of their steady affection to the mother country, as for their strenuous efforts to support the government, and advance the general interests of the whole British empire." The sacrifices during the French war were fresh enough, even in British minds, to render this reference both forcible and pathetic. Not as a favor, but as a right, New York demanded " exemption from the burthens of ungranted, involuntary taxes, as the grand principle of every free state." For " without such a right vested in the people themselves there can be no liberty, no happiness, no security." " And if conquered vassals upon the principle even of natural justice may claim a freedom from assessments unbounded and unassented to, without which they would sustain the loss of everything, and life itself become intolerable, with how much propriety and boldness may we proceed to inform the commons of Great Britain, who to their distinguished honor, have in all ages asserted the liberties of mankind, that the people of this colony, inspired by the genius of their mother country, nobly disdain the thought of claiming that exemption as a privilege."

The evil policy of the imposition of involuntary taxes is urged ; and while the authority of parliament is recognized " to model the trade of the whole empire," duties as well as internal taxes enforced by its arbitrary order will prove pernicious to Great Britain as well as to the colony. The address protests that the assembly cannot be guilty of a " desire of independence upon the supreme power of parliament," but in behalf of its constituents " cannot avoid deprecating the loss of such rights as they have hitherto enjoyed, rights established in the first dawn of our constitution, founded upon the most substantial reasons, confirmed by invariable usage, conducive to the best ends ; never abused to bad purposes ; and with the loss of which liberty, property and all the benefits of life tumble into insecurity and ruin : rights the deprivation of which will dispirit the people, abate their industry, discourage trade, introduce discord, poverty and slavery: or by depopulating the colonies, turn a vast, fertile, prosperous region into a dreary wilderness, impoverish Great Britain, and shake the power and independency of the most opulent and flourishing empire in the world." With this protest against taxation were included appeals for permission to maintain paper money to meet the stress caused by the French war. So audacious were these petitions and addresses regarded that no member of parliament could be found formally to present them. They were left to have such effect as private circulation would command.

The careful student of the petitions of 1763 and 1764 does not need to seek elsewhere for the clear expression of the principles which led to the Declaration of Independence. The documents are not only akin in spirit, but rest on the same solid foundations. New York pleads natural justice and the rights of men against taxation by parliament and interference with the colonial courts, and asserts with bold courage, that without such rights there " can be no liberty, no happiness," and " life itself would be intolerable." Livingston and Bayard and

Phillipse and the New York assembly were in the forefront of the struggle for the liberties which king and parliament were foolishly and criminally crippling.

The attempt to impress sailors for the British navy added to the popular indignation. A press-gang seized, June, 1764, four fishermen in the harbor; but in return the captain's barge was captured, and although the men were set free, the boat was hauled on shore and burned, and the courts could not discover the captors.

Mr. Bancroft testifies truly that the "spirit of resistance was nowhere so strong at this moment" as in New York. The assembly responded to the popular feeling, and took the first formal step towards colonial union against Great Britain, by a resolution, October 18, 1764, clothing a committee previously appointed with power to "correspond with the several assemblies or committees of assemblies on this continent, on the subject-matter of the act commonly called the sugar act; of the act restraining paper bills of credit in the colonies from being a legal tender; and of the several other acts of parliament lately passed, with relation to the trade of the northern colonies; and also on the subject of the impending dangers which threaten the colonies of being taxed by laws to be passed in Great Britain." This committee, established to conduct the colony's correspondence with its agent in London, and now to seek united action with the other colonies, consisted of John Cruger, Philip Livingston, Leonard Lispenard, William Bayard, and Robert R. Livingston. They were the recognized leaders in the assembly, and were all, except the last named, members from New York city; Livingston sat for Dutchess county. A conference between the colonies had before occurred, in furtherance of British policy. This is the beginning of official action in behalf of American union for American interests, and the honor of it belongs to New York.

www.ingramcontent.com/pod-product-compliance
Lightning Source LLC
Chambersburg PA
CBHW030910270326
41929CB00008B/642